Letters to Cristina

Letters to Cristina

Reflections on My Life and Work

~

Paulo Freire

Translated from the Portuguese
by Donaldo Macedo
with Quilda Macedo and Alexandre Oliveira

ROUTLEDGE
NEW YORK AND LONDON

Published in 1996 by

Routledge
29 West 35th Street
New York, NY 10001

Published in Great Britain in 1996 by

Routledge
11 New Fetter Lane
London EC4P 4EE

Printed in the United States of America
Design: Jack Donner

Library of Congress Cataloging-in-Publication Data

Freire, Paulo, 1921 –
    [Cartas a Cristina. English]
    Letters to Cristina / Paulo Freire: translated from Portuguese to English
by Donaldo Macedo, with Quilda Macedo and Alexandre Oliveira.
        p.   cm.
    ISBN 0–415–91096–X. — ISBN 0–415–91097–8 (pbk.)
    1. Freire, Paulo, 1921 –   —Correspondence. 2. Educators—Brazil—
Biography. I. Macedo, Donaldo P. (Donaldo Pereira), 1950 –   . II. Title.
LB880.F732A413 1996
370'.92—dc20   96–7429
    [B]   CIP

Contents

Foreword

≈

FOR ME, WRITING HAS BECOME A DEEP PLEASURE just as it has also become a duty that I cannot reject, for it is a political project that must be met. The joy of writing fills all my time. It fills my time when I write, when I read and reread what I have written, when I receive the first galleys to be corrected, and when I receive the first still-warm copy of the book from the publishing house.

To write, I read and reread written pages, essays, and book chapters that deal with the same theme I am writing about, or with other related themes; this represents a habit in my personal experience. I never live exclusively to write since, for me, writing also implies reading and rereading. Every day, before I begin writing, I have to reread the twenty or thirty pages of the text that I last wrote and presently, little by little, I feel obliged to reread the entire text that I have written thus far. I never do one thing at a time. I live intensely the impossible relationship of the false dichotomy between writing and reading. To read what I have written makes it possible for me to improve what I have already written, while stimulating me and animating me to write what I have not yet written.

To read critically in the very process of writing redirects my attention to whether or not I have achieved my desired goals. Critical rereading also tells me whether or not I am writing with enough clarity. It is in the process of reading and rereading what I have already written that I become better able to write more effectively. We learn how to write when we react vigorously to what we have written, discovering in the process that we are able either to improve our writing or to feel satisfied with what we have written.

As I mentioned before, however, writing should never be viewed only as a question of personal satisfaction. I do not write simply because it gives me pleasure. I write because I feel politically committed, because I would like to convince other people, without lying to them, that what I dream about and what I speak about and what causes me to struggle are *worth* writing about. The political nature of the act of writing, in turn, requires ethical commitment. I cannot lie to my readers by deliberately hiding the truth; I cannot affirm that which I know is false. I cannot give the impression that I am knowledgeable about this or that subject if I am not. I cannot quote a single phrase that intimates to my readers that I have read the entire work of the quoted author. I will lose the authority to continue to write or speak about Christ if I, at the same time, discriminate against my neighbor because he or she is black or because he or she is a blue-collar worker.

One should not define the act of writing by alleging that it is a pure, divine act of the angels. No. Women and men write and are subject to limits that they should recognize. There are epistemological, economic, social, racial, and class limits. I should, whenever possible, keep in mind the fundamental ethical requirement of knowing my own limits. I cannot authentically accept a professorship if I do not teach or if I teach by confusing or falsifying. In truth, I cannot teach what I do not know. I cannot teach clearly unless I recognize my own ignorance, unless I identify what I do not know, what I have not mastered.

Only when I fully know what I do not know can I speak about what I do not know, not as an object of knowledge, but as an absence that can be overcome. Thus, I can begin to know better what I do not know.

It is very difficult for me to meet such requirements without humility; that is, if I am not humble enough, if I refuse to recognize my incompetence and the best path to overcome it. The incompetence that I dismiss and disguise ends up unveiling itself, unmasking me.

What is expected of those who write with responsibility is a permanent and continuing search for truth that rejects puritanical hypocrisy or veiled shamelessness. In the final analysis, what is expected of those who teach by speaking or writing, by being a testimony, is that they be rigorously coherent so as not to lose themselves in the enormous distance between what they do and say.

In keeping with my old promise to write *Letters to Cristina* about my childhood, my adolescence, my youth, and my maturity, in which I talk about what I did with the help of others and the challenge of reality, I have to understand that I have to be loyal to what I have lived as well as to the historical time of my lived experiences. That is, when we write, we cannot ignore our condition as historical beings. We cannot ignore that we are beings inserted into the social structures in which we participate as objects and subjects. When I step back today from the moments I lived yesterday, I should, on one hand, be as truthful as possible while I reminisce in describing the plot and what happened. On the other hand, I should also be truthful to the moment in which I describe my lived experiences. The eyes with which I review the past are not the same eyes with which I saw in the past. No one can speak about what has happened unless it is through the perspective of what is now happening. What seems invalid to me is to pretend that what occurred could possibly have happened under the different conditions that are present today. In the end, the past is to be understood and not to be changed.

It is with this perspective, for example, that—while I do refer to the authoritarian traditions of the society—I recognize that today we live in a more significant historical moment in our political life with respect to our democratic experience.

For the first time in thirty years of discretionary military rule, we were able to prevent the election of a president[1] who would betray his own people. Although things did not occur with the expected rigor and have not reached their ultimate consequences, we have to realize that we are living a process. What behooves us is to recognize the nature of this process. We need to recognize the resistance to seriousness, to decency, that has characterized the dominant among us so that we can strengthen our democratic institutions.

Our preoccupation should be with the ways in which we can make our democracy better, not with throwing rocks at it or suppressing it because shamelessness is still to be found in it. Our preoccupation should be to strengthen Congress.[2] Those who act against its existence and attempt to close it down are the enemies of freedom. There is just as much a chance of finding men and women who are corrupt as there are possibilities to find men and women in Congress who are decent. There are also corrupt individuals in other institutions. Considering that we are finite beings who are subject to temptation, we should aim to make our institutions better by diminishing the opportunities that lead to unethical practices.

Wherever in the world one finds corruption unveiled, along with the punishment of those who are guilty, it is the practice of democracy and not the work of dictatorships. Let's reiterate that what we need to do is to strengthen democracy by making it more effective—by diminishing, for example, the distance between the elected official and the voter. The district-level vote reduces such distance and makes it possible for the voter to examine the candidate he or she voted for. It also makes the process less expensive while injecting it with more seriousness. We cannot teach democracy to anyone with regimes based on exceptions; it is not with a gagged press that we learn the meaning of a free one; it is not by being mute that we learn to speak; and it is not through greed that we learn how to be ethical.

There is something that is almost accidentally being realized among us and that should become common practice, for it is an obvious necessity: the pragmatic unity of the Left. We cannot continue to explain our continued separation as due to only minimal divergences. Through these divergences, we help the singular Right strengthen itself due to the fragility among us on the Left.

A progressive, postmodernist requirement is that we not be too certain of our certainties, that we operate contrary to the exaggerated certainties of modernity. The dialogue among differences means that we can, with the possibility of victory, contradict the antagonists. What we cannot do is transform our divergences into substantial ones. To elevate polite disagreement into an insurmountable obstacle is to treat differences on the Left as if we were on the Right. The development of different parts on the Left represents a means through which we can deepen necessary dialogue.

[4]

Introduction

~

MY EXPERIENCE IN EXILE WAS ENRICHED BY THE LETTERS I wrote to friends. My correspondence with students and teachers was far more intense, however. When they came through Santiago, or when they heard about the literacy work that I had done in Brazil and Chile, students and teachers would write to me, either to continue a dialogue or to begin one; in some cases, these conversations continue even today. This process was part of my ten years in exile in Chile, the United States, and Switzerland.

It does not matter why we woke up one day in a foreign land. Exile, over time, allows new situations to reinsert us in the world. The same thing happens to those people who stay in their own country. History does not stop for them, does not wait for our absence to end so that we can tell them upon returning that it was not really a reencounter.

Things change, as we do. At this point, I feel that I should warn readers who have read my other reflections on exile that I might seem to contradict myself. I do not think I actually do so. In the intimacy of these necessary repositionings in the world—in the world of those who had to leave and in the original world of those who were able to stay—something I have been talking a lot about takes place: the drama of being uprooted. There is all the need, lived out in anguish, to learn the great historical, cultural, and political lesson that, in attending to our business in a borrowed context, we create another context that we have not quite psychologically abandoned. And yet, we are forced physically to leave our preoccupation (as I discuss in my book *Pedagogy of Hope: A Reencounter with Pedagogy of the Oppressed*, published in 1992).

When the reasons that push us from our context into another are ostensibly of a political nature, the correspondence between those who leave and those who stay behind runs the unquestionable risk of creating problems for both sides. One of these risks involves persecution, not only for those who are exiled and their families, but also for those who stay behind. This issue would take up many pages of writing (in a style that we could call "believe it if you want") concerning the persecution suffered by those exiled from their families and by Brazilians who stayed in Brazil. Those individuals who received unwise letters from careless friends, or letters that were "extremely well written," were the subjects of persecution since the letters were not correctly understood by the masters of censorship.

I will never forget, for example, a communication we had one afternoon in Santiago, Chile. A ham operator, who was a sociologist and who worked for the United Nations, offered us the opportunity to speak with our relatives in Recife, Brazil, through contacts with another ham operator there. We were extremely careful. Our words were very reserved. Our conversation was purely affective.

On another occasion the same friend offered his services to make it possible for an exiled politician from São Paulo, Plínio Sampaio, to speak with his family through another ham operator in São Paulo. Coincidentally, the São Paulo ham operator was a friend of Plínio's. I was next to Plínio and I remember, as if it were today, how he told his friend that he missed their serenades together and that he was sure they would soon sing together again and listen to serenades.

One of the geniuses of Brazil's secret intelligence was listening to the conversation. I can imagine the joy with which he communicated the news to his superior that Plínio Sampaio was preparing to return to Brazil to unleash a guerrilla war on São Paulo. Of course, it would have been the first guerrilla war made up of serenaders and would certainly have included the singers Silvio Caldas and Nelson Gonçalves. As a result, Plínio's friend in São Paulo had his ham operator license revoked, ending his weekend entertainment. Above all, he lost the chance to help others who dreamed of becoming ham operators. From that afternoon on, he became the subject of the irrational surveillance of the impressive services of the Brazilian intelligence.

Because of such incidents, I was always careful to respect the contexts of the friends in Brazil to whom I wrote while in exile. I was very discreet. I feared that my letters might create difficulties for my friends if of any sentence had not been carefully thought out.

Even if it were only a postcard, I used to write almost weekly to my mother, who died before I could see her again. I corresponded with my brothers and sisters, a cousin, my brothers-in-law, and two nieces, one of whom was Cristina. I also wrote, every once in a while, to about a dozen friends.

I am convinced that men and women who lived through the tragic experience of losing their freedom—from the right to have a passport and return home to the right to correspond with friends without having to worry about the consequences—should constantly tell the youth of today, many of whom were not yet born, that these things are true. That all these things, and much, much more, happened.

The self-censorship we exercised was a limit on our right to write letters, and it was only diabolical and stupid fantasies that made these letters feed the units of repression because of this or that noun, this exclamation or that interrogative mark, or the innocent omission of periods. Using such letters as evidence, the military kidnapped, imprisoned, tortured, beat prisoners until they bled, and then returned them to their cells, half alive. Their hobbling bodies were, however, full of dignity as they returned, walking naked down the prison halls past their friends' cells, who waited for their turn to be tortured. It is necessary to say, and to say again, a thousand times, that these things happened. It is necessary to say with force that these things happened, so that in this country,[1] we never again have to say that these things happened.

One day, on a winter afternoon in Geneva, I received a letter from my mother. Sad and hurt, she told me that she did not understand why I had stopped writing to her. Somewhat naively, she began asking if she had said something wrong in previous letters. She did not understand that some bureaucrats had intercepted my letters and postcards to her. In those letters, I never, not even metaphorically, made any reference to politics in Brazil. This censorship had to be pure meanness.

I then wrote six letters to my mother, sending them to friends in Africa, the United States, Canada, and Germany. I asked my friends to please send the letters to my mother's address in Campos in Rio State, explaining the reason behind my request. Sometime later, she wrote saying how very happy she had been to receive my letters from so many different parts of the world.

By then my mother had probably understood the meanness that had caused my silence and that later was interrupted by the solidarity of my friends. I wrote to every one of them, thanking them for the fraternal and loving gesture they had made in helping me recontact my mother.

At one point, the repression intensified so much that correspondence diminished and almost disappeared. This period was inaugurated by the government with AI-5—Institutional Act, No. 5—on December 13, 1968.[2] Only my mother and other members of my family could write to me.

During this period, those who came to Geneva avoided visiting us. They were afraid that upon returning to Brazil they would be interrogated about what I had said to them—if I was thinking of returning to Brazil, if I was planning to unleash a guerrilla war. One of the results of arbitrary power is that people internalize fear and allow it to take over, thus policing themselves. They begin to control themselves and become dual and ambiguous beings in whom the oppressors live. Many other people, however, would look us up, and not only those who agreed with us. Many people who did not agree with our political position visited us to show their solidarity. In case I should forget one, I will refrain from naming those who comforted us with their presence in our home in exile. Those who came to our house, sharing their friendliness, we will remember. To all of them, I again send thanks after such a long time.

One of those visits caused us much pain. A young couple, with a young daughter who was three or four years old, arrived in Geneva from Paris and spent an afternoon with us. The husband was a medical doctor without much political commitment but in complete solidarity with his wife. She had been imprisoned for her political activities against the dictatorship. To a great extent, she was destroyed emotionally. Sometimes, while talking to us, she would abandon the current experience she was narrating and would, just as vehemently, talk about past situations. All of a sudden, she would recoil into her own body, almost disappearing into the chair in front of us. Sometimes she would say things whose meaning we could only guess at. They were extracts of conversations from the cell of her terrible experiences.

She was Catholic and had worked in a clandestine movement[3] that was the only political activity that the military would allow youth at that time. The military closed all doors and opportunities for political expression to those who had opposed the coup d'état, excepting the opposition party that the military had created to give the impression of democracy. Ironically, actually more than ironically, dialectically, history saw to it that this false party of opposition became the real opposition party.[4]

She was imprisoned and immediately tortured[5] in capricious and varied ways. She spoke to us for more than three hours about what she had gone through. We listened as it was our duty as friends to listen. We listened without even insinuating that she had told us enough; we knew that our suffering paled in comparison to her pain, the beatings she relived by relating the story to us, as she reincorporated into her body what she had suffered.

Still today, this woman represents, in my life experience, the person that I most needed to talk to concerning her suffering, her humiliation, her negation, the zero to which she had been reduced. In listening to her I was shaken by a profound surprise that all the things she was telling us were possible. I could not believe that people were capable of committing such atrocities. She spoke, almost always, as if she were narrating a work of fiction. What was tragic for us to realize, during that afternoon in our apartment in Geneva, was that in the Brazil of those days, the fiction was treating prisoners with dignity and respect.

At one point, she began to cry discreetly. She recouped her composure and said, in a quiet and easy manner that belied the intensity of her experience, "One day, Paulo, I was already in the position to be whipped. I spoke and said, 'Calm down: Think of how God must be viewing you right now. Armed, not particularly brave, ready to continue to destroy my small, fragile, indefensible body.'"

The guards became visibly uncertain. These men did not believe in God but, just to be sure, they decided to believe in God a little. Indecisive for a second, they then untied her while they murmured among themselves. One of them risked saying, "Very well, we are going to spare you today, but God has changed. We cannot understand how he could help subversives like you and the type of priests and nuns who are out there."

At the end of the afternoon, already standing up and ready to hug us, she uttered a sentence that moved me the most: "It is terrible, Paulo. The only time that these men gave any sign that they were human was when they were shaken by fear. It was only due to their fear of going to hell that they backed down from their meanness and ceased torturing me."

What was most important that afternoon was that the young couple, in the face of unquestionable and ongoing suffering, did not reveal, not even once, a negative or fatalistic vision of history. They did not dwell on the history of meanness, the history of cruelty, or the history of injustice. They both understood that cruelty existed and exists. They were objects of this cruelty, but they refused to accept that there was nothing to do but cross their arms and bow their heads to the chopping block.

It was around this time, at the beginning of the 1970s, that I received the first letters from my niece Cristina, who was then still an adolescent. She was curious about how we lived in Switzerland and about the country's beauty, democracy, education, and level of civilization. Her assessment of Switzerland contained some truth but also some myths. There is real beauty: lakes, mountains, pastures, landscapes that belong on postcards. But there is also real ugliness: discrimination against women, blacks, Arabs, homosexuals, and immigrant workers.

Furthermore, although I respect punctuality and see it as a virtue, I also see subservience to a schedule as a bureaucratization of the mind, a form of alienation.

I wrote to Cristina about all of these issues, to the extent that one can to an adolescent. I talked about other things as well: my longing for Brazil while in exile, principally in Chile, and my efforts to limit my longing so as not to allow it to become nostalgia; my work at the World Council of Churches; some of the trips I took; and my routine in Geneva.

Before I wrote to Cristina—during the very first days of my exile in Chile, after having spent two months in Bolívia—I corresponded with Natercinha, Cristina's cousin. I shared with her how surprised I was, feeling a child-like joy, when I saw snow for the first time in my life, near the mountains in Santiago not too far from where we lived. On the street with my kids, I felt like a child again myself, making snowballs and play-ing in the white flakes that covered the grass as well as my tropical body.

Time passed. Cristina's letters continued to arrive. Her questions increased. Her first year at college was approaching when, one afternoon in the summer, I received a letter from her displaying a predictable curiosity. "Until now," she said, "I knew you, my uncle, only through stories my mother, my father, and my grandmother used to tell me." Now, a timid intimacy with the other Paulo Freire began to take place—Paulo Freire, the educator. And, she made a request, one I began responding to a long time ago and am just now finalizing. "I would like," she said, "for you to write me letters about your life, your childhood and, little by little, about the trajectory that led you to become the educator you are now."

I still remember how that letter challenged me and made me begin to think of how to respond. I had in front of me, on my desk, an intelli-gent letter from my niece that represented a viable and interesting project. I thought it would be interesting, in writing the solicited letters, to expand my analysis of the issues. Writing so that a young person could understand would enable me to practice my pedagogical thinking as well. It was then that the idea emerged to collect the letters and to publish them in the future. In such a book I could not fail to refer to the changes in my educational practice throughout the years.

I then began to collect data and to organize my files of observations made over the years of my practice. I also began to speak with friends concerning the project, getting feedback and critiques. Coffee tables in Geneva, Paris, and New York mediated these conversations, which began to shape the book before it was put on paper. I began to understand, on the one hand, the need to be clear that the experiences about which I would talk did not belong to me, and, on the other hand, the need to, without writing a collection of autobiographical texts, refer to certain events in my childhood, adolescence, and young adulthood, avoiding any rupture between the man of today and the child of yesterday. These events, at least in some respects, inform the work that I have been doing as an educator. For this reason, it would be naive to pretend to forget them or to split them from my more recent activities, creating rigid walls between different experiences. To separate the child from the adult, who has since his youth dedicated himself to the work of education, could not provide a better understanding of the man who, in trying to preserve the child that he was, searches also to be the child that he could not be.

In truth, these letters are constituted by putting on paper today memories of what took place a long time ago. It is possible that the very distance at which I find myself from the original events will interfere; I may alter the exact manner in which they took place. At any rate, I have made serious efforts to be as truthful to the facts as I possibly can in these letters, as in the *Pedagogy of Hope* where I refer to the old plots in which I was involved. I would not, for example, in this type of book, write that our family had moved in 1932 from Recife to Jaboatão if we had moved only from one neighborhood to another in the same city of Recife. It is possible, however, that in describing the move, I added details that have been incorporated into my memory from what happened later in my life, details that surface today as concrete events of unquestionable recollection.

In this way, it is impossible to escape fiction in my experience of remembrance. It was something like this that I learned from Piaget in his last television interview in Geneva before my 1980 return to Brazil from exile. He spoke about certain betrayals to which the memory is subject when people are at a distance from the original events.

For instance, it would be very difficult to speak about Jaboatão and forget about the existence of two musical bands, the Paroquial and the Rede Ferroviaria Federal, and their outdoor concerts. However, in remembering them, I may have introduced some elements that incorporated themselves into my memory for some reason.

Or, in referring to "Mr." Armada and describing what this schoolmaster represented to children who ran the risk of being matriculated in his school, it may be that I have fantasized about one moment or another. Mr. Armada, however, existed, as did his fame as an authoritarian and hard schoolmaster.

While insisting that the reader remember these risks of memory, I would like to say that they do not inhibit me, I only feel a duty to underline them. I would not have to do so if the letters I have written to Cristina were works of fiction. Cristina Freire Bruno, my niece, is today a psychotherapist in Campos, State of Rio. I am now fulfilling a promise I made to her a long time ago.

Better now than never.

First Letter

~

For me to return to my distant childhood is
a necessary act of curiosity.

THE MORE I RETURN TO MY DISTANT CHILDHOOD, the more I
realize that there is always something there worth knowing. I continue to
learn from my childhood and difficult adolescence. I do not return to my
early years as someone who is sentimentally moved by a ridiculous
nostalgia or as someone who presents his not-so-easy childhood and
adolescence as a form of revolutionary credentials.

In my own case, the difficulties I confronted during my childhood
and adolescent years caused in me—rather than an accommodating position before challenges—a curious and hopeful openness toward the
world. I never felt inclined to accept reality as it was, even when it was
still impossible for me to understand the roots of my family's difficulties.
I never thought that life was predetermined or that the best thing to do
was to accept obstacles as they appeared. On the contrary, even in my
very early years I had begun to think that the world needed to be
changed; that something wrong with the world could not and should not
continue. Perhaps I wanted the world to change because of the negative
context in which my family lived. Finding myself immersed in predicaments that did not affect the children around me, I learned to compare
my situation with theirs. This led me to conclude that the world needed
to be corrected. This active outlook later resulted in two significant
beliefs:

1. Because I had experienced poverty, I never allowed myself to fall into fatalism; and

2. Because I had been born into a Christian family, I never accepted our precarious situation as an expression of God's wishes. On the contrary, I began to understand that something really wrong with the world needed to be fixed.

Since early on, my position was one of critical optimism. In other words, I held the hope that seldom exists apart from the reverses of fate. Perhaps it was during my distant childhood that I developed the habit that I still carry today of occasionally surrendering myself to profound contemplation, as if I am isolated from everything else, the people and things that surround me. I like to think I find myself in the play of losing myself. I often find myself in this contemplative state while doing research or in my office. I also become contemplative in other spaces and at other times.

Therefore, for me to return to my distant childhood is a necessary act of curiosity. In doing so, in stepping back from it, I become more objective while looking for the reasons I involved myself and these reasons' relationship to the social reality in which I participated. It is in this sense that the continuity between the child of yesterday and the man of today is clarified. The man of today reflects in order to understand how the child of yesterday lived and what his relationships were within the family structure, in the schools, and on the streets. On the other hand, however, the afflictions of the child of yesterday and the activism of the man of today cannot be understood as isolated expressions, even when we cannot negate either reality. Neither is sufficient to explain the more profound meaning of my doings. My lived experiences as a child and as a man took place socially within the history of a dependent society in whose terrible dramatic nature I participated early on. I should highlight that it was this terrible nature of society that fostered my increasing radicality. It would be a mistake for people to see my radicality, which never became extreme, as the traumatic expression of a child who was not loved and felt desperately alone.

My radical rejection of a class-based society, which is necessarily a violent society, could provide a rationale for some analysts to argue that my radicality has its roots in a supposed affective disconnectedness during childhood.

In truth, however, I was never alone or unloved. I never doubted my parents' affection for me or their love for each other and my brothers and sisters. The security of the love in our family helped us to confront the real problem that afflicted us during the greater part of my childhood: the problem of hunger. It was a real and concrete hunger that had no specific date of departure. Even though it never reached the rigor of the hunger experienced by some people I know, it was not the hunger experienced by those who undergo a tonsil operation or are dieting. On the contrary, our hunger was of the type that arrives unannounced and unauthorized, making itself at home without an end in sight. A hunger that, if it was not softened as ours was, would take over our bodies, molding them into angular shapes. Legs, arms, and fingers become skinny. Eye sockets become deeper, making the eyes almost disappear. Many of our classmates experienced this hunger and today it continues to afflict millions of Brazilians who die of its violence every year.

Many times, with no means to resist, I felt defeated by hunger while doing my homework. Sometimes I would fall asleep leaning on the table where I was studying, as if I had been drugged. I tried to fight this hunger-induced sleep by opening my eyes really wide and fixing them, with some difficulty, on the science and history texts that were part of my elementary school work. It was as if the words became pieces of food.

On other occasions, after tremendous effort, I could read the words one by one without, however, understanding the meaning of the text composed of those words.

At that time, I was very removed from the educational experience in which students and readers become aware that they are also producers of knowledge, in which authors do not simply deposit comprehension of their texts into students. Understanding the text, in my school days, meant memorizing them mechanically. The capacity to memorize texts was seen as a sign of intelligence. The more I failed to memorize the texts, the more convinced I became of my insurmountable ignorance.

It was necessary for me to live through many such experiences, but it was more important for me to eat more frequently. Sometime later, I realized that my ignorance was not as marked as I had thought. My perceived ignorance was, at the very least, less than my hunger.

Some years later, as the director for the Department of Education of a private school in Recife, it became easier for me to understand how difficult it was for sons and daughters of poor families to achieve satisfactory educational results. They were vulnerable to a greater and more systematic hunger than I had experienced and were without the advantages I had had as a middle-class child.

I did not need to consult scientific studies to determine the relationship between a lack of nutrition and learning difficulties. I had a first hand, existential experience of this relationship.

I could see myself in the children's stunted frames, their big and sometimes sad eyes, their elongated arms, and their skinny legs. In them I could also see some of my childhood friends who, if they are alive today, will probably not read this book of letters to them. They will probably not know that I am writing about them with much longing and respect. I am referring to Toinho Morango, Baixa, Dourado, and Reginaldo.

In describing the relationship between unfavorable concrete conditions and children's learning difficulties, I should make my position on the subject clear. I do not think such conditions create in students a nature that is incompatible with the ability to learn in school. What has been happening, however, is that the elitist, authoritarian schools do not take into account, in their curricular organization and their treatment of program content, the knowledge that is generated by social classes that are subjugated and exploited. It is never considered that difficult conditions, no matter how devastating, engender in the kids who experience them the knowledge to survive. In truth, the dominated popular classes generate knowledge and culture, and they experience different levels of exploitation and the consciousness of the exploitative order. This knowledge becomes, in the final analysis, an expression of resistance.

I am convinced that educational difficulties would diminish if the schools took into consideration the culture of the oppressed, their language, their efficient way of doing math, their knowledge of the world. From their own knowledge, students could move to the more systematic knowledge taught by schools. Obviously, this challenge is not to be carried out by the schools of the dominant classes but rather by the schools of the dominated classes and by progressive educators who live by connecting their discourse and their practice.

During my frequent visits to schools, when I would talk to teachers and administrators, I saw how difficult it was for students to learn when they were challenged by a consuming hunger.

On one of these visits, a worried teacher spoke to me about one such student. Discreetly, the teacher directed my attention to a skinny student in the corner of the room who acted as if he were absent and who was oblivious to what was going on around him. The teacher said, "He spends part of each morning sleeping. It would be a form of violence to wake him. What do you think? What should I do?"

We learned later that Pedrinho was the third son in a very large family. His father, who worked as a laborer in a local factory, did not earn enough money to provide the basic material necessities to his family. They lived on top of one another in a ramshackle hut.[1] Pedrinho rarely ate, and he had to work to help the family survive. He sold fruits on the streets, ran errands for people, and he carried merchandise to the market in his neighborhood.

For him, school represented a parenthesis, a time-out in which he could rest his tired body. Pedrinho was not the exception. There were worse, even more dramatic situations than his. On seeing and talking to such students, I remembered what studying while hungry had meant for me. I remember the wasted time that I spent closing my eyes and repeating from the notebook in my hands: "England, the capital is London. France, the capital is Paris. England, the capital is London." "Repeat, repeat so that you will learn," was the general suggestion when I was in school. How could I have learned, however, if the only possible geography was the geography of my hunger? For instance, the geography of somebody's backyard with fruit trees—mango trees, breadfruit trees, cashew trees, Surinam cherry trees—geography that my older brother, Temístocles, and I knew by heart, inch by inch. We knew all of its secrets and our memory held all the quickest paths to the best fruit trees.

We knew all the places between the dead leaves to carefully hide the not-so-ripe[2] bananas so they could ripen protected from other hungers, such as those of the "rightful property" owners.

One of the fruit orchard owners caught me one early morning while

I was trying to steal a beautiful papaya from his backyard. He unexpectedly appeared in front of me, giving me no opportunity to flee. I must have turned pale from surprise and shock. I did not know what to do with my shaking hands, from which the papaya fell to the ground. I did not know what to do with my body—if I should be stiff or relaxed before this serious, rigid person who embodied censure.

At that time, stealing the fruit was necessary but the man gave me a moralistic sermon that had little to do with my hunger.

Without saying a word—yes, no, I'm sorry, or I'll see you later—I left the yard and returned to my home much diminished, devastated, and withdrawn. What I wanted was to find a place where I couldn't even see myself.

Many years later, and under different circumstances, I experienced anew the strange sensation of not knowing what to do with my body: "Captain, another one for the cage," the security guard from the military base in Recife said. It was after the coup d'état of April 1, 1964, that the police brought me there from my home.

Both the police officer and the captain looked at me with ironic, vengeful smiles. I found myself again not knowing what to do with my hands and my body. One thing I knew—this time I had not stolen any papaya.

I don't remember what they taught me in school the day that I was caught with the neighbor's papaya in my hands. What I do know is that if I had difficulty solving some arithmetic problems, I had no difficulty in learning to calculate how long bananas took to ripen under the protection of the leaves in our hiding places.

For us, our geography was, without a doubt, not only a concrete geography, if I may say so, but a geography that had special meaning. In our geography we interpreted the two worlds in which we lived intensely: the world of children (in which we played soccer, swam, and flew kites)[3] and the world of premature men (in which we were concerned with our hunger and the hunger of our family).

We had friends in both of these worlds. Among them, some never knew the meaning of spending the whole day on a piece of bread, a cup of coffee, and a little rice and beans; or of looking for available fruit in somebody else's yard. Even when some of them participated with us in stealing from people's yards, they would do so for different reasons, for solidarity or for the thrill of adventure. In our case, there was something more pressing—our need to kill our hunger. This does not mean, however, that alongside our pressing needs was not the pleasure of adventure. In truth, we used to live a radical ambiguity: we were children prematurely forced to become adults. Our childhood was squeezed out between toys and work, between freedom and need.

By my eleventh birthday I had full knowledge of my family's precarious financial condition, but no means to help through a gainful job. Like my father, I could not just do away with my necktie, which was more than an expression of masculine style. It represented my class position, which did not allow me, for example, to have a job in the weekly market carrying packages or to do odd jobs in someone else's household.

In more developed societies, members of the middle class can, especially in difficult situations, work at manual jobs without the threat of losing their class status.

Second Letter

~

The piano in our house was like the tie around my father's neck. In spite of all our difficulties, we did not get rid of the piano, nor did my father do away with his necktie.

BORN INTO A MIDDLE-CLASS FAMILY that suffered the impact of the economic crisis of 1929, we became "connective kids." We participated in the world of those who ate well, even though we had very little to eat ourselves, and in the world of kids from very poor neighborhoods on the outskirts of town.[1]

We were linked to the former by our middle-class position; we were connected to the latter by our hunger, even though our hardships were less than theirs.

In my constant attempt to recollect my childhood, I remember that—in spite of the hunger that gave us solidarity with the children from the poor outskirts of town, in spite of the bond that united us in our search for ways to survive—our playtime, as far as the poor children were concerned, marked us as people from another world who happened to fall accidentally into their world.

Such class borders, which the man of today so clearly understands when he revisits his past, were not understood by the child of yesterday. Those borders were expressed more clearly by some of our friends' parents. Immersed in the alienating day-to-day routine, not understanding the causes behind the circumstances in which they were involved, the parents of these children were, by and large, existentially tired men and women who were historically anesthetized.

I cannot resist the temptation of making a parenthetical comment in this letter, calling attention to the relationship between class violence, class exploitation, existential tiredness, and historical anesthesia; that is, the fatalism among dominated and violated people before a world that is considered immutable. For this reason, the moment such people commit themselves to their political struggle, they begin to assert their position as a class. They transcend the fatalism that had anesthetized them historically. Such fatalism caused the parents of our poor friends to look at us as if they were thanking us for being friends with their sons and daughters. As if we and our parents were doing them a favor. To them, we were the sons of Captain Temístocles, we lived in a house in another section of the city, and our house was not like their huts in the woods.

In our house, we had a German piano on which Lourdes, one of our aunts, played Chopin, Beethoven, and Mozart. The piano alone was enough to distinguish our class from that of Dourado, Reginaldo, Baixa, Toinho Morango, and Gerson Macaco, who were our friends in those days. The piano in our house was like the tie around my father's neck. In spite of all our difficulties, we did not get rid of the piano, nor did my father do away with his necktie. Both the piano and the necktie were, in the end, symbols that helped us remain in the class to which we belonged. They implied a certain lifestyle, a certain way of being, a certain way of speaking, a certain way of walking, a special way of greeting people that involved bowing slightly and tipping your hat, as I had often seen my father do. All of these things were an expression of class. All of these things were defended by our family as an indispensable condition of survival.

The piano was not a mere instrument for Lourdes's artistic enjoyment, nor were my father's neckties just a clothing style. They both marked our class position. To lose those class markers would have meant losing our solidarity with members of the middle class in a step-by-step march toward the poor people on the outskirts of town. From there it would have been very difficult to return to our middle-class milieu. It therefore became necessary to preserve those class markers in order psychologically to enable our family to deal with our financial crisis and maintain our class position.

Lourdes's piano and my father's neckties made our hunger appear accidental. With those markers, we were able to borrow money. Even though it was not easy, without them, it would have been almost impossible. With those markers, our childhood fruit thefts, if discovered, would have been treated as mere pranks. At most, they would have been a minor embarrassment for our parents. Without them, they would certainly have been characterized as child delinquency.

Lourdes's piano and my father's neckties played the same class role that the tropical jacaranda trees and fine china play today among Northeast Brazil's aristocracy, who are in decline. Perhaps aristocratic class markers are less effective today than Lourdes's piano and my father's neckties were during the 1930s.

I highlight the issue of social class because the dominant class insists, in eloquent discourses full of deceit, that what is important is not class, but the courage to work and be disciplined, and the desire to climb and grow. Therefore, those who triumph are those who work hard without complaining and are disciplined; that is, those who do not create problems for their masters.

It is for this reason that I have emphasized our origin and class position, explaining the gimmicks[2] that our family developed in order to transcend our economic crisis.

I will never forget one of our gimmicks. It was a Sunday morning. Perhaps it was ten or eleven o'clock. It doesn't matter. We had just teased our stomachs with a cup of coffee and a thin slice of bread without butter. This would not have been enough food to keep us going, even if we had eaten plenty the day before, which we hadn't.

I don't remember what we were doing, if we were conversing or playing. I just remember that my two older brothers and I were sitting on the ledge of the cement patio at the edge of the yard where we lived. The yard contained some flower beds—roses, violets, and daisies—and some lettuce, tomato, and kale plants that my mother had pragmatically planted. The lettuce, tomatoes, and kale improved our diet. The roses, violets, and daisies decorated the living room in a vase that was a family relic from the last century. (Of these relics, my sister Stela still has the porcelain sink that was used to give us our first baths upon arriving in the world. Our sons and daughters were also bathed in the same porcelain sink. Regretfully, our grandchildren have broken with this family tradition.)

It was then that our attention was attracted by the presence of a chicken that probably belonged to our next-door neighbors. While looking for grasshoppers in the grass, the chicken ran back and forth, left to right, following the movements of the grasshoppers as they tried to survive. In one of those runs, the chicken came too close to us. In a split second, as if we had rehearsed it, premeditated it, we had the kicking chicken in our hands.

My mother arrived shortly after. She did not ask any questions. The four of us looked at each other and at the dead chicken in one of our hands.

Today, many years after that morning, I can appreciate the conflict that my mother, who was a Christian Catholic, must have felt as she looked at us in perplexity and silence. Her alternatives were either to reproach us severely and make us return the still warm chicken to our neighbors or to prepare the fowl as a special dinner. Her common sense won. Still silent, she took the chicken, walked across the patio, entered the kitchen, and lost herself in doing a job she had not done in a long time.

Our dinner that Sunday took place some hours later without any exchange of words. It is possible that we were tasting some remorse among the spices that seasoned our neighbor's chicken. The dish killed our hunger, yet the chicken was an accusatory "presence" that reminded us of the sin, the crime against private property, that we had committed.

The next day, our neighbor, upon noticing the loss of his chicken from the pen, must have cursed the thieves who could only have been the "little people," poor lower-class people, the kind who steal chickens.[3] He would never have imagined that the authors of the theft were close, very close to him indeed. Lourdes's piano and my father's neckties made any other conjecture impossible.

Third Letter

~

In truth, I was not the type of kid who spoke much of his upright world, characterized by coat, necktie, and heavy starched collar, or who repeated adults' words.

WE MOVED, IN 1932, like people looking for salvation, to Jaboatão, a small city about eighteen kilometers from Recife.

Until March of that year we had lived in Recife, in a medium-sized house, the house where I was born and that was surrounded by trees. Some of those trees were like people to me, such an intimacy had I developed with them.

The old house—with its hallway, rooms, narrow patio, and backyard filled with trees—represented the world of my first life experiences. In this world I learned to walk and talk. In it I also heard my first scary stories about ghosts who pulled people by the legs, blew out candles, revealed the hiding places of stone jugs full of silver, and told why ghosts suffered in the other world.

Many of these stories made me tremble from fear when I lay down to sleep. I would close my eyes, my heart beating, and cover myself completely with the sheet, waiting, believing, that at any moment a ghost would appear and speak with a nasal twang. In the stories, the ghosts from another world generally began to appear after midnight and always spoke with a nasal twang.

Many times I spent the night hugging myself under the bedsheet as if to protect myself from fear. The big clock in the dining room would interrupt the silence with its sonorous bells. For this reason, I developed a special relationship with the big clock. Mysteriously reinforcing the conditions of my fear, the clock's ticktock was a wakeful presence registering the time I hoped would pass quickly. In a strange way, the large clock made me feel better. I always felt like telling the big clock, "Thank you very much, because you are here, alive, awake, almost looking after me."

Today, a long time after those nights and sensations of fear, in writing about what I used to feel, I relive the magical affection I had for the clock. I listen to the clock here, and I remember, all of a sudden, the faint clarity of the oil lamp that only highlighted the darkness of the house, the house's geography, the bedroom, and the distance between the bedroom and the dining room where the clock comfortably rung its bells.

One very difficult month in our house, marked by financial problems, imposed silence on our dining room. I saw the clock being taken away by its new owner. Today, in remembering it, I understand that the sale of the clock alleviated my family's financial problems but I also know that the clock's absence left me alone with my fear.

I never said anything to my mother and my father. I did not want to reveal my magical intimacy with the big clock. Above all, I did not want to reveal the reason for my magical intimacy with it.

It took me a long time to get used to the absence of the big clock that had diminished my fears, that had watched over me in the unending nights.

I don't know the history of the big clock. All I know is that when I was born the big clock was already there, occupying a special place on the privileged wall of the dining room. It came into our family toward the end of the last century and all of us had a special affection for it.

It could not have been easy for my parents to sell the clock. I still remember the sadness on my father's face when he looked at the big clock for the last time, as if it were a person. My father almost talked to it, almost asked the clock for forgiveness for the act we were committing. I could tell by the way he looked at the man carrying the big clock away. If the clock could have spoken it would have said something about our ingratitude.

Fortunately, the first signs of daylight pushed away the ghosts. The sun would filter through the grass roof of my room while the birds brought back my tranquillity. My fear was not bigger than me. I began to understand that, even though fear was life's manifestation, it was necessary to establish fear's limits. In reality, I was attempting to educate my fear, an education that is necessary for the development of courage.

I think that, at home, no matter how much I tried to hide my fear, people suspected its existence. Especially my father. Every once in a while I would hear his steps walking toward my bed. Guided by the oil lamp light, he would check to see if I was asleep. Sometimes I talked to him and told him all I was well. Other times, I swallowed my fear and pretended to be asleep. On both occasions, his care for me made me happy.

I would like to highlight here how important it was for me to be the object of my parents' care. It is worth saying that it was important to know that I was loved by them. Unfortunately, we are not always able to express, without constraint and with maturity, our necessary love for our sons and daughters by using various forms and ways, among them giving special attention. Sometimes, for a number of reasons, we do not know how to let our children know how much we love them. We fear letting them know how much we love them. In the end, we work against them when we hide within us, because of an unfortunate shyness, our affection and love for them.

Little by little, however, as I have mentioned before, I began to transcend my fears. At about eight years of age, I became more or less calm. Before, any sound signaled something extraordinary, even the possibility of a visit from another world; after, I began to look for plausible reasons for each sound I heard. Why believe immediately that something abnormal was taking place? Why not think about the coconut tree swinging in the wind? The next day I would try to identify sounds that during the day seemed innocuous but at night became suspicious.

By refining my perception during daytime play, I began to understand, sometimes surprisingly, the variety of sounds. I began to distinguish a number of noises that before were imperceptible. This exercise strengthened me so I could confront the fears that used to consume me at night. The challenge of my fear, and my decision not to allow myself to submit to it, led me, at a very young age, to transform my bed and the silence of my room into a unique theoretical context. I began my first critical reflections about my concrete context, then limited to our backyard and the three hundred meters that separated my house from the primary school I had just begun to attend.

Early on, I exercised myself in the search for raison d'être, even if I could not always understand the real and profound meaning of such a process.

The search became almost a game and I started to learn the most minute details of our backyard. The banana tree leaves; the majestic cashew tree with its branches trailing on the ground, its roots curving up through the dirt like the veins of old hands; the coconut tree; the various types of mango trees; the breakfast tree and the strong wind that moved the tree branches; the singing of the birds: all of these things expanded my curiosity as a fascinated child.

The knowledge that I was gaining of my childhood world—such as the wavy shadows, like dancing bodies, projected by banana tree leaves—began to secure in me a form of calmness that other children my age did not have. The more I tried to understand during the day how things worked, by attempting to determine varied noises and their causes, the more I began to feel liberated from my ghostly nights. My efforts to know did not kill, however, my childlike spontaneity or replace it with a deformed rationality. In truth, I was not the type of kid who spoke much of his upright world, characterized by coat, necktie, and heavy starched collar, or who repeated adults' words.

I lived my world intensely. From my experiences I began to learn about the world's day-to-day routine without losing sight of the world's beauty. Simply put, I began to move through the world with security, whether by day or by night.

My father played an important role in my constant search for understanding. Being affectionate, intelligent, and open, he never refused to listen to us talk about our interests. He and my mother were a harmonious couple whose union did not lose them their individuality. They exemplified for us what it means to be understood and to understand, never showing any signs of intolerance. Although my mother was Catholic and my father was a spiritualist, they always respected each other's religious opinions. From them, I learned early on the value of dialogue. I never was afraid to ask questions, and I do not recall ever being punished for disagreeing with them.

They taught me how to read my first words and then how to write them on the ground with a wooden stick under the shade of our mango tree. My first words and phrases were linked to my experiences and not my parents'. Instead of a boring primer or, worse, an "ABC Table" for memorizing the letters of the alphabet (as if students learn how to speak by sounding out letters), I had my backyard as my first primer, my first world, my first school. The ground, protected by tree leaves, was my blackboard and sticks were my chalk. By six years of age, when I arrived at the little school where Eunice Vasconcelos was my first professional teacher, I already knew how to read and write.

I have never forgotten the joy with which I welcomed the exercises called "sentence forming" that our teacher gave us. She would ask me to write in a straight line all the words that I knew. Afterward, I was supposed to form sentences with these words and later we discussed the meaning of each sentence I had created. This is how, little by little, I began to know my verbs, tenses, and moods; she taught me by increasing the level of difficulty. My teacher's fundamental preoccupation was not with making me memorize grammatical definitions but with stimulating the development of my oral and writing abilities.

There was no rupture between my parents' teaching at home and the pedagogy of my teacher Eunice at school. At home, as in school, I was always invited to learn and never reduced to an empty vessel to be filled with knowledge.

No barrier existed between the way I was raised at home and the work I was given at school. Thus, school work never was a threat to my curiosity but rather was a stimulus. The time I spent playing and searching in my backyard was not the same as my experiences in school, but school was not my opposite point of reference, something that made me feel uncomfortable. Time spent in my backyard overflowed into time in school, making me feel happy in both spaces. In the final analysis, even though school had its own conditions, it did not limit my joy in life. It is the same joy in life that has characterized my entire life. It is the same joy in life that I experienced as a child in Jaboatão and which I continued to experience, as a man, during my time in exile. This joy has a great deal to do with my optimistic outlook on life, which means that, as a critical person, I am never paralyzed by life. This is why I always push myself toward forms of engagement and action that are compatible with my political beliefs.

Unfortunately, the happiness I had experienced in my backyard and at the little school where my teacher Eunice stimulated me, was not to be continued throughout my schooling.

Only two other teachers besides Eunice, from whom I learned how to form sentences, marked me: Áurea Bahia in Recife and Cecília Brandão in Jaboatão. The other elementary schools that I attended were boring and mediocre, although I have no bad feelings toward the teachers in those schools.

In referring to the small private school where Eunice taught, I cannot forget to mention her great-uncle, Adelino, whom I saw every morning when I went to "form sentences."

"Jau, Jau, I put the knife in your stomach," he would say, almost singing it, half-smiling with affection when I approached him somewhat timidly and curiously, not understanding the meaning of the sentence he sang. He was roundish and possessed of a big belly. With his ostentatious mustache, which enabled him to be recognized from far away, his small but lively eyes, Adelino was a distinguished figure. He was an old man who called attention to his ominous role as a retired government functionary. When he was angry, four-letter words spewed forth from his mouth, draped by the bushy mustache. My childhood memories are filled with his presence, his personal courage, his sincerity, his friendliness, his openness, and his quixotic way of being in the world, like Sancho Panza. All of these qualities speak of him and constituted his profile.

I have never forgotten one event. It was night time and raining heavily. The rain pocked the ground with holes, making its own geography of islands, lakes, and puddles. Lightening and thunder followed one another, filling the world with noise and brightness. There was only one difference among the lightening, thunder, and Adelino's song, "Jau, Jau, I put a knife in your stomach"—I was not afraid of the song.

Adelino had anticipated the storm but Martins, who was then an employee of the identification office of the Pernambuco Civil Police, had not. Martins was, in some respects, the opposite of Adelino. He was short and fat, but not as fat as Adelino. He smiled at appropriate moments, but he loved cigars, which he used to smoke down to the very tip. His reason for living was bureaucratic routine. Without this routine—his papers, the schedules, and the rest—life would lose its meaning. It was, perhaps, an uncomfortable journey through the world.

Martins was a character out of a novel. Many times after having arrived home from work—tired but composed, silently rocking in his chair, gazing at the arbitrary designs made by the smoke of his cigar—he would think about the papers that had gone through his office and that he, after meticulously studying them, had sent to section A or B. He reviewed his actions as if he had not only solved somebody's problem but had saved the world.

Shortly after I got married, I visited Martins for the last time in his humble house in a neighborhood of Recife. I wanted my first wife, Elza, to meet him. Adelino died shortly thereafter.

Martins was weak, but more because of a consuming illness than his age. He retained the same serenity in his eyes, although he no longer smoked his beloved cigars. He received us in a small living room whose walls were filled with pictures of family members, some faded and yellowed with age.

The decor was characteristic of the living rooms of middle-class families of medium income and was later copied by lower-class families. Colored photos filled the walls of the living room, always displayed under the picture of the heart of Jesus. Pictures rarely missing were the engagement or marriage pictures of the owners, often placed close to pictures of their children's first communions.

Martins spoke of his past, which for him was a better time than that of our visit. He spoke of my father, mother, uncles, and aunts. Above all, he spoke of my Uncle Rodovalho as, he said, "a friend always." He spoke of Adelino with a smile and a look that faded away, indicating a soft nostalgia. He spoke about some of Adelino's exploits, his courage, and loyalty.

During that night of heavy rain, my father, Martins, Adelino, and Zé Paiva, the husband of one of my father's aunts, prepared a poker table. To the side of the table, but not far away, my mother and one of my aunts embroidered and conversed. Next to them was my sister Stela.

Near the table, my older brothers and I curiously observed the exchange of cards, but my interest in the game was diminished by my fear, provoked by the loud thunder and bright lightening, which to this day I still dislike. Cards exchanged hands, words filled the time as the cards were dealt.

Adelino began to lose. One, two, three times. If he had a pair, somebody else had two pairs. If he had three of a kind, somebody else had a straight.

All of a sudden, with rage in his eyes, his hands curled into fists, he threw his cards on the table and said, in macho language that was offensive to the women, "Your mother is a whore."

The heavy silence that followed left him embarrassed. He got up, uneasy, almost losing his composure—he no longer knew what to do with his hands. Visibly embarrassed, he hitched his pants up his belly to where his belt could hold them more comfortably. He looked around, his eyes sparkling with a different shine. His eyes were like those of a child sorry for doing something bad. He spoke timidly even though he had a forceful character. Given the social context, he knew that he had made a big mistake: He should not have spoken those words in the presence of women or girls. He knew that he had committed an unforgivable action and had no other choice but to apologize. He said, "Forgive me."

"You are forgiven," replied my father.

Shortly after, without saying a word, he crossed to the door, opening it softly. It was raining heavily. The rain poked holes in the ground, making its own geography—islands, lakes, and puddles. Adelino left by himself. The rain soaked his body, his soul, his anger, and his regrets.

At home, the game was over. A conversation without much color was attempted but it could not be maintained. Adelino's words, which had filled the entire room, now emptied it. A heavy silence took over, hanging over everyone, covering the table, contouring the walls, and underlining the sound of the thunder.

Some years later, my Grandmother Adozinha returned a book by José Lins do Rego to my Aunt Esther, who was like a second mother to me, for reasons of the same morality that caused Adelino to leave the poker table on that stormy night. In remembering that distant night, which involved all those present in the living room, I now think that even though I had been socialized to be open, creative, and critical, my socialization was also characterized by such limitations as the censoring of language considered impure or even remotely sexual. This was one of the contradictions I experienced while growing up. On the one hand, I was stimulated to grow; on the other hand, I experienced a repressive puritanism that, I must admit, was not too overwhelming. Other families were much more rigid than ours. Those families were tormented by the affliction of pursuing the shadow of sin in everything and everybody. I believe that the openness in my family was decisively due to my father's influence.

At any rate, when I was seven years old I broke my leg while swinging on ropes with my brothers in the late afternoon. Because the fracture was quite high, near my hips, I was taught to say in a well-mannered tone, "I fractured my femur." To say "hips" was not considered proper. It connoted sensuality and was part of the geography of sin. During my mother's generation, the demands of morality were much worse. She could not speak of anything above her ankle. In those days, to speak during a family reunion in somebody's living room about the beauty of a woman's legs was an infraction of high social cost to anyone who should dare it.

Under such circumstances, I learned early on that certain terrains could not be traveled by my childhood curiosity. Answers to our sexual questions were, little by little, found among my brothers and their older friends.

If some naively established a radical connection between knowledge and virtue, the mature generation of my time, on the contrary, established our ignorance concerning sexual questions and our distorted comprehension as the best road to virtue. A child was that much more pure if he or she believed, or pretended to believe, that we were delivered into this world by the serviceable stork.

As I am writing, I remember an incident that a great friend of mine who is a German theologian told. He belonged to a younger generation than mine. I think the story he relayed is worth citing as the ultimate example of puritanism, of an ancient and universal sexual repression that is suffocation, and against which we should fight more and more. My friend and I were sitting at a table talking about sexual repression and the inhibiting taboos that marred almost every woman and man of our generation. He then told me a story about a classmate from a Protestant theological seminary he attended. The young classmate of my German friend, full of doubts concerning his father's behavior, repeated to my friend a dialogue he had heard one night from his parents' room, which was next to his bedroom.

What he heard was the following. "No, no, not today," his mother had said, begging, while his father, categorically, had responded, "I have a call from God that I must obey—I have to bring more shepherds into this world." In the sexual relations of that couple, there was no way to admit the possibility of pleasure and sexual play since these represented only the wickedness of sin. What they had in their sexual encounter was the fulfillment of a "bureaucratic" duty to bring more shepherds into this world.

The new generation of urban youth is now so open that they could not live such a distorted sexuality. While sexuality is not limited to the act of lovemaking, the new comprehension does not leave out the full expression of a right—the legitimate right to have pleasure. The new generation cannot accept the baseless and sick dichotomy between the body and the soul. They can no longer accept the notion that the body is the fountain of imperfection, of sinful desires, while the soul is the purity that may be lost through the temptation of the sinful body, which leads the soul to be overcome by desire.

I am not surprised nor do I feel threatened by the new generation of youth, who may sometimes exceed not only in their understanding of sexuality but also in their practice of it. There is no necessary rebelliousness that does not advance discourse and action. Once in a while, as part of a language of critique, rebellion searches to transcend outmoded puritanical distortions. In order to rectify what has been exaggerated, one sometimes also exaggerates.

The role of educators, in such moments, should not be to accept peacefully what is exaggerated by uncritical rebelliousness. Nor should educators merely reject rebellious denunciation, since such a posture would place them alongside reactionary traditionalists. The role of the educator, who is critical and who understands the phenomenon, should be to embrace the rebellious critique while pointing out its tactical mistake. And he or she should not reject the strategic adroitness of those who err tactically. To reject a critique because of a tactical mistake represents a form of opposing the strategic dream while giving the false impression of adhering to the dream. On the other hand, to accept the tactical mistake without a fight, without protest, represents a friendliness with the mistake that works against utopia. A coherent, progressive educator has to be attentive to the always tense relations between tactic and strategy. We must learn about these relations since without the knowledge of them we may fall into a form of incoherence that leads us to sacrifice our strategic dream.

Fourth Letter

~

More than anything else, I felt like I was being expelled, thrown out of my sense of security.

LEAVING RECIFE IN 1932, leaving the relatively large house where I was born and my first world, to go to Jaboatão was a traumatic experience, although I was curious about the changes the move would create. We left Recife due to the difficulties our family had begun to experience two or three years earlier; one of my maternal uncles, Rodovalho, was forced to propose the move. These difficulties would have been felt earlier if it had not been for my uncle's help when my father became inactive due to his health. The move that April morning so long ago yanked me from my preferred world, separating me from my beloved trees, the canary that sang every early morning from the roof of our house, and the friends with whom I used to play. Albino Fernandes Vital was one of them and remains a brotherly friend to this day. He is well known, more outside Brazil than among us, as a scientist in his field of phytopathology. And there were Pedro and Sérgio, sons of Mr. Zuza, who was the music leader of a band that never got beyond the rehearsal stage. There was a tall, very beautiful girl of whom, every day on my way to school, the School Group Mathias de Albuquerque, I would dream, planning to tell her, "You are beautiful and I like you." But I never had the courage, and I went on being content with the desire to tell her rather than actually telling her. The desire to tell her that she was beautiful was so strong that at times it was as if I had told her so. Sometimes, the entire route from my house (she was my neighbor) to school felt like part of a long conversation in which she would say that she also liked me. In those days of 1932, this tall girl had for me the same importance that Tereza had for Bandeira (as he speaks of it in his *Poesias*, published in 1955).

The move yanked me from a new experience in my schooling: It cut short my three months in school with Aurea Bahia, one of the teachers I have already referred to. She has a strong presence in my memory.

More than anything else, I felt like I was being expelled, thrown out of my sense of security. I experienced a fear that I had not felt before. It was as if I were dying a little. Today I know that I was feeling, in those instances of fear, a second experience of semiconscious exile. The first was my arrival into the world after leaving the security of my mother's uterus.

The two trucks that my father had contracted to move our belongings arrived early. The movers almost immediately began their task while I silently assisted them from a corner of our old house's terrace by not obstructing their hurried coming and going. I watched the furniture, piece by piece, being moved out of our house.

In those days, the organization of work had been created by the people, with rudimentary techniques that the workers strictly followed called *calungas de caminhão*,[1] which made the workers more efficient. The driver understood these techniques well and placed the truck near the door for the best access to the furniture. These techniques also determined what piece of furniture had to be taken out of the house first and positioned on the truck bed to make the best use of available space and to maintain balance.

Before the move I had participated in another one that had been less important since it involved moving within the same neighborhood. What impressed me most about the movers' technique was how they carried the piano on their heads, protected by beautiful and well-made cushions, and sang at the same time, establishing a body rhythm that distributed the weight among themselves, four strong men sweating. A relationship linked their body rhythm, the speed with which they walked, and the distribution of weight among the men, which was mediated by the cadence and speed of their movement, and determined by the musicality of the song.

I watched all the furniture, piece by piece, leave the house. Lourdes's German piano, the straw chairs, the old drawing table from the last century, the pestle for grinding roasted coffee beans, and the copper pans for the corn soup on the feast of Saint Johns.[2] The hands[3] of sweet corn were always bought the day before. We all took part in preparing the corn husks, getting the ears ready to be shaved. The shaved sweet corn was added to a portion of coconut milk and put over the fire in copper pans that had been rigorously cleaned. Once on the fire, the patient work of mixing the corn would begin. Although the entire process of making the corn soup was pleasing to me, I was most curious when little by little, the liquid mass began to thicken and then, all of a sudden, change from liquid to a near solid. This signaled that the corn soup was ready.

Another moment is impossible for me to forget. With spoon in hand, we used to argue over what remained in the pan after the corn soup had been transferred to the old serving bowls of my grandmother. At night, we added cinnamon powder to some of the bowls, making designs on the corn soup. We gave these to our closest neighbors who had brought plates of food to us on other occasions. Under the rubric of courtesy, each family participated in a kind of culinary competition, a competition that was not expressed out loud, to make the best corn soup on the street.

With the intensification of the economic crisis, the production of corn soup diminished. It diminished, but it always continued.

All of this cooking took place under the rigorous but effective direction of Dada. Dada had raised my mother and was now raising my sister Stela. Dada's love for Stela and her preoccupation with her were such that she often would wake Stela to make sure that she was sleeping.

Three years after we arrived in Jaboatão, Dada died of tuberculosis. Fortunately, this happened in our house and not at the hospital, despite our economic crisis. She died surrounded by the comfort of everyone. I remember a serious conversation, balanced and not sentimental, in which my mother explained to us the need to struggle to provide Dada with all the things she needed to fight for her life. This required that we reduce the little that we were eating in order to help her, consciously acting on the commitment that our family had to her, and demonstrating to her, in her last moments in this world, the love we had for her.

I do not know if Dada knew that she was dying. Perhaps she thought she was just tired and old. On a calm afternoon, in the same room in which my father had died the year before, Dada died.

I watched the furniture, piece by piece, leave the house. But it was not only the house that was being emptied out. I also felt empty, still sitting quietly, on the terrace, from which I moved only to enter one of the trucks with my father, who also was quiet. As the truck began to move slowly, he looked, for the last time, at my mother's garden, a garden she had defended so many times against the attacks of rats. He only looked, he did not say a word. Nor did he speak during the entire trip from Recife to Jaboatão, which was, in those days, quite a long trip.

Fifth Letter

~

To this day, I never point out someone's mistakes twice,
nor can I stand it when people do so to me.

BORN IN RIO GRANDE DO NORTE, my father migrated to Recife
while still young, at the beginning of the century, bringing with him only
a certificate of his studies in the humanities and a taste for adventure. It
seems that his taste for adventure was paired with a distaste for forced
coexistence with an authoritarian stepfather, who wanted nothing to do
with my father's open nature.

Shortly thereafter, he "settled" in the army, which he left after attain-
ing the rank of sergeant. He transferred to the Pernambuco Military
Police with that rank, at a time when a new state government was
invested in reforming the police.

It wasn't until three years after I was born that he retired, with the
rank of captain, due to a case of arterial sclerosis, which caused his death
in 1934.

One of his examples, which greatly influenced us, his sons and
daughter, in our formative years, and of which we spoke at home, was his
lack of hypocrisy. For instance, he was not involved in certain developments among the officers of the Pernambuco Military Police back in the
1920s. I am referring to the military personnel who—disguised as "poor
bums" while being in fact murderers—joined the so-called "handkerchief
gang,"[1] a group known for its violent attacks on and persecution of jour-
nalists who opposed the government. Not before one of these acts of

violence, still common today—our recent history is filled with the tortured and the disappeared—resulted in a famous journalist being killed was the shameful violence put to an end.

My father was usually sent on some mission outside Recife whenever the police planned to beat a journalist. Because they could not count on him—never even going so far as to approach him on the topic—the top command responsible for the atrocious acts removed him every time there was to be a new attack.

I remember that, in spite of our early years, we felt good that our father was not dirtying his hands with such filthy business.

As a result, we most valued our family's experience with the difficulties we had to face. One day, I surprised my father sitting in his bedroom next to my mother and crying due to his powerlessness before the obstacles he faced in providing his family with a minimum of comfort. It was worth a great deal to me to get a hug from him, to feel his wet face on mine, and to be certain of the reason why he cried.

All we suffered gives us today the invaluable comfort of being able to speak about our father without any arrogance or grandeur, it is true, but with legitimate satisfaction in a serious and honorable man.

His forced retirement brought him closer to all of us. He would take every opportunity he had to engage one of his sons or his daughter in conversation. Never did he indulge in erudite lecturing, nor did he force conversation on a topic which did not interest us. He questioned and challenged us while introducing us to different topics.

He was available to us at all times, including those hours he dedicated to his studies or to his carpentry work in an improvised and somewhat precarious workshop.

At various times he tried to supplement his limited income as a retired captain with whatever he could get for his work as a "carpenter." He made artistic birdcages; lawn chairs; stools; and backgammon, checkers, and domino sets. Failure was often the result, and he would give his work away as gifts to friends.

One day, inspired by the weekly trips a friend took to Recife to bring merchandise from the interior—a town called Belo Jardim, where my Uncle Monteiro had become mayor after the 1930 revolution—my father came up with the idea of "importing" pumpkins, brown sugar,

his conversations with my Uncle João Monteiro, a government opposition journalist who, due to his bravery and conscience, seemed to spend
three days in jail for every two at home.

I remember his constant comments about the disrespect for liberty,
the abuse of power, the arrogance of the rulers, the silencing of the
people, the disrespect for public property, and corruption, which he
called "out-of-control pillage."

He taught us about democracy not only through the example that he
set—his respect for us, our rights, and his way of establishing necessary
limits to our freedom through his authority—but also by the sensible and
fair criticism he offered of the abuses of the powerful. Still, there were
some practical portions of those lessons on democracy. One of them was
the concrete opportunity he had to show us the opposite of freedom, as
lived by himself.

With loose and prematurely gray hair, exuding the peace of those who
have done their duty, he would almost weekly cross our backyard—he
lived next door but our backyard gave him access to two streets—accompanied by the moron who escorted him on his visits to the "refrigerator."
That is what we called the cell where the regime would "put him away" for
the "crime" of advocating the right to criticize the abuses of the powerful.
The nickname was derived from the "generous" act of the police, who in
defense of the rights of "subversive agitators" would flood the cells with
cold water at short intervals.

João Monteiro was as much a victim of the "handkerchief gang"
spirit, which killed Trajano Chacon, as Wladimir Herzog, Rubens Paiva,
Miriam Verbena,[3] and millions of Brazilians killed in the most cowardly
manner during the 1964 military coup.

So many weekends did he spend in the "comfort" of the cell reserved
for him by the violent general inspector of the Pernambuco Civil Police,
Ramos de Freitas, that João Monteiro came down with tuberculosis and
went in search of better air in the interior of the state. Still, he died of the
disease in 1935.

I used to live in Jaboatão, and I remember going to the train station
to see him for the last time during a five-minute stop on the São Caetano
train, as it was known.

He was broken spirited: his shoulders hunched in, his voice hoarse and difficult. He looked at me, smiled. "God bless you. Come see me," he said, the train already in motion.

In 1928, I listened to my father and my Uncle Monteiro say that it was not only necessary to change the state of things, but urgent. The country was being destroyed, robbed, humiliated. They used that notorious phrase, "Brazil is right on the edge of the abyss." These are the kinds of things they would talk about: "They won't speak, and if they do, they won't be heard; they'll be oppressed."

They referred here to Vieira.

In a greeting to the marquess of Montalvão, viceroy of Brazil, at the Misericórdia Hospital in Bahia in 1638, Vieira said, in the most political of all his sermons, that the silence imposed by the crown was one of Brazil's worst predicaments.

> We well know, those of us who speak the Latin language that this word *infans, infante,* means one who does not speak. That was the state the boy Baptist was in when Our Lady came to visit him. This is also the state in which Brazil has been for many years, which, in my view, has been the major cause of its troubles. Since the patient cannot speak, all conjectures are difficult medicine. That is why, of all the sufferers Christ cured, none required so much time or care as the dumb possessed man: the worst accident Brazil suffered in its infirmity was that of doing away with its own voice. Many times it may have wanted to righteously complain, many times it may have wanted to ask for the medicine to cure its condition, but respect or violence has always drowned the words in its throat, and if ever a word has made it to the ears of those who should provide a remedy, so have the voices of power, to ensure victory for the claims of reason.

Brazil wastes away, My Lord, (let us say it in one word) because some ministers of His Majesty do not come here to seek our welfare, but rather to seek our wealth.[4]

Vieira played with the meanings of "taking," at times using it to mean the act of accepting responsibility, control, and at times to mean

the act of possessing what belongs to others, robbery. Vieira went so far
as to say to the Marquess of Montalvão and his entourage:

> The King orders them [the ministers] to take Pernambuco, and
> they are content to take it. This taking possession of what is
> others', whether by the King or by the peoples, is the source of
> [Brazil's] disease. And the various arts and ways and instru-
> ments of taking are the symptoms that, being extremely
> dangerous by nature, make the disease even more lethal. I ask,
> just so the causes of the symptoms become better known: In this
> land, does the minister of justice take? Yes, he takes. Does the
> minister of finance? Yes, he takes. Does the minister of the
> republic? Yes, he takes. Does the minister of the militia? Yes, he
> takes. Does the minister of state? Yes, he takes.[5]

Joaquim Nabuco in 1879, giving a speech about a project for consti-
tutional reform, said:

> Gentlemen the project being currently discussed comes to this
> registry under the saddest of auspices. It is a project that has
> been debated by a council of ministers, resolved in ministerial
> conference, and for that reason, I said, and the honorable repre-
> sentative from Piauí [Mr. Dória] seconded my expression, that
> the investigative record on this parliamentary initiative has
> languished on the minister of justice's desk. The project was
> discussed with the emperor, was the object of transactions
> within the ministry leading to the termination of two of its
> most prominent members, and, only after having gone through
> all these procedures and investigations, arrived at this house,
> where it was endorsed by a vast majority on the same day.[6]

In the 1954 gubernatorial race in Pernambuco between industrialist
João Cleofas and General Cordeiro de Farias, in which the communist
supported the former, the Recife Front was divided between voting for
Cleofas and voting for "blank," says Paulo Cavalcanti.

Two days prior, the stretch of Imperial Street at the Sérgio Loreto Square, the location of the newsroom and press for *Folha do Povo*, a communist-controlled newspaper in Pernambuco, was without electricity. Complaints to the competent department at Pernambuco Transways yielded no results. It was said that unidentified technical difficulties were the cause of the blackout. Electricity service was resumed the day after the elections. Between the eve of the election and the election on Sunday, a false edition of *Folha do Povo*, a perfect replica of the paper, with the usual titles and clichés, was circulated. The headlines read, in huge letters: "Communists Should Vote Blank." An alleged manifesto by Prestes followed, recommending that no one vote for industrialist Cleofas. All sections of the city were flooded with this false edition of the paper. Police cars were in charge of delivering the paper to the doors of all electoral sections; hundreds of investigators were mobilized for the job.... In spite of using such sneaky tactics, General Cordeiro de Farias lost the election in the capital, the "Cruel City" once again experiencing a moment of invincibility.[7]

Authoritarianism continues today, as does disrespect for public property, looting, and palace scandals. The Collored or de-Collored PC's[8] move on, devastating the country with a shameless lack of accountability. They steal, they kill, they violate, they kidnap, and nothing or almost nothing happens. A whole population of prisoners is slaughtered in a most cowardly manner;[9] the dead are blamed and the semantics of the word "carnage" discussed.

To them, deceit is a virtue, dirty business the model. Shamelessness is the example to follow.

None of these tragedies, however, in spite of the force with which they are repeated or the lack of accountability, should constitute a reason for apathy or fatalism. On the contrary, they should push us into the hopeful fight, and with no option of surrender.

It is incredible how the dominant classes of this country, even in their most advanced capitalist sectors, repeat the habits and procedures that reek of colonialism.

The dominant classes' arrogance in dealing with the popular classes—their contempt; their greed; their exploitation; their authoritarianism; their hypocritical discourse, shamelessly in opposition to their actions; and their unsustainable excuses for discrimination—has, over time, silenced or attempted to silence the Brazilian people.

Today, as they were yesterday, my father and my Uncle Monteiro would be against the oppression of the working class, for the protection of the weak, and against the arrogance of the powerful. They would be shocked by their insensitivity. They would be fighting side by side with the millions of Brazilians who have repudiated dictatorial rule throughout our history. Today, they would be against those who believe that workers' strikes are the expression of subversives who, eternally dissatisfied, seek to destabilize the government, which is supposedly democratic and loves all workers.

Many times, under the shade of the trees at the house where I was born and which I left to live in Jaboatão, I heard them talking, even if I could not always understand everything they said about the need for change in Brazil.

That rainy morning, in the departing truck, submerged in silence, my father was a different man. His silence, however, which in other circumstances might have affected me, did not matter then. His silence coincided with my own. We both had the same reason, just felt on different levels. I did not ask him anything, as the truck slowly lumbered away, and I was glad that he did not ask me anything either.

The driver also respected our pact. He didn't ask anything either. He said nothing, except for a thank-you when my father offered him a cigarette.

Sixth Letter

~

Today, from the vantage point of my seventy-two years of age, I can look far back into the past and clearly see the extent to which language and its comprehension have always been of concern to me.

JABOATÃO, A SMALL MUNICIPALITY, was a provincial town when we arrived. Today it is part of what is called greater Recife. In 1932, the town was already beginning to experience the expansion of the big city, which enfolded Jaboatão as one of its suburbs.

Jaboatão's industry consisted of sugarcane farms, reduced to supplying two or three medium-sized sugar plants; a paper factory belonging, at the time, to a German group; some small and primitive gravel factories; the repair bays of the old Great Western, today the Federal Railroad Company; a small retail industry; and two or three company stores[1] that supplied the farms and sugar plants. These were the main sources of employment for the municipality's rural and urban populations, in addition to an incipient municipal and state bureaucracy.

A few small elementary schools, precarious in every sense, were scattered, as if sprinkled, around the rural area. A few state schools existed in the urban center which, in spite of being run by teachers with degrees and having more resources, were mediocre.

An exception to the educational feebleness of the place were two outstanding educators, Cecília Brandão and Odete Antunes. The former, previously mentioned in these letters, patiently and effectively helped me to overcome some of the gaps in my schooling. In public and private schools, throughout their long lives, both made an indisputable contribution to the generations that passed through their classrooms. Both deserve to have their lives and practices as educators studied.

An extraordinary woman, Cecília was a blend of tradition and modernity. She combined, at sixty years of age, full-length dresses, long sleeves, and high necklines with a curiosity about the sciences and the world. She graduated from the University of Recife's law school at the age of sixty, respected and well liked by all of her colleagues and teachers. A lover of Latin and grammar (without being a grammar freak), she was also a pianist with an equal fondness for Brazilian *chorinhos* and the classical music of Beethoven and Mozart.

Many times, visiting us on sunny afternoons, she would play Lourdes's German piano, giving short recitals for the family which I always attended.

She knew the financial difficulties we went through, and many times she helped in one way or another. During one of her visits, she told my mother before she started playing that she would love to have me as one of her students. In a delicate and yet direct manner, she made it clear that she expected no payment for her work. She just wanted to help me, teach me, reviewing the things I already knew and working on those I didn't.

Cecília Brandão and Aluízio Pessoa de Araújo[2] had a lot to do with my education. Without Cecília, I hardly would have made it to Osvaldo Cruz High School. Without Aluízio, I would not have gained as much life experience as I did. Cecília awoke in me the almost limitless longing for language, which still accompanies me today. My interest in language included, initially, a joy in studying grammar, without ever giving into grammaticism. This inclination would later be reinforced and deepened at the Osvaldo Cruz High School[3] under the influence of Professor José Pessoa da Silva, then a young law student at the University of Recife.

Today, from the vantage point of my seventy-two years of age, I can look far back into the past and clearly see the extent to which language and its comprehension have always been of concern to me. It is interesting to note, for example, that the first significant influence I received in this area, which I can see clearly today, was from Eunice Vasconcelos, previously mentioned in these letters. Eunice was my first professional teacher, the one who taught me how to "make sentences." She paved the way for Cecília, José Pessoa, and Moacir de Albuquerque.

It was José Pessoa who, while I was still a student at Osvaldo Cruz School, suggested to his director, Aluízio, that I teach Portuguese.

Pessoa loaned me his books to study, and he introduced me to famous professors from around Recife, among whom were José Lourenço de Lima and José Brasileiro. A learned a great deal in unguarded, brotherly conversations with these masters.

Moacir de Albuquerque, brilliant and passionate in everything he did, not only loved the literature he taught—if indeed it is possible to teach literature—but also loved the act of teaching itself. He instilled something in me that Pessoa had hinted at in his classes. He instilled an awareness of how joyful and important it is to seek the aesthetic moment, the beauty of language.

Not only in his classes, but also at his house, to which he would invite me for lunch or dinner once in a while, he called my attention to the zealous study of discourse. He would refer to those like Gilberto Freyre, Machado de Assis, and Eça de Queiroz as scholars who corrupted the Portuguese language, "de-boned" it. He always mentioned Graciliano Ramos, Manuel Bandeira, Carlos Drummond de Andrade, and Lins do Rego. The last I was introduced to in Rio by my friend Odilon Ribeiro Coutinho, who today is a writer—something that would delight Moacir de Albuquerque if he were alive. Odilon Ribeiro Coutinho is a writer and talker as very few are. Whether he is talking or writing about the "wet mysteries" of Lins do Rego, or about the dry elegance of Graciliano Ramos, or about the sensual contours of Gilberto Freyre, or about Picasso, Matisse, Lula Cardoso Aires, Brenand, or Rego Monteiro, it doesn't matter, Odilon never talks for talk's sake nor does he write just to prove he is a writer.

Gilberto Freyre once told me with admiration—in a seaside conversation on the Itamaracá Island; the first and last conversation I had with him after my return from exile—about the unconventional manner in which Odilon treated language, both in writing and in speaking.

But, allow me to go back to reliving Jaboatão, some of its peoples, and some of the plots in which I became involved. It is not possible to do so without talking about Jaboatão's rivers, one of which—the one which bathed me the most, the Duas Unas—came from afar, snaking through the city, and was full of beautiful spots, including small quasi-bays we called "bowls" surrounded by Ingá trees that made the water golden with pollen, where boys bathed, swam, fished, and stared, their hearts pound-ing, at women bathing naked. The Duas Unas river ran into the Jaboatão river right at the site of the paper factory and two sugarcane plants, which dumped into the rivers all their juices. The paper factory and the sugar plants polluted and disfigured the rivers.[4]

When we arrived in Jaboatão, the rivers had not yet been degraded in the name of a perverse notion of development and as a function of the power of the powerful. The rivers were still alive. We used to bathe in them without any fear; on the contrary, their waters were clear and warm, rarely cold, they almost caressed us. They did hold, it is true, a great and then unknown threat for marginal populations: Lyme disease. But they were free of all the dirt that has now taken over so many Brazilian rivers, free of those white foamy borders that increasingly form on the banks of condemned rivers.

There was life in them, fish, shrimp, lobster, and fresh-water weeds. And in the rivers we experienced intense life.

It was because of our proximity to the Duas Unas that my brothers and I changed, though not suddenly of course. Moving from a tree-shaded urban backyard to a new sociological context—that of river-bank dwellers—changed our whole psychology.

We changed because the new contours challenged our bodies and our sexuality with new stimuli. Previously, in Recife, we lived among large shady trees and very close to grown-ups. In Jaboatão, by the river, we had the opportunity to see naked women's bodies.

We left the enclosed backyard of a house to live with all that the water "road" of a river implied, including the road's invitation for us to expose ourselves to it. Soon, in particular my brother Temístocles and myself, we became explorers of the road of the river.

Our financial crisis, which simply moving from Recife to Jaboatão we could not expect to overcome, taught us very quickly to make our own toys and fishing rods with safety-pin hooks. The water road, the same river that called and attracted us, offered banks filled with birds (*sabiás, sanhaçus, frei-vicentes,* and water-chickens) and water filled with different kinds of fish (*gundelos, piabas, carás, camarões, aratanhas, pitus,* and *aruás*).

A boy named Ubaldino Figueiroa, whom we called Dino, today a prosperous and honorable trader in Jaboatão, was one of the best friends we made and his friendship continues as well today as it did in 1932. He was the one who introduced us to the adventure of sneaking into the riverside backyards along the water road that was the Duas Unas.

We used to fish in its waters and hunt in the backyards along its banks. We played soccer in fields—sometimes improvised, sometimes institutionalized—in lots along the river.

One field, the most famous one, was located along the most beautiful stretch of the river. At that point, the river was a straight line for about two-hundred meters and banks were covered by Ingá trees and green, round bushes. Grammy was the name of the field.

We played incredibly lively soccer matches there and then would swim in the popular swimming style, with no set style or rules.

That beautiful stretch of the river was an attraction for children and adults alike, who came from different points in the city. The fresh water and the green of the banks, the opportunity to swim, whether classic swimming or popular style, all that made the place a people's club, a little beach.

It was always possible to make new friends there. We heard many stories about ghosts—their cries of pain, derisive laughter, even the creaking sound of their bull cart—that inhabited the darkness of the nights in the land of old sugar-cane farms surrounding the city of Jaboatão.

One of the opportunities the oppressed have—in dominated cultures and pretechnological cultures that conceive of an imaginary level—is to attribute suffering and divine punishment to the oppressor's soul. Cruel foremen's souls, it is often said, make "appearances" in the form of loud lamentations during nights of the crescent moon, crying or growling with remorse. For the oppressed, given this level of comprehension of history, imagining, even knowing, that the cruel foreman's soul weeps and wanders, lost because of the evil it practiced while living and protected by the lord, is a certainty that consoles.

It is possible that some of the ghost stories[5] I heard in my childhood, especially the ones I heard in Jaboatão rather than the ones I heard in Recife, may have operated through me, without my knowing it, in shaping my comprehension of struggle in history. The stories may have shaped my understanding of the right and the duty to fight, which the oppressed must seize in order to overcome oppression. Ideally, the oppressed's mobilization, organization, and struggle will begin to change the quality of their culture and of history. Damned souls will begin to be replaced by the live presence of the oppressed, of the popular classes, in the transformation of the world. Ideally, by exercising their right to believe in God, in God's goodness, in God's justice, in God's presence in history, the oppressed, as a class and as individuals, will take history into their own hands and will recognize that making history and being history is the duty of men and women; it is theirs. The ideal lies in punishing the perverse—the killers of popular leadership, of country folk, and forest people—here and now. The ideal is to punish them in history, not in the imagination, effectively and with justice. The ideal is in overcoming our weakness and impotence by no longer concerning ourselves with punishing the souls of the unjust, by "making them" wander with cries of remorse. Precisely because it is the live, conscious body of the cruel person that needs to weep, we must punish them in society, which reinvents itself to humanize itself.

On a certain sunny Sunday morning, Temístocles, Dino, and myself were warming our bodies in a moment of rest from our swimming. A boy our age engaged us in conversation. He came from an area deep in the city, a very populated area that was almost rural in its lack of amenities.

Entre Rios was the name of the neighborhood. I haven't seen Entre Rios in many years. No doubt it has changed as much as the Duas Unas changed, as much as my body has changed.

I do not remember the boy's name, and I regret not creating a closer friendship with him. But his memory stayed with us because of the story he told. It was about his experience in school and his fear of the rough teacher whose profile the boy tried to demonstrate by holding his hands and arms out to suggest the teacher's roundness. "Mr." Armada was his name. The doings of Mr. Armada, his foreman way of being a teacher, his authoritarianism, his violent methods, were well described by the boy.

Today, whenever I remember this story, I feel that the boy's narrative was his way of purging his fear so that he could face the threat of Mr. Armada the following day. It was as if he needed to become more intimate with the danger. To speak as he did of Mr. Armada was a magical way of reducing the risk. And he did it so well that he inspired in us—

Temístocles, Dino, and myself—an uncontrollable desire to go to the area of domination. That was what we did, two days later, helped by the directions our friend had given us.

Mr. Armada was a tall man, a man of the people, of little education, and as fat as Adelino, but a lot younger than him and certainly without the moments of kindness with which Adelino softened his roughness.

None of the children who lived in the area had any peace just thinking that they might end up enrolled at his famous school. It was a private school in the small living room of his house, with more children than space.

"Move it Pedrinho, hurry up, boy. If you continue like this I'll end up throwing you in Mr. Armada's school." This must have been how mothers and fathers encouraged their Pedrinhos and Carminhas to behave.

Just from hearing the stories about the teacher, I strongly reacted against him. On hearing the stories our friend had told us at the river, I dreamed of seeing Mr. Armada prohibited from owning a school and being made to kneel down on corn kernels, so mean was he to the kids.

As we got closer to Mr. Armada's "village," we knew we were in the right neighborhood. We could hear an oral drill, sounding like the tones of rosary prayer.

"A B plus A makes BA, a B plus E makes BE, a B plus I makes BI, a B plus O makes BO, a B plus U makes BU.

"BA, BE, BI, BO, BU. BA, BE, BI, BO, BU.

"BA BA, BE BE, BI BI, BO BO, BU BU, BA, BE, BI, BO, BU."

We stopped about ninety feet from the little school, in the shade of a tree, not knowing exactly what to do. There was a silence and then another drill began. "1 plus 1, 2; 1 plus 2, 3; 1 plus 3, 4; 1 plus 4, 5; 1 plus 5, 6; 1 plus 6, 7; 1 plus 7, 8; 1 plus 8, 9; 1 plus 9, 10."

We heard Mr. Armada's strong, booming voice, "4 plus 2, 6; 4 plus 2, 6."

All of a sudden we heard an unusual noise and saw this skinny boy, quick as an arrow, almost fly out of the house. Behind him, with an irate face, enraged eyes, and waving arms, Mr. Armada and his kilos came running at a disadvantage. The boy shot by us like a bullet, at least thirty or forty feet ahead of Mr. Armada. All of a sudden, as if he had run over his own anger, Mr. Armada tripped and fell straight down to the ground. His blue jeans ripped at the knee and he bled from the fall of his full weight against the hard, dry ground. Mr. Armada yelled at the boy, saying that the boy would not escape his anger, his punishment, his violence. Half-sitting, he turned to the little school, which had emptied of children. Scared, they stood on the street looking at his fallen body and anger. Mr. Armada, for his part, yelled and screamed, threatening everything and everybody.

Mr. Armada had fallen only four feet away from us. We could see the full extent of his anger. Anger at the boy who had provoked him, anger at the humiliation of his heavy body tumbling to the ground, anger at the pain of his bleeding knee, and anger at the boy's temporary victory.

I could see all those angers on his face, the rage in his eyes.

The neighbors came quickly and helped Mr. Armada up, while the kids, overtaken by a great fear, returned silently to the school.

Perhaps Mr. Armada's fall, his big body striking the ground, his failed effort to sit up, his defeat by the accident, helped the kids understand that Mr. Armada was also vulnerable. He had tripped, tumbled, and fallen.

That might explain the rebelliousness with which the children of the area were seized by after the episode. Our friend told us, another time by the river, that Mr. Armada was now harassed every time he walked the streets of his neighborhood. Some kid was always hiding around a corner, behind a tree, to yell, "Did Mr. Armada fall? Yes, he did. Did Mr. Armada cry? Yes, he did."

The more the soft voice of the oppressed makes fun of the oppressor (while the body of the oppressed is hidden, unreachable), the more the voice becomes capable of robbing the oppressor of peace. At some point, the oppressor becomes feeble.

Mr. Armada began to feel afraid of walking the streets, in spite of his power, his fame.

It is even possible, though I can't say for sure, that he softened up in his classes.

Mr. Armada was no exception or cultural deviation. There are plenty of other Armadas whose iron-handed discipline of students is well liked by parents who feel that harsh discipline will make their children serious people.

Years later, in Recife, when I worked at the Social Service for Industry (SESI), I spent fifteen days visiting hills and small rivers in popular areas. I entered as many popular schools as I could find to talk with the teachers. Authoritarianism remained. I found many spanking paddles with the inscription "Calms the heart."

The Brazilian authoritarian tradition, the experience of slavery, the abuse of power that cuts through all social classes, all explain Mr. Armada. Mr. Armada could not exist if he were an unpleasant exception.

Mr. Armada did not oppose, quite the contrary, he affirmed our authoritarian tradition.

Today, sixty-two years after Mr. Armada's adventure, the "pedagogy of hitting" is still defended and practiced by a number of families, regardless of social class. In contrast, a second pedagogy rises, just as negative, the pedagogy of permissiveness, according to which kids can do whatever they want.

By denying both the pedagogy of hitting and of permissiveness, let us hope that a new democratic practice will take root, one where authority does not surpass its limits and drown freedom nor is nullified by hypertrophied freedom. Let us hope, instead, that by limiting freedom we will limit authority.

There were two musical bands, one called the Railway Band, made up of office workers from the Great Western Railways in Northeast Brazil; the other called Banda Paroquial, organized and directed by an extraordinary artist and priest, Father Cromácio Leão. On most Sunday nights during the summer these bands would alternate playing. These celebrated evening roll calls would bring to the city's modest plaza boys and girls, men and women, young and old to applaud their favorite band.

Musical bands, no matter where in the midland cities, had, among other roles, the important purpose of bringing people out onto the streets where they would meet one another and talk. During one season of the year, the musical bands competed against one another. They would take each other's measure, rehearsing in front of their decorated gazebos.

In January they celebrated, and they continue to celebrate to this day, the patron saint of the city, Saint Amaro. It was a time to show off new clothes, new shoes. I will never forget the striking colors, mostly shades of red, that characterized the clothes of the dark-haired peasants who came to pay homage to their saint and, of course, ask him for a better year.

"The greatest adversary of Banda Paroquial," the scholar Van-Hoeven Veloso would say, "was the Railway Band." The two bands always engaged in the hottest disputes. One day, as Veloso remembers,

> a civic commemoration ended with an evening roll call by these two bands in the Plaza Dantas Barreto. As the roll call began, so began the musical dispute between the two bands. In the end, neither band wanted to come down from the gazebo first. It was getting late, and the end result was that the local judge and the police had to intervene, ending the evening roll call in the following manner: a Railway musician should leave the gazebo followed by a Banda Paroquial musician until the last musician left the gazebo. And still there was a problem to deal with: which musician would leave the gazebo first? From which of the two bands?[1]

Early on, I began to favor the priest's band, as it was also called. Father Cromácio like my father, was from Rio Grande do Norte, and he

Seventh Letter

~

Many times, Temístocles and I loitered near the movie theater door, hoping that the fat, kindly porter would let us sneak in to catch the last ten minutes of the film.

JABOATÃO, 1932. There was no high school. Students who had the means to enroll in high school commuted daily on a slow train that made the eleven-mile trip in forty-five minutes.

The center of the city was populated predominantly by a middle class made up of public functionaries who worked in local, state, and federal offices; other office workers; some liberal professionals; and a few of the city's working elite who owned mills and factories.

There was only one movie house, little better than the tiny movie house in the town of Recife where I was born. I remember how, like most kids of my generation, I applauded Tom Mix and his white horse as well as Buck Jones and Rin-Tin-Tin.

Many times, Temístocles and I loitered near the movie theater door, hoping that the fat, kindly porter would let us sneak in to catch the last ten minutes of the film. His expression was always friendly when, after checking his bulk pocket watch, he would let us in. He did this often, not only with us, but also with other neighborhood kids. One day he had to stop. He broke the news to us with a sadness bordering on shame, as if he were asking us for forgiveness. His boss had found out what he was doing and had threatened to fire him.

From that night on, we saw the Porter's friendly face only occasionally. Seeing it was a sign that there were some leftover nickels at home.

visited us just after he arrived in Jaboatão. He had a long talk with our family during that first visit, and an open friendship developed between the priest and our family. Many times when I was still a boy, and later as a young man, I would go to his house and on every one of those visits he would greet me with the same care and attention. It was never a forced greeting, never a formula or a ritual. He was always human and passionate when speaking about music in general, about his band in particular, and about the excellent glee club he had also created.

As I am writing now, I can see myself with him on one of those visits. It was three o'clock in the afternoon on his birthday. I went to wish him a happy birthday from my family. He greeted me with great happiness by offering me a piece of *bolo de rolo* cake, baked by some devout "daughter of Maria." Today, bolo de rolo is still a specialty of Recife and the surrounding areas. He asked me how I got to school, if I continued to like Jaboatão, and if I had gone to the last evening roll call in which his band had played.

Suddenly, he stopped talking and tilted his head toward the window. He stood up, alert to some piano music that had entered his living room without his permission. Still silent, but visibly angry, he strode back and forth across the living room, swerving to avoid hitting the furniture. Then, he stopped in front of me, staring at me, and said, "Paulo—Beethoven, Bach, Chopin, all the great musicians are in heaven. But that young lady," and here he pointed to one of the houses across the street, "she runs the risk of going to hell. No one can do what she does to music without punishment."

After seating himself, he looked at me again. He smiled mildly and spoke less emphatically, attempting some self criticism. "Perhaps I am too demanding. At any rate ... " He did not finish the phrase, as if he were sorry for having played down his criticism. Meanwhile, the young lady continued to disturb the silence of the street in the heavy and hot afternoon.

In addition to being a maestro and a composer, Father Cromácio was a Latin specialist who had taught my teacher Cecília so well. He was also an expert in the Portuguese language. He guided my initial studies while I was still a student at Osvaldo Cruz High School. When I was twenty or twenty-one years old, and again living in Recife, I visited him frequently.

We would talk for a long time. I spoke with an adolescent joy in my slow-paced and methodical studies about Ernesto Carmeiro Ribeiro's evening discussions on grammar and about the rebuttals of Rui Barbosa. This was my exposure to Portuguese and Brazilian grammarians.

On remembering those visits, my readings, and my activities as a teacher of Portuguese, I am reminded that—through the influence of writers such as Pessoa da Silva and mostly Moacir de Albuquerque, and through reading Machado de Assis, Eca Manuel Bandeira, and Drummond—I ended up teaching myself that there can be no antagonism between "writing correctly" and the joy of writing, since the joy of writing is, in the final analysis, writing correctly (see my *Pedagogy of Hope* for more on this).

For this reason, at a particular stage of my intellectual development, I began to feel uncomfortable with grammar rules that stated that it was not possible to begin a Portuguese sentence with an objective pronoun. Father Cromácio and Cecília, I was sure, would never write in nonstandard Portuguese. This, however, would not have diminished, and never did diminish, my admiration and respect for him and her.

The outdoor concerts of Jaboatão. Christmas and New Year's feasts. The feasts of Saint Amaro. The 7:00 A.M. train. The trip from Central Station to Osvaldo Cruz High School, stopping at Pedro Augusto and Our Lady of Carmo, where I left behind a piece of my happiness.

The girlfriends of my youth. I never thought, in those days, that I would suffer so from the difficulty of talking to one girl or another, or that after so many years, I would continue to miss them. I am certain that I would be very happy to see them again.

The 7:00 A.M. train, the students feeling happy or worried about their exams—Dulce, Teo, Selma, Iracy, Carneiro Leão, and Toscano. Among them was me, although perhaps they did not notice; I was poor, skinny, awkward, and ugly. I often felt inhibited. If I had a toothache, I would do everything to hide it. Letting on that I had a toothache would have provoked the suggestion that I go to the dentist, but we could not afford it. Then, because I did not go to the dentist, the condition would worsen. The pain would become more acute as the cavity reached some depth. My insecurity would increase and take on new forms with the continued deterioration of my teeth. I would, for example, change the way I smiled.

In my struggle against such understandable insecurities, I found security in the seriousness with which I approached my studies of Portuguese. None of my school mates tried, either through words or gestures, to put me down. It was not necessary that they do so. It was enough that they could. They were the ones who could hurt me. This was the difficult reality in which I found myself. It is for this reason that I helped them overcome their difficulties regarding the use of the Portuguese pronoun *se* and the infinitive. By explaining the Portuguese vowel contractions, I could find the strength that I was lacking. My knowledge of the syntactical rules governing the use of the pronoun se offset my image of myself as bony and ugly.

I was then a student at Osvaldo Cruz High School, one of the best institutions for learning in Recife at that time. After a week of visiting the high schools of Recife looking for one that would accept me for free, my mother had met Dr. Aluízio Araújo, who gave her the much sought after "yes."

She had left Jaboatão early that morning with the hope that, when she returned in the afternoon, she would bring with her the happiness of having gotten me a scholarship for my high school studies. I still remember her face smiling softly as she told me the news while we walked from the train station to our house. I'd known what time she would arrive, and so I was waiting there for her. She told me about the conversation that she had with Dr. Aluízio and his proud decision to offer me the opportunity to study. He had only one requirement: that I really dedicate myself to my studies.

I soon felt linked to the school, its courtyards, its classrooms, the mango trees under whose shadow we spent our recess, and some of my classmates who, for various reasons, I began to admire: Frígio Cavalcanti, Maria Lúcia, Jaime Gamboa, Paulo do Couto Malta, Albino Vital, and Euler Maia. I became close to such teachers as Amaro Quintas, Moacir de Albuquerque, Valdemar Valente, Pessoa de Silva, Júlio de Melo, José Cardoso, and above all, to Aluízio and to Genove, his wife and collaborator.

I learned a great deal from my relationships with my teachers, my classmates, and, later, my students of Portuguese, but I learned most from Genove and Aluízio's humble benevolence and their constant availability. Even though I never stopped showing my gratitude to them, it is nonetheless possible that Aluízio died without realizing the extent to which I'd admired them.

As people, Aluízio and Genove occupied as important a place in my life as the house where I was born and the city of Jaboatão. For this reason, whenever I go to Recife for a few days, I always stop by to talk to Genove. I also visit Jaboatão to relive in its streets, its plazas, a little of the past. I take refuge in occasions that, by stimulating my memory, resituate me in the past.

Morro da Saúde is the name of the house where I lived and where my father died, something I talk about in *Pedagogy of Hope*. I returned there a short time ago. I wanted to show it to one of my daughters, Maria de Fatima. I looked at it quietly. I had lived many moments inside and outside of that house, but in seeing it I was overtaken by memory.

Suddenly, I saw before me a soft and careful figure, that of Fraterno—a competent cabinetmaker who had befriended my father during the first few months after we arrived in Jaboatão. He lived next to our house, Morro da Saúde, toward the back of the house, next to the kitchen.

Once in a while we would go to Fraterno's house. We would have a cup of coffee, which Fraterno's wife Júlia would almost immediately offer us, while my father chatted with Fraterno about what he was doing or hoping to do in his somewhat ill-equipped wood shop. Fraterno gave my father not only his technical advice, but also the loan of his tools.

To the right of Fraterno's house was a quasi farmhouse whose owner was an arrogant person with pretensions to power.

"Captain," Fraterno greeted my father on one of our visits to his house. "I had a problem with our neighbor over there, the one who thinks he owns the world because of my little pig. The beast got away and started rummaging through his garden. He called me over, raging like a powerful man, and told me that the next time he would kill my little pig, just to see what I would do about it."

Fraterno talked with a careful smile on his face, the same careful smile he probably had on his face when he talked with this powerful neighbor, the distrustful smile characteristic of those who are powerless but who don't want to give in right away. "I looked at him," confessed Fraterno, almost reexperiencing the fearlessness with which he had responded to his neighbor, "and said, 'Sir, you are not going to kill my little pig, I can tell you that.'"

Seated next to my father, I followed Fraterno's story with excitement, already taking his side in a fight that I knew would be unequal.

"Why won't I kill your little pig, Mister?" the powerful neighbor roared, angry at being challenged by our peaceful friend.

"Why," answered Fraterno, "because I am going to catch my little pig."

From that day on, we applied the little pig's story to all kinds of situations in our house. Sometime later, after the death of my father, Fraterno moved away. He went to live somewhere far from our house. We lost touch with him for a long time.

Years later, Fraterno looked me up. He looked older, but he possessed the same love he'd always had for us. He greeted me with the familiar smile he always carried, but which now had a different air. He had with him a letter from a secret and forbidden girlfriend of mine; one I used to meet at the train at seven o'clock.

He was then working as a cabinetmaker in her house and, while talking to her, discovered her secret. She talked about her forbidden romance, the obstacles to her love, and in the course of the conversation Fraterno was able to identify me as the second character in the secret romance. Even though he ran the risk of losing his job, Fraterno offered to help us, the girl and me, by breaking the silence that had been imposed on us.

While visiting the house where my father died and where I had lived, I felt like I was seeing Fraterno in front of me, generous as always, with a letter in his hand that broke a month-long silence.

Jaboatão, May 13, and Barão de Lucera Street, where I used to stroll once upon a time. I still feel nostalgic thinking about the girlfriends I had at the end of my adolescent years. I still miss them as I speak with mixed emotions about the soccer games at Portela, our swims in the river, and the Sunday outdoor concerts. In the nine years that I lived in Jaboatão, I rarely skipped those outdoor concerts. They had a special meaning for me, accompanying the band from its headquarters to the plaza and back, along with the other kids. That's how I began to learn the *os dobrados* songs that the band used to play. I often repeated them, whistling all the way home.

Today, even though so many years have gone by, I still remember fragments of some of those songs, which I whistle in the intimacy of my home office every once in a while.

While the musical bands alternated in offering their concerts to the urban population, two soccer teams, which played clubs from other cities, gave real meaning to Sunday afternoons. Due to our passion for soccer, my brothers and I at a young age began to play in the courtyard of our house in Recife. It was always torture when we could not see a game because we did not have the money for tickets.

One time, there was a very important game. A famous soccer club from a neighboring city came to Jaboatão for a rematch. Temístocles and I spent a week looking for ways to go to the game, which had already taken on the air of a duel. Saturday night came, and we still had little hope. By Sunday morning we became certain of the impossibility of attending the game—at least legally, by paying for the tickets. We had only one chance left: to outfox the guards and gatecrash.

The major game would begin at 4:00 P.M., preceded by a preliminary game. That's what the games were called among the soccer clubs in the area. The preliminary games began at 2:00 P.M.

Around noon, we were in full gear, ready to invade the stadium. We easily entered the stadium through the back, on the side of the field near the river Duas Unas. Hardly anyone was there at that time. Optimistic and full of high spirits, we spent a long time quietly squatting behind the branches of a big tree limb. Our intention was to exit our hideout discreetly when the first game began and then to disappear into the mass of spectators.

An hour before the game, our adventure came to an end. We never imagined that the openness of the stadium would multiply the vigilance and efficiency of the guards. One of them caught us buried in the leaves of the hideout that had seemed so safe.

We left the stadium feeling very frustrated and went outside to join the other kids with no money. For them and us, watching the soccer match was reduced to hearing the wild screams of the spectators inside.

We missed seeing any soccer games until we became friends of Lamenha, a young soccer idol who was the best goalie of the local club. He had a lot of prestige due to his excellent soccer techniques and he would take us into the stadium without any difficulty. The stadium door was always open for him and those who came with him. His hands on our shoulders were worth more than the money we would have had to pay to see him play.

The first months in Jaboatão were normal. They did not add to or subtract from any of the difficulties that we had begun to experience in Recife and which had caused us to move to Jaboatão.

Very near our house were the field where we played soccer and flew kites and the river where we went swimming and fished so that we could eat. The surrounding area, with its trees, shadows, fruits, and friendly areas, little by little became outmoded. Jaboatão became a new world for us, far vaster than what we had known up to that point, which was the courtyard of our house in Recife. Our new world was full of green sugar-cane and the smell of its molasses, a world full of the moaning of oxcarts pulled by tame animals. Or perhaps they were more fatalistic than tame, if I may say so.

The oxcart driver, out of habit castigating his oxen Mimo, Pintando, and Fandango, would get them to plod ahead, eyes filled with resignation. It was also a world in which the exploited peasants' misery revealed itself to us with drama. It is in this world that one can find the deepest reasons for my radicality.

Friendship and comradeship began to grow through the soccer games with Dino, Armindo, Itararé, Júlio, Van-van (today's historian of the Jaboatão of the 1800s), Baé, Joãs Romão, Reginaldo, Dourado. Friendship and comradeship also began to grow in the public schools that we attended and in the ravines and hills where our forays took us. In a short time, we became the "connective kids," with friends among those who ate and those who hardly ate.

I often chatted by the river with Dino, a middle-class boy like me whom I have referred to several times in these letters. We would chat about our difficulties while we fished in the shadow of the *ingazeiros*, tropical shrubs. He was the one who introduced me to a delicious dish that was affordable, given our financial constraints, and which became a regular in our diet: fried papaya. He used to say with certainty, "It is necessary for the papaya to be ripe—not too ripe and not too green—just ripe." He would repeat this so that I wouldn't make a mistake. Our neighbor's papaya trees were open to us, as were the chicken eggs we found here and there.

Today, so far from my childhood, I understand that the outdoor concerts of Jaboatão, the soccer games, and the forays into the hills and hidden ravines were where I faced truly dramatic situations. I was marked by the river where I swam and fished and in which, like Manuel Bandeira says in *Poesias*, "One day, I saw a young girl swimming in the water. I stopped, my heart pounding. She laughed. It was my first enlightenment."[2]

Eighth Letter

～

An abandoned hope.

IT WAS A RAINY SATURDAY, LIKE MANY OTHER SATURDAYS in Jaboatão. When I was a child, we humorously called Jaboatão "the chamber pot of heaven"[1] because of the high rainfall. My mother and I were returning home with the little amount of food that, God knows how, she had been able to purchase at the market. We were passing Barão de Lucera Street when my mother saw a wooden sign on a two-story building at the corner which said "Jaboatão High School" and listed the school hours.

Promptly at eight o'clock on the following Monday morning, my mother and I arrived at the high school to speak with its director. Her goal was to get a job there as a secretary. I suspect she had come up with this idea over the weekend. She and my father probably began fantasizing by building this castle in the air: Tudinha Freire, secretary of the first high school in Jaboatão. I can imagine how, in her fantasy, she saw herself entering the same meat stores where she was so often belittled and this time receiving the treatment she deserved. "Good morning, Senhora Tudinha, how much meat are you going to take home with you today?"

Until then, her experiences with a lack of money and material goods had sharpened her sense of deprivation and withered her expectations. Now, with much spirit and hope, she was arriving at the high school to speak with its director. The director of the high school was young, possibly a law student at the time, who had just arrived in Jaboatão with far hungrier dreams than my mother's.

During the forty or fifty minutes that it took the train to travel from Recife to Jaboatão, the high school director probably imagined himself as the future chancellor of the University of Jaboatão, the university that he would soon create by expanding his high school. He dreamed that his high school would represent the best pedagogical methods in the entire region. It would attract students from the dry midlands and the remote arid interior of Northeast Brazil, all coming to the famous high school in Recife. Even then, in 1933, the young director could imagine the high school leading the first regional conference, debating educational themes that were just as current then as today, including school dropout rates, purposeful and inadvertent truancy, quantitative and qualitative school failures, the National Education Center location, and so on. He saw himself in his office, chancellor of the future University of Jaboatão, meeting with the chairs of such fields as engineering, medicine, and education. He probably saw himself dressed formally in his academic gown, overseeing the graduation ceremonies, and surrounded by dignitaries.

We could hear hints of the great chancellor, here and there, the morning we visited him.

"Good morning, Senhora," he greeted my mother.

"Good morning, Senhor," she answered.

He gestured for us to sit down while asking how he could help us.

"I found out Saturday," my mother said, "by reading the sign on your house, about the existence of your high school. So I thought I would come to talk to you about the possibility of becoming a secretary here, although I don't have any experience in this line of work."

The director could have said that he also did not have any experience in beginning something new, but he didn't. He had arrived in Jaboatão without knowing anyone and, without asking anyone, had rented a house and posted his sign as if the school already existed. He did not get in touch with the local authorities nor did he contact local educators such as Cecília Brandão, Odete Antunes, or Clodoaldo de Oliveira, so that he could exchange ideas with them and determine if his dream was viable or not. He may not even have known about the ministry of education's legal requirements for high school accreditation. All he knew was that in Jaboatão there were no high schools and, for him, that was enough.

"I don't know if you know, but it's only been a week since I opened this high school to see if its development is possible. I have to find out, first, if I will have enough students; second, if I will have any teachers. If I have both, I am thinking of establishing some sort of arrangement to make my high school an extension of another high school in Recife, which has already been accredited by the ministry of education. Students will take the official exams in Recife, where they will be officially registered. So far, I have been contacted by three teachers but no students. It would be my pleasure to have you as my secretary, but I must inform you that during this trial period I won't have any way to pay you. If things work out, we can discuss your salary."

The director's comments must have cut deeply into my mother's dream. She had to think fast in order to respond. It was necessary for her to take a risk. Perhaps it would be better to tie up some of her time while waiting for something to happen. Perhaps it was better to gamble than not. Who knew if students and teachers would suddenly begin arriving at the high school, making it a reality? For those people who have little or nothing, any possibility deserves a try.

"I understand. I accept your proposal," my mother answered, already assuming the secretarial manner although she wasn't going to get paid.

They agreed on a schedule and tasks. My mother returned home later that day. From that day on, my mother endured a month of conflict, torn between her desire to overcome her economic difficulties and her fear that it would be impossible to succeed. At some point during that month, my mother began to count on a minimum sum with which she could diminish her and my father's anguish about the financial needs of the family. At the same time, it was likely that the young director was beginning to contemplate a high school with a humble interior where he would not be organizing any educational conferences or expanding into a university.

My mother's schedule during this initial phase of the high school's life was from 9:00 A.M. to noon and from 2:30 P.M. to 5:00 P.M. One day she returned home at 10:00 A.M. Her weary body bore a face filled with suffering, the heart-break of a broken dream, an abandoned hope. The director had closed the high school.

P.S. Today, August 5, 1993, I lost one of my best friends, Albino Fernandes Vital.

In our childhood, when we were five or six years old, we developed a friendship that was never once even slightly wounded over all these years. We started our friendship in the soft grass covering the front yard of his small and humble house almost next door to the house where I was born on Encatamento Street in Recife. We were classmates during elementary school and at Osvaldo Cruz High School, of which I have spoken in other letters. We went our separate educational ways when he chose the field of agronomy. He became a noted researcher in the area of phytopathology and was better known abroad than among us here in Brazil. As the popular adage says, "House saints don't perform miracles."

Albino was an extraordinary man. Over the years, I never heard him make a single negative comment about anyone, just as I never heard him praise someone who didn't deserve it. We find ourselves today—Jardina, his beloved wife, and all of us who had the privilege of being intimate with him—burdened by the emptiness that inaugurates the first day in this world without him.

Ninth Letter

~

Someone took me out of the room and to a corner of the
house where I heard the moans, each time weaker, with
which my father said good-bye to the world.

OCTOBER 31, 1934. SUNDOWN ON A SUNDAY full of blue sky. My
father had been suffering from an abdominal aneurysm for four days. He
was suffering intensely and approaching death without sign of an appeal.
Even we, the young ones, could perceive the end, about which we could
do nothing.

My mother rarely left the room where my father was. She sat by the
head of the bed, caressing his forehead while telling stories full of the
faith and hope that he would soon recuperate and live out his days in joy
and tenderness. That hope, on Sunday, was strengthened by my father's
marked improvement.

Popular knowledge has an expression for the well-being that termi-
nally ill patients often experience before death: "health's visit." During
this last experience of life, it is as though the patient says good-bye to
hope and joy, to feeling things, to seeing or listening to friends. The
patient enjoys life as though he or she does not know that the end is near.
No one sees "health's visit" as a death notice; everyone sees it as a sign of
life, even those who have observed it before.

I remember the indescribable, fantastic joy that I experienced on that
Sunday in October of 1934. Each time I went into my father's room, I felt
good. My father, laying serenely on the bed without pain, smiled and
played with me. Next to him was my mother, gentle, full of tenderness,

saying words that expressed her near peace in view of my father's improvement. She was betrayed, along with all of us, by the falsehood of "health's visit."

When I returned to the room between 5:00 and 5:30 P.M. I saw my father struggling to sit up, screaming with pain. His face was twisted as he fell back in agony. I had never seen anyone die, but I was sure then that my father was dying. I was overwhelmed by a sensation of panic mixed with anticipated nostalgia, an enormous emptiness and an inexpressible pain.

Someone took me out of the room and to a corner of the house where I heard the moans, each time weaker, with which my father said good-bye to the world. These last moments of his life, the contortions of his face, his moaning due to pain—all of this is fixed in the memory of my body with the same sharpness as a fish fossilized in rock.

For two or three days after my father's funeral, the women in my family were engaged in a chore characteristic of closed societies with rural traits and untouched by technological advances. They threw themselves into a task that revealed a certain taste for death—the task of dyeing all their clothes black, a symbol of mourning.

The widow suffered the most strictures of what was called "closed mourning." These observances could only be eased two years after a husband's death. My mother fought against ever easing the self-enforced severity of her "closed mourning" until, under the influence of my sister Stela, she acquiesced many years after my father's death. She finally eased out of "closed mourning" and adopted "open mourning," which she maintained until her last days when she was seventy.

It is not always easy to bury our dead. Only when we assume their absence, no matter how painful this acceptance may be, does the pain of their absence diminish and we begin to return to being fully who we are. Only in this way can we wholesomely have, in the felt absence, a presence that does not inhibit our ability to love.

In a healthy mourning experience, we cannot simply shovel dirt over the absence of a loved one nor can we simply pretend and reduce our lives to the past. The experience of mourning, which results from death, is only valid when it is expressed as a struggle for life. To experience mourning with maturity is to live the tension between the desperation caused by the loss and the hope of reinventing ourselves. No one who suffers a substantive loss continues the same. Reinvention is a requirement for life.

It is important to know that no one is born prepared to love life through the experience of mourning. The experience of mourning, in spite of its specificity, is one of the many hard experiences we will have in our lifetime.

What I want to say is that the sequence of learning in which we all participate inculcates the love of life or the love of death in us, shapes the way that we relate from a young age to animals, plants, flowers, toys, and people; the way that we think about the world; and the way that we act in the world. If we treat objects with meanness, destroying them or devaluing them, the testimony we give to our offspring is a lack of respect for the powerless and a disdain for life. We learn to either love life or to reject it.

My father's death, along with the emotional emptiness with which it left us, meant the worsening of our family situation. On the one hand was the absence of the head of our family, on the other was the drastic reduction of my father's small pension, which my mother received when she became a widow. It was an insignificant sum.

It was only between 1935 and 1936, a year or two later, that things got better with the help of my older brother, Armando, who got a job in the city hall of Recife; my sister, Stela, who began to work as a first grade teacher; and my other brother, Temístocles, who spent his entire day in Recife running errands for a business office.

In these letters to Cristina, I am happy to have a chance to declare publicly how grateful I am to them. Their help and dedication gave me immeasurable support so that, with the collaboration of many people, I could do the things that I have done.

Tenth Letter

~

The informal knowledge that was born of my life experience in Jaboatão yielded to the more critical reflection born of my return to Recife.

WE HAD LIVED IN JABOATÃO FOR NINE YEARS, from April 1932 to May 1941, when we returned to Recife. Our return took place under far better circumstances than our move to Jaboatão nine years earlier had, when we thought that a mere lateral move would magically solve all our problems and difficulties.

The constant contributions and solidarity of three sons and a daughter, Stela, enabled our family to meet the normal costs of running the household. I was the one who contributed the least. I received a small salary from the Portuguese classes that I taught at Osvaldo Cruz High School and, later, in other schools, and I earned some money tutoring students privately.

Each of us took care of our individual needs with a part of what we earned. The remaining, largest share, we gave to our mother for running the household. When there were extra expenses, we split the cost.

From 1941 to 1944, the year I got married for the first time, I was intensely dedicated to reading, as critically as possible, the Portuguese and Brazilian grammarians. I used part of my salary to buy books and old specialized journals.

These journals and books always put my acquisition of clothes at a minimum. Only when I could leave it no longer would I buy some inexpensive piece of clothing. During that inspiring period, in which I found myself passionately bewitched by my job at Osvaldo Cruz High School, I rarely spent as much money buying clothes as I had before. At the urging of my uncle's competent tailor, I agreed to his making me a white linen suit that I paid for in installments. Although my clothes were never dirty, they were ugly.

My usual attire, though not my favorite, was a tropical-style suit, maroon with white stripes. Through constant wear and abuse, the color faded to a shade resembling green. The suit would have been warm in a temperate climate. You can imagine what it was like to wear it during the summer in Recife, when temperatures reached the eighties.

One day, toward the end of my class at noon, an intelligent and lively soul, one of those bright youngsters with an almost angelic naiveté, suddenly asked me, as if she could not save her question for tomorrow, "Paulo, aren't you hot with those clothes on?"

"I am," I responded. "I just don't have any other clothes."

After class, she came to her senses, approached me, and apologized unnecessarily. I was the one to be forgiven for the neglectful, careless way in which I dressed. For me, however, the journals and books I bought were worth much more. Reading them challenged me. I was learning how to study, and I was preparing myself to practice my teaching more effectively. Those journals and books were worth far more than elegant clothes. Clothes would come later, when they did not compete with the fundamentals: journals and books. Better yet, they would come when clothes and books could be purchased without counting to ten before I made the final choice on what to buy.

Some afternoons in Recife included, as obligatory stopping places, two or more bookstores that satisfied my taste for reading and the pleasure of perusing the books of a number of Recife's intellectuals. Secondhand bookstores offered older books that were out of print.

The Imperatriz Bookstore, which belonged to Berenstein, was where Melckzedec, the best bookseller in Recife, worked. Melckzedec later became the owner of an excellent secondhand bookstore, the National Bookstore, where Mousinho and, most important, Aluízio worked. They were just as sensitive and competent as the master booksellers Berenstein and Melckzedec.

We, the young intellectuals, all very curious, would meet at the bookstore in our pilgrimage along the shelves as we examined the indexes of books and read their descriptions. There we would exchange ideas. The National Bookstore had a large open space, with a long table and chairs all around it, where we sat after going through the bookshelves and freely discussed ideas with one another as if we were in an academic seminar.

At the back of the store was a space where they opened the big boxes of imported books. I in my body still feel the joy I experienced when Aluízio would invite me to watch them open the boxes of books in Melckzedec's National Bookstore or the Imperatriz Bookstore.[1] I still feel the emotion I experienced while looking through the pages of the new books before they were put on the book shelves.

Odilon Ribeiro Coutinho, Waldemar Valente, Amaro Quintas, and José Lourenço de Lima were some of the friends who accompanied me with childish curiosity to the ritual opening of the boxes of books.

What books would appear? What surprises would we have, what publications would end up in our hands, and what recently published texts would challenge our capacity for reading? These urgent questions were part of the emotions I felt while I waited. First, I was enveloped in the smell of new books. Second, my hands and curious eyes would gently encounter the books with more than just superficial contact. Third, I would take some of them home and read them in the special study corner of my house.

This box-opening event would sometimes take place on the same afternoon in both the National and the Imperatriz bookstores, which were about two or three buildings apart.

Opening boxes of books provoked surprise, eagerness, and happiness, which developed into challenges. Challenges to my ability to buy these books and challenges to my capacity to read them.

At that time, I mostly threw myself into the study of grammar, punctuated by readings in the philosophy of language and introductory linguistics essays. These books eventually led me to education. In truth, my passion was never centered around grammar for grammar's sake. I never ran the risk of falling into a merely technical study of grammar. My passion was always directed toward the mysteries of language in a never anguished but always restless search for its substantive beauty. Hence, you can understand the pleasure with which I immersed myself, without any concern for time, in the readings of Gilberto Freyre, Machado de Assis, Eça de Queiroz, Lins do Rego, Graciliano Ramos, Drummond, and Manuel Bandeira.

I don't mind repeating here that the idea that the aesthetic dimension of language should concern only artists, not scientists, is false. It is the duty of all those who write to write beautifully. It does not matter what one writes or writes about. It is for this reason that I always recommend that my master and doctoral students, when they are about to write their thesis, should vigorously read authors who write well and beautifully, even if the authors are not in their area of concentration.

Having seen examples of good writing helps you when deciding on this or that word during the writing process, or when trying to work out the relationships among groups of words in a discourse. These examples become models. This does not mean, however, that writers should not struggle to develop their own ways of writing, even though they may be influenced by some models.

Perhaps you have noticed that whenever people are asked about their professional background, they tend to answer by emphasizing their academic preparation. Rarely do people take into consideration their more existential experience. That is, even though we are most influenced by people, this remains little discussed. The influence of people—with whom we deal all the time, such as teachers who were coherent and serious, humble people who practiced competence—is never announced. In truth, professional development takes place in existential experience, conceived in and influenced by it.

Regarding my development as an educator who thinks about educational practice, I would never dismiss my experience of walking through Recife and going from bookstore to bookstore, becoming intimate with the books, or of traveling through Recife's narrow roads and hills conversing with local groups about their problems.

During the ten years I spent at the Social Service of Industry (SESI), I lived the tension between practice and theory and ended up learning how to deal with this tension. I also learned how to deal with it during all my years of study, both as a student and as a teacher.

The informal knowledge that was born of my life experience in Jaboatão yielded to more critical reflection born of my return to Recife.

Eleventh Letter

~

The mistake of the Left is its dogmatic and aggressive discourse, its mechanistic proposals and analyses; the mistake of the Left is also its fatalistic understanding of history, essentially antihistorical, in which the future is so inflexible it is never problematized.

IN 1947, I ARRIVED at the Social Service of Industry (SESI), Regional Department of Pernambuco, where I stayed for ten years and was involved in the most important political-pedagogical practice of my life, something I talk about in *Pedagogy of Hope*.

I should point out that my arrival at SESI made possible my reencounter with working-class reality. I call it a reencounter because the first encounter had taken place during my childhood and adolescent years in Jaboatão, where I dealt intimately with rural and urban kids, the sons and daughters of rural and urban workers.

I became part of the first SESI education committee to be organized by its president, the engineer Cid Sampaio. He convened the group and discussed with them his ideas concerning how the institution should provide service and education. His vision of service and his politics of action were actually liberal in orientation, but so much more open than the politics of half his industrial colleagues that they could be considered progressive.

Today I can see that I was right in supporting him in his campaign for the governor of Pernambuco State in 1958. It was a progressive act in the same way that, four years later, it was a progressive act to support Miguel Arraes, who was jailed shortly afterward. Cid Sampaio lost his political rights during the April 1, 1964 coup d'état, when he was in the middle of his mandate as the governor of Pernambuco State.

Even though I recognize the enormous influence that my time at SESI had on my political and pedagogical formation, in this letter I will describe only the most important aspects. It is possible that, later on, if I have the time and predisposition, I will do a more detailed analysis of that period, which I have called, in *Pedagogy of Hope*, the foundation time.

Here I will analyze the political-pedagogical aspects of that time, which necessarily implies ethical, ideological, historical, and sociological dimensions.

Given the interests of the dominant class, the SESI was an intelligent move by its leadership to create a benefactor institution whose fundamental role of providing assistance was turned, unfortunately, into a paternalistic, bureaucratic service. The pedagogy that informed the provision of services never took a form that allowed anyone to problematize it. Therefore, nothing about the provision of medical, sports, judicial, or educational services could encourage those being served to unveil truths, reveal reality, or become more critical in their understanding.

From the perspective of the dominant class, SESI was a service organization that was to restrict its function to the bureaucratic mode of providing services. For this reason, any practice that might result in or imply a democratic presence was to be eschewed by those responsible for coordinating the nucleus of social agencies. Even minimal participation by the workers in the process of providing services was viewed as dangerous and subversive and thus to be rejected. It would be naive to think that the creation of SESI represented an expression of goodwill on the part of the dominant class who, touched by their workers' needs, created the institution to help them.

On the contrary, SESI was an intelligent move on the part of paternalistic leadership to further its contradictory relationship with the working class.

It was more of an attempt to ease class conflict and stop the development of a political and militant consciousness among workers. Hence, those practices that stimulated critical knowledge were sooner or later restricted.

I vividly remember the story of an experiment that took place in Geneva, recounted by someone who participated in the experiment. A religious women's group organized itself around educating children and adolescents, the sons and daughters of immigrant parents. One day, the group's leadership visited some industrialists who agreed to help the group to continue and expand their activities. Two months later, having received some financial aid to defray their costs, the group initiated one of the projects, a sexual education project involving fifteen to twenty girls. The women responsible for the project then received a visit from an industrialist sponsor.

The women gave him a detailed account of the project because they were happy with the results they had obtained. The young girls learned to discuss freely their preoccupations concerning sexuality with the educators. They learned to dialogue without feeling inhibited, even going so far as to realize that they were free to engage in sexual activities.

When the meeting ended, the woman said that the industrialist spoke dryly. Without beating around the bush, without half-measures, he announced that he was going to cancel his support, declaring categorically, "If these young girls are freely discussing questions of sexuality, what will they discuss tomorrow regarding questions of social justice? I want domesticated workers, not inquiring workers." This was the comment of a modern industrialist in Switzerland during the 1970s. The practice of service provision is steeped in this kind of thinking.

Even though I spoke very little about social classes, it was at SESI, because of its contradictions, that I began to learn that the classes exist in a contradictory relationship. I learned that they have conflicts of interest and are permeated by antagonistic ideologies.

The dominant class, deaf to the need for a critical reading of the world, insists on the purely technical training of the working class, training with which that class should reproduce itself as such. Progressive ideology, however, cannot separate technical training from political preparation, just as it cannot separate the practice of reading the world from reading discourse.

From the dominant point of view, the more we proclaim the lie that educational practice is neutral in the provision of service, the more we can diminish resistance to this lie, and the easier we can achieve dominant goals.

I cannot contain here an important commentary. Perhaps never before has the dominant class felt so free in exercising their manipulative practice. Reactionary postmodernity has had success in proclaiming the disappearance of ideologies and the emergence of a new history without social classes, therefore without antagonistic interests, without class struggle. They preach that there is no need to continue to speak about dreams, utopia, or social justice.

Weakened religiosity and the inviability of socialism have resulted in the disappearance of antagonisms, the postmodern reactionary triumphantly says, suggesting in his pragmatic discourse that it is now the duty of capitalism to create a special ethics based on the production of equal players, or almost equal players. Large questions are no longer political, religious, or ideological. They are ethical but in a "healthy" capitalist sense of ethics.

We, therefore, don't have to continue to propose a pedagogy of the oppressed that unveils the reasons behind the facts or that provokes the oppressed to take up critical knowledge and transformative action. We no longer need a pedagogy that questions technical training or is indispensable to the development of a professional comprehension of how and why society functions. What we need to do now, according to this astute ideology, is focus on production without any preoccupation about what we are producing, who it benefits, or who it hurts.

I cannot see myself as one of those intellectuals who not too long ago were progressives and who now are surrendering to the lies and entrapments of this astute ideology. I don't see why I should feel at all inhibited in declaring myself a progressive man of the Left. The leftist and rightist ideologies are still alive, but it is necessary for the rightists to preach that ideologies no longer exist so as to invigorate the Right.

The mistake of the Left, or a sector of the Left, today and yesterday, has been the desire for authoritarianism, a by-product of the Left's dislike for democracy, which it views as incompatible with socialism.

The mistake of the Left is its dogmatic and aggressive discourse, its mechanistic proposals and analyses; the mistake of the Left is also its fatalistic understanding of history, essentially antihistorical, in which the future is so inflexible it is never problematized.

In the attempt to prevent the suffering of subordinated classes, the progressive educator should avoid limiting the marginalized classes' universe or their epistemological curiosity about objects that have been depoliticized. In other words, I should not depoliticize their comprehension of the world and their subsequent intervention in it just because it would be charitable to help them avoid knowing the truth behind the facts. I should not eschew a type of politicization that results in more suffering because the subordinated classes haven't the means to fight or because I allow myself to be enchanted by the present neoliberal ideology—an ideology of privatization that never speaks about costs, the costs are always absorbed by the working class.

Let's now return to the SESI in Recife around the end of the 1940s and the beginning of the 1950s. It is important to highlight that, even though we are now separated from 1950 by several decades, the question of the rights of the subordinated classes—their rights to a voice, to mobilization, to organize, and to education that unveils the truth—is just as timely today as it was in the 1950s. It is a question still discussed and debated by the upper classes while the Brazilian common masses are kept out—that is, those Brazilians who have been denied the right to be. The neoliberals who proclaim the death of social classes and class struggle foam at the mouth when their statements are not believed. I never foam at the mouth when I hear others deny the existence of social classes and class conflict. The reason that I don't is because I rely on greater historical truths than on fragile declarations that disregard those truths.

One of the advantages I have had over intellectuals who are intellectualists is that certain ideas were never poured into me as if they came from nowhere. On the contrary, my knowledge came from my practice and my critical reflection, as well as from my analysis of the practice of others. Because of my critical thinking abilities and my profound curiosity, I was led to theoretical readings that illuminated my practice and the practice of others and explained the level of success or confirmed the level of error that took place.

On the one hand, my progressive perspective has an implied ethical position, an almost instinctive inclination toward justice and a visceral rejection of injustice and discrimination along the lines of race, class, gender, violence, and exploitation. On the other hand, my character also tends to reject knowledge that is antibook or antitheory. I prefer a knowledge that is forged and produced in the tension between practice and theory.

I was not a progressive educator simply because my readings of some authors suggested I should be. I was a progressive educator because I was offended by the perversity of an unjust reality that denied the ontological vocation of all human beings: to be more. (I have talked at length about this in my previous books.)

I was not a progressive educator because I was certain that the future would bring socialism. On the contrary, I was a progressive educator because I rejected a mechanistic comprehension of history and was certain instead, that the future would be constructed by us, men and women who struggled to transform the evil present. I was certain that the future would be constructed by progressives like us through a substantive transformation of the present or by reactionary forces through superficial changes of the present.

These changes would demand and generate a knowledge of transformation as well as a knowledge of conservation—class knowledge. In other words, on one hand you have the knowledge of the dominated class and, on the other hand, you have the knowledge of the dominant class. These ways of understanding, however, never exist in a pure state with respect to one another.

My reading of revolutionary thinkers, specifically the nonoligarchic ones, helped me a great deal while offering me scientific bases for supporting my ethical and political beliefs. I always believed that a democratic position was part and parcel of progressive practice, which is rejected by authoritarian structures for this very reason. Hence, we must have coherence. It is impossible to reconcile a progressive discourse with an authoritarian practice.

Something else explains my political pedagogical beliefs, something that cannot be underestimated, much less rejected; something that was never understood by authoritarian Christians, who are contrary, sectarian, and fundamentalist: my Christian upbringing.

I was perceived as a diabolical thinker by some while others tried to dismiss me as an idealist bourgeois. From them, however, and their unmeasured hatred for difference, I learned the fundamental virtue of tolerance, which never leads us, if it is authentic, into a form of collusion.

I never understood how to reconcile fellowship with Christ with the exploitation of other human beings, or to reconcile a love for Christ with racial, gender, and class discrimination. By the same token, I never could reconcile the Left's liberating discourse with the Left's discriminatory practice along the lines of race, gender, and class. What a shocking contradiction: to be, at the same time, a leftist and a racist.

During the 1970s, in an interview in Australia, I told some greatly surprised reporters that it was the woods in Recife, refuge of slaves, and the ravines where the oppressed of Brazil live coupled with my love for Christ and hope that He is the light, that led me to Marx. The tragic reality of the ravines, woods, and marshes led me to Marx. My relationship with Marx never suggested that I abandon Christ.

For those who understand history as a language of possibility, for those radicals who reject sectarianism and learn from difference, for those who democratically reject all forms of repression, it is not difficult to understand my position; a position that was rejected yesterday and today by dogmatic thinkers who believe that they are the owners of the truth and who have lost touch with themselves through their excess of certainty.

For these reasons, I was convinced that the present was tainted by a historical, cultural, and ideological past that was aggressively authoritarian and which required that progressive educators develop a practice that involved participants. That is why I gave my all to the work at SESI. Those experiences of decision making did not exist outside the conflict concerning comparison, evaluation, rupture, and belief.

One of our tasks as progressive educators, today and yesterday, is to use the past that influences the present. The past was not only a time of authoritarianism and imposed silence, but also a time that generated a culture of resistance as an answer to the violence of power.

The Brazilian present has been enveloped by these colonial legacies: silence and the resistance to it—the search for a voice—and the rebelliousness that must become more critically revolutionary.

This was the central theme of my academic thesis, "Education and Present-Day Brazil," which I defended in 1959 at the University of Recife. Today this university is called the Federal University of Pernambuco. I incorporated parts of this thesis in my first book, *Education as the Practice of Freedom*. My thesis reflected my experiences at SESI, which had significantly affected me. I combined my experiences in SESI with critical reflection and extensive reading from a foundational bibliography.

As you can see, what moved me required practices contrary to the politics of service provision. Those practices were not coherent with the spirit of SESI and the objectives for which SESI had been created.

I should mention that although I did not clearly understand the contradictions in SESI, I was not unaware of them. On the one hand, I knew that I could not convert SESI or save it from its "original sin," as a good friend and colleague of mine, who worked as a social worker in Rio de Janeiro, used to put it.

On the other hand, I was certain that there was no reason why I should not attempt to do what I could do to be loyal to my dream. So, I struggled to make a democratic school that would stimulate the students' critical curiosity, that would transcend the educational rigidity that calls for mechanical memorization. It was a school where teaching and learning were viewed as inseparable parts of the same process of knowing. Teaching involved the recognition that what the teacher already knows the student begins to know. The student learns to the extent that he or she apprehends the object of knowledge that the educator is teaching.

Finally, I was proposing, along with my coworkers, to implement an administration that was fundamentally democratic, an administration open to the participation of workers and their families. Through this process, all would learn the meaning of democracy through the democratic practice of participation, the experience of decision making, critiquing, denunciating, and praising.

I want to highlight in this letter two projects along the political pedagogical lines that I mentioned before. One of these projects was developed by me and a group that worked with me when I was director of the SESI Division of Education and Culture. The other project was my leadership as the superintendent or director general of SESI.

In both instances, I developed programs that reflected my political pedagogical beliefs and which were consonant with my analysis as previously discussed in this letter.

Let's look at the first project, which was implemented at the Division of Education and Culture. My point of departure will be our comprehension of education and schooling and how we put it into practice.

I was heavily influenced by my personal experience at home, my relationship with my parents and my brothers, which I have spoken about in the previous letters. My relationships at home had a strong democratic character. The environment in which we lived was characterized by our freedom and our respect for the authority of our parents. Because of it, I recognized a Brazilian past that was authoritarian and revolved around the exaggerated power of the master as contrasted with the powerlessness of subordinates, who either accommodated or rebelled. All of this directed me toward democratic schools in which educators struggled to change the traditionally authoritarian climate of Brazilian education.

The democratic experiences in my household, and my personal past, contradicted the authoritarianism that was the base of Brazilian society.

It was obvious to me that, given a choice between the despotic security of the traditional school and the openness of the democratic movement of the New School, I would opt for the latter. Thus, I familiarized myself with European, North American, and Brazilian thoughts aligned with this democratic movement. For this very reason, I am never offended when some people criticize me for being a New School groupie. I am surprised, however, that not all my critics realize that when I criticize the authoritarian relations between educators and learners, I also criticize the authoritarian relations generated by the capitalist mode of production. My criticism of the traditional school, inspired by the influence of thinkers from the New School and my personal experience, led, little by little, to my criticism of the very system of capitalism.

The fact that I was not satisfied with the political and ideological position of such people as Anísio Teixeira, Fernando de Azevedo, Lourenço Filho, and Carneiro Leão does not lead me to say, simplistically, that they were "has-beens" or that they "never were." The fact that I had different dreams does not prevent me from acknowledging their contribution toward pedagogical reflection, which also involved reflection on practice.

On reviewing, after many years, the pedagogical practice of that time and in rethinking the major points of our program, I now understand its timeliness and validity. But understanding its timeliness today does not necessarily mean, regrettably, that my colleagues and I were precursors of some real change. It means only how little we have advanced on the terrain of democratizing education. We had completely committed ourselves to the task of democratizing education in the

Division of Education and in the school itself. We wanted to democratize the relations among educators, learners, parents, custodians, school, and community. We wanted to democratize the school by understanding the patterns in the act of teaching. We wanted to put our efforts toward overcoming the mechanical transference of content so that we could embrace a critical way of teaching. We wanted to respect the knowledge that learners brought to school as well as their cultural identity.

The struggle today is against the alarming rate of school retention, which pushes a scandalous number of children out of our schools.[1] These children many educators call, either naively or maliciously, school dropouts. These educators, either naively or maliciously, misunderstand the concept of school retention. In reality, the concept of dropping out is an expression of the dominant ideology and its powerful position, which blames students for dropping out without analyzing the true causes of school retention. Students are always blamed for their learning deficiencies; the system never bears any responsibility for its failures. It is always this way. The poor and the oppressed are blamed for their precarious state. They are lazy and useless.

Our understanding of school dropout and school retention was different. We believed that a democratic school would have to rigorously evaluate its own evaluative measures.

Students' ability to learn has a great deal to do with whether they confront hardships at home, whether they have enough to eat or wear, whether they have a place to sleep and play, and whether they confront obstacles to intellectual experience. Students' learning depends on health and emotional stability.

It also depends on teachers' instruction—their seriousness in tackling teaching, their scientific competence, their love, their sense of humor, their political clarity, and their coherence. All of these qualities determine teachers' respect for their students.

Because of all of these things, we paid great attention to the permanent preparation of teachers and to the education of parents. We learned a great deal from our initial mistakes, both in the preparation of teachers and in our work with parents. In both cases we were absolutely correct in the objectives of our practice and wrong in the method we used to achieve our objectives. We contradicted ourselves. We opted for an education that called for the development of critical postures, that favored choices and decision making, and relied on the rigorous analysis of facts. We contradicted ourselves, first, by not listening to the people with whom we were working concerning what they would like to discuss and, second, by choosing ourselves the lecture themes, as I discuss in *Pedagogy of Hope*.

Although we insisted for a long time on this mistake, we evaluated our practice by thinking about it and reformulated our procedures, which led to the development of a necessary coherence between our objectives and the paths that lead to them.

While trying to overcome our mistakes and errors, we heard a mild, almost polite, criticism of our work from a parent of one of our students. This criticism had an extraordinary impact on my colleagues at SESI in Recife and me.

At a meeting we had finished talking about the duty of the school to respect the knowledge that students bring to school. Seated in the front row was a young father who, uninhibited, got up and said, "If you ask me if I like this meeting, I am not going to say no because I learned some things from the professor's words. But if you ask me if this is what I wanted to learn today, I would say no. What I wanted to learn today is how to discipline, since my wife and I are having problems with the kids at home and we don't know how to solve them."

The same thing would happen at the teacher training sessions. We would discuss the same themes debated in the circles for parents and teachers. The themes were not arbitrarily chosen by other persons in the group or me; they would emerge from our visits to the social nucleus of SESI, the schools, and talks with teachers. But, the fact remained that it was only coincidence when the theme we talked about coincided with the expectations of the participants.

From that night on, we understood that we would have to deepen our democratic experience. We began to ask the participants, teachers and parents, what fundamental themes should make up the agenda for the next meeting.

The next day, in the office of the Division of Education, we began to prepare what we started to call the "Thematic Letter," to be signed by the students' teachers and sent to each parent. Generally, in the letters, we would propose a theme and two or three challenging questions concerning the theme.

We would suggest at the end of the letter that parents discuss the theme for the next meeting with their peers in the factory, those who were close to them, and their relatives. Thus, they could bring to the circle not only their own opinions but also those of their friends.

This way, we took a step forward—in that the school attempted to extend its area of influence and involve students' parents and the community within which the school was located. The teacher training seminars became more dynamic too, because the participants of the organization had input concerning the theme to be discussed.

At the suggestion of one of the teachers, all the teachers began to discuss with their students ways to make the themes more accessible during the seminars. The same discussions took place with parents. This led parents to feel a higher motivation toward their children's education and enhanced their participation in meetings.

With the greater participation of parents encouraged by the ability to suggest themes for the meetings and prepare for these meetings, and with the critical involvement of teachers and students, circle attendance by both parents and teachers rose substantially. We also began to observe marked differences in the student's behavior in school.

Schools and parents began to understand each other better because they knew each other more, which diminished their mutual lack of trust.

At that point, we had to confront two big difficulties. The first was in the area of discipline. Because of our culture's authoritarian characteristics, we received many requests that we be harder on children in school. Parents would say, with a smile, sure of what they knew and not at all insecure or embarrassed, "What makes a man serious, straight, and conscientious is punishment and severe discipline." The second difficulty was in the area of literacy. For them, learning how to read and write could be done no other way than with the ABC primer.

There were families who would take their children out of our schools for the two reasons discussed above and enroll them in small private schools available throughout the poor areas of the neighborhood. I myself spent two weeks, when I first arrived at SESI, going through the poor sections of town in Recife and visiting these small private schools to talk to their teachers. Almost all of them applied rigorous corporal punishment. Only a few of the schools I visited did not have on the teacher's desk a paddle used for striking the fragile hands of students.[2] I never forgot the carving on one paddle that said, "Calms the heart."

How many hearts of mischievous or oppressed children were beating just as hard in their skinny bodies after their punishment, in spite of the obscene inscription on the paddle?

Early on I understood from talking with parents that we would have little success if we appeared to be defending licentiousness. Permissiveness in the name of freedom would end up working against freedom, due to the lack of established authority. In truth, what most concerned parents was the fundamental question of limits. That is, the limit of freedom, authority. Parents were not able to understand the dialectical tensions between authority and freedom, but rather believed that freedom died out without authority, thus exacerbating the tension.

Therefore, it was necessary to be calm and confident in our conversations with parents. It was necessary to defend positions without ever falling into the trap of appearing licentious.

Our criticism of the parents' model of discipline and our refusal to accept it did not mean a total negation of authority, since without authority there is no discipline, only licentiousness. By the same token, however, we knew that without freedom there is no discipline, only authoritarianism.

Our struggle to understand what constituted true discipline, which is engendered through contradictory and creative relations between authority and freedom, was furthered by the results of research on these relations among the parents of our students. We were shocked by how violent punishment was in Recife, in the rural areas, and in the hinterland. This was in contrast to the almost total absence of violent punishment in the beach areas of the state, as I discuss in *Pedagogy of Hope*.

It was not difficult to discuss discipline at meetings regardless of the agenda to be debated. And we could do it without manipulating the parent-teacher meetings.

During that time, I sometimes met privately with parents who sought to vent their anguish concerning a process of punishment that they felt led to the loss of their son or daughter. "Professor, sometimes we think there is no other recourse. It appears we are fooling ourselves. Physical punishment does not resolve anything."

Many years have passed since those meetings but I still have them fixed vividly in my body's memory. If I were a painter I could easily draw some of those pained faces, whose strong traits reappear in my memory as I write.

The second difficulty, which I mentioned earlier, had to do with the parent's demands that we teach their children with the ABC primer, a demand I also discuss in *Pedagogy of Hope*. This demand involved us in debate for a long time. Every once in a while one of the parents would return to the same old argument. "My grandfather learned this way. My father learned this way. I learned this way. How come my son cannot learn the same way?"

This argument, which had robbed us of some students, began to lose effectiveness when, one day in a parent-teacher meeting, I asked the following, "Who here has seen a child begin to talk by saying the letters of the alphabet?"

The silence that ensued indicated the negative answer, "Nobody." In truth, no one begins talking by pronouncing letters. When a baby says, "Mama," he or she wants to say, "Mama, I'm hungry, I'm wet." If this is how we all, men and women, begin to talk, how can we learn to read and write by starting with the letters of the alphabet? Think about that.

Everything pointed to the fact that parents did think about my question. The arguments for the primer began to decline and, as a consequence, little by little, the criticisms leveled against us for not teaching the ABC table did too.

Through the experience I gained over this time I finally became the superintendent of SESI. If during my directorship of the Division of Education and Culture I made every effort to democratize the school by expanding the participation of students, educators, and parents and by fighting (sometimes without success) to raise salaries, when I became superintendent, I also tried to democratize the administration of the institution.

I will briefly speak about some major projects that I led, assisted by a small group chaired by Heloisa Jacques Bezerra, a dedicated and competent social worker.

The first project was an attempt to create a structure through which the leaders of the SESI divisions, service sections, and other institutional sectors would begin to know each other. For what it is worth, the directors and assistants of the divisions did know each other and, in some cases, were friends. Unfortunately, when it came to professional relationships, they hardly ever knew what the others were doing. Thus, we duplicated services by accident and contradicted the practices of other divisions. We also had unnecessary expenditures, for example, in the purchase of materials. Sometimes, cars from the separate divisions would bring technical experts to the same social center when, if there had been some planning, one car would have sufficed. Planning would prevent wear and tear on the cars and save fuel.

Encouraging mutual knowledge among the directors of the various divisions created a larger vision of service delivery, which facilitated solidarity among those responsible for the many programs located throughout the city of Recife and the rural areas of the state.

At that time, public offices and private organizations were open Saturdays until noon. At one of my first meetings with the directors of the divisions and their assistants, I discussed having our project meetings on Saturday mornings. The SESI offices would close to the public on Saturdays while the directors and their assistants took advantage of the freed-up time to get to know each other better. Once the proposal was accepted, we had a second meeting with the entire personnel of the division, including the janitors. Only after general approval of the proposal did we begin our work. We organized the four first meetings, in which we chose those divisions that would describe their practices while the rest of the personnel participated in the debate that followed. I could say, parenthetically, that during the 1950s I was never cut off from thinking theoretically about how to improve practice.

At the fourth meeting, Francisco, the janitor with the most seniority, was chosen to lead the discussion. He was to talk about his work, his day-to-day routine, the positive or negative aspects of his work, and how the directors, in general, related to him.

The relationships among personnel became so much better that during the meetings we advanced to analyzing our practices. These relationships enhanced our work so much that we unveiled the theory embedded in our practice.

First, I learned early on that it was necessary, at the very least, to bring the nucleus coordinators from the capital city to these meetings. Second, we had to follow the same process with them. In other words, we had to discuss their descriptions of their leadership with the general personnel and how they implemented various projects in their nucleus. These meetings tended to turn into serious personnel training seminars while avoiding becoming purely "academic." They were academic in the best sense of the word.

It is worth describing the emotion and self-assurance with which Francisco, the senior janitor, spoke and the impact that his words had on everyone. He began by saying that, "I don't have much to say about my day's work in D.R. [the regional office of SESI]. I am only a janitor doing my job, cleaning rooms and desks, buying cigarettes for the professors, serving their coffee, taking documents from one office to another. Only when I found out that I was to speak to all these people today, either by ad-libbing or by reading, did I begin to ask what it is that I do during a day at work and in life.

"I do a lot of things. First, by adding one day to another, I create a month during which I earned, with much sweat, my family's sustenance. Second, I work because I don't know how to live without work. My day is like those of millions of Brazilians and better than those millions of others who don't even have the little I have.

"I am happy with my day-to-day life. I am humble. But there are some things that I don't understand and should mention to all of you. For example, when I enter a director's office with the coffee tray and he is in a meeting with other professors, no one looks at me or answers when I say good morning to them. They only grab their coffee cups and never once say, even to be different, thank-you. Sometimes I am called in by a director and he gives me money to buy him a pack of cigarettes. I go, I go down the stairs if the elevator is taking too long, I cross the street, I buy the cigarettes, I return, I give the cigarettes to the director. 'Here,' another director will tell me, giving me some change, 'bring me some matches.' Why don't they discuss what they want so I can take care of it in one trip? Why go up and down, down and up, just to buy a little bit each time?

"I think that these meetings are going to help make things better. I understand much more about the work of a lot of people. I did not know what many of them did.

"I hope that those who never said good morning or thank-you don't become angry with a humble janitor. I told these stories because they are part of my day-to-day routine as a janitor here in the D.R."

One could sense in the silence, in the fidgeting of bodies on chairs, the discomfort that Francisco's comments had caused those who had never said good morning to him or thanked him for his services. His social claims are as relevant today as they were yesterday. When I watch certain television programs today, I never see the waiter who serves coffee to the guest or interviewer being looked at courteously or thanked for the service. Sometimes, the television guest is someone who is considered progressive, yet it is as if the waiter is not a human being, just a robot programmed to serve others.

Our elitism does not allow us to perceive the lack of coherence between our liberatory discourse and our indifferent attitude toward people, who have been reduced to almost thing-like status. This is not a minor problem.

The next step we took was to organize and develop meetings with the nucleus coordinators and their assistants, using the same training spirit and objective. These meetings actually represented evaluations of the practice that took place in their areas.

Along the same lines as those in the parent-teacher circles were debates about the organization of agenda themes. The coordinators prepared the agenda of the meetings through discussion with directors and technicians in a prior meeting.

Each nucleus would guide me with their prior suggestions, which my secretary, Eremita Freitas, the directors of the division, and I studied. These suggestions were then discussed during the scheduled meetings.

Positive results did not take long to be achieved. We developed a better knowledge base, created the concrete possibility of interchange, fostered mutual help, and promoted greater effectiveness of the divisions within each nucleus. The openness to dialogue led to a better comprehension of the limitations of each one of us.

Another step remained to be achieved that was as difficult as it was important: to use similar methods to develop a democratic practice in the

SESI clubs with the workers' leaders. Each nucleus had its club and gaining directorship of the club happened through open election.

The SESI clubs were the idea of a young journalist, José Dias da Silva, who was finishing his law degree when he arrived at SESI to take part in the first group that engineer Cid Sampaio organized. The initial dream was to develop the SESI clubs into a space where the clubs' associates could democratically have a voice. The clubs worked against the "original sin" of the SESI organization, which conformed to institutional paternalistic aid norms.

It is in this sense that the administration of the industrialist Sebastião de Holanda Cavalcanti was as open as his peer Cid Sampaio. The clubs were how I ended up as the superintendent of SESI. The SESI clubs used to receive everything from the regional divisions, including the money for their festivals, their celebration of May 1, and their sport competitions. The regional division, through its superintendent, would determine how much each of the SESI clubs should receive for this or that endeavor.

My dream was to rupture the authoritarian structures so prevalent in my own education so we that could transcend the paternalistic institution of aid provision, which I had called in one of my reports at that time "The Santa Claus Syndrome." We hoped to democratize our practice as much as possible.

I was not and am not now against the assistance we provided. I am against the paternalistic mentality of assistance programs, which anesthetize the political consciousness of those who receive assistance. Assistance is good, necessary, and at certain times, indispensable. But the paternalism that generally informs the politics of assistance represents an ideological trap of the dominant power and manipulates the dominated popular classes.

I once again relied on the competent and dedicated social worker Heloisa Bezerra to carry out the systematic meetings with the leadership of the SESI clubs in Recife as well as in the rural areas of the state. Heloisa was a well-respected ex-student of the Social Workers School of Pernambuco, which was later incorporated into the University of Recife. Today it is part of the Federal University of Pernambuco. Teachers and ex-students of the university, who did or did not work at SESI, were Lourdes Moraes, Dolores Coelho, Hebe Gonçalves, Maria Hermínia,

Evany Mendonça, Lilia Collier, Deborah Vasconcelos, Glória Duarte, and Maria Amália, among others. Heloisa was the one who organized the meetings, chaired them, and wrote up the minutes. Her minutes enabled the theoretical reflections with which we prepared for the next meeting.

Heloisa and I visited each of the SESI clubs throughout the city in order to prepare for our first meeting. On our visits we talked about the importance of the increased participation of the SESI clubs in shaping the destiny of the social nuclei. We spoke of the leadership's need for information and training so that they could more effectively participate in the democratic process.

I was convinced during that time, and my lived experience later confirmed my belief, of the fundamental importance of education in the process of change. In other words, knowledge guides change. Thus, it became necessary to add educational practice to our attempts to expand the sphere of decision making within the SESI clubs. This educational practice was informed by the stimulus of epistemological curiosity. It was necessary to keep our eyes open to avoid the development of dichotomies between doing and thinking, between practice and theory, between acquiring skills and knowing the raison d'être behind the technique, between politics and education, and between information and education.

In reality, all information holds the possibility of expanding into education if the information is critically received by the informed and not simply swallowed by him or her. Information should communicate through words as a link between the content of the communication and its receiver.

Information is communicative, or generates communication, when receivers learn the content of what was communicated in such a way as to transcend the act of receiving. They do this by recreating the received communication and transforming it into knowledge concerning what was communicated. The receiver becomes the subject of the process of communication, which, in turn, leads to education as well. Education cannot take place within the suffocating limit of specialization. Education can only take place when we go beyond the limits of purely utilitarian knowledge.

For this very reason, educators who are mesmerized by the neoliberal pragmatic discourse are not educating in the full sense of the concept. When these educators accept the notion that what is important is the acquisition of facts without the educational background to critically analyze these facts, they produce a type of training that reduces students to narrow technical professionals. It is worth saying that an educational practice void of dreams, dissent, and pronouncements is neutral and accommodating.

On the other hand, we should highlight what is also true. That is, an educational practice reduced to only dissent and pronouncements and the inspiration of dreams while minimizing the technical preparation of students for work readiness is not worth much.

The goal should be toward information that is educational, which leads to critical knowledge, which implies the technical domain as well as political reflection, which asks the following: for whom, for what, against whom, and against what will these technical instruments work?

One of our problems is relying on memory when discussing the details of our past practice so that we are prone to minimize those details.

We cannot escape this process. Even when I write today about the past, I recognize the temptation to overlook some details. However, I want to be loyal to my past educational practice. I am talking now not only about what I did but also about what moved me. I was moved by the growth of my institution and the knowledge guaranteed by our rich practice. I never rejected those institutions as impure even though I never took them as absolute truths. I always put my institutions to the test by critically analyzing and evaluating them. I incessantly searched for the raison d'être of the institutions in order to determine what had caused them. My epistemological curiosity was always at work. Let's now return to discussing the relationships of the SESI clubs.

Once my work proposal was accepted by the director of the clubs throughout the city of Recife, I wrote a letter inviting all the directors of the divisions and nuclei to attend a meeting at my house at 8:00 P.M. on a Friday. The office of the superintendent would provided transportation to facilitate the success of the meeting. In the letter I proposed an agenda of five topics.

1. The meeting would open with a brief description of the spirit of the project by the superintendent, brief since the project had already been discussed at preliminary meetings in each office;

2. the superintendent would describe the objectives of the new SESI administration under the leadership of the entrepreneur Holanda Cavalcanti;

3. the SESI administrative director would discuss the institution's collection of funds, hiring of personnel, material expenses, deficits, and economic aid received from the national division;

4. the SESI director would ask whether he had the approval to continue the project (in the case of approval, suggestions would be made concerning the operation of the project, meeting dates, etc.);

5. the meeting would adjourn with juice and sandwiches.

Writing about these happenings, I remember the feelings that I experienced that night. The feelings return to me with such realism and intensity that I almost experience them anew. This is what happens when I am happy to have seen my expectations realized, to have heard the expected comments, to have intentions evaluated. Even though there were naive moments, the critical climate of that meeting ranked it as a high point in my life. I went on to participate in hundreds of meetings with the same leaders. In the process of our participation together, our knowledge of the world and our political vision grew accordingly.

All the workers' leaders and the SESI clubs' directors signed up to speak. The first speaker, who was frank and articulate, announced that he would begin his speech with some apprehension by making a declaration. He stated that it was the first time that the SESI administration had gambled on democracy, agreeing to discuss budgets and deficits with the SESI clubs with all the documents in hand. This made him uneasy, thinking that something had to be behind the proposal.

"What does the administration really want in offering us this democratic space? As the people say, 'a blind person is always afraid of big charity.' Only our practice can give an answer to my restlessness," he said. "I vote for the continuation of these meetings and for the acceptance of this project."

A second speaker congratulated the administration for its decision to listen seriously to community-based people and to begin to discuss issues with them. The project was voted in and it was decided to hold a monthly meeting with the superintendent's office and the SESI leadership. Each meeting would take place in different social settings. The meeting site would be decided at the previous meeting.

After the intervention of the two speakers and the unanimous approval of the project, the clubs also approved the motion that the meetings be held monthly on Sundays from 8:00 A.M. to 1:00 P.M.

It was also agreed that the process of holding meetings would teach us to make the best of them as we learned to prioritize. For this reason, we decided that the best approach to take was to never establish a form that would determine how we conducted the meetings. That way, both the SESI leadership and the office of the superintendent would have to prepare for the meetings. The only thing defined and established was the right to speak, the right to critique, and the right to be respected by all.

The first meeting ended with overall general satisfaction. Fifteen days after, we met again at 8:00 A.M. at President Dutra's nucleus in Vasco da Gama, in Casa Amarela.

The meeting in Vasco da Gama tested my coherence, tolerance, and patience, indispensable qualities for a progressive educator to develop, something I discussed in *Professor Sim: Tia Não*. That meeting added to my experience a political know-how, a know-how that became pivotal in defending various proposals, in developing a critique of errors. My office of the superintendent generally won the proposals put forth concerning the theses debated.

One of the theses that I began to defend at that meeting had to do with ensuring a greater democratic posture at the SESI clubs. This involved doing away with the SESI free medical and dental care, sports activities, legal assistance, and education. I knew that the workers' leadership and some patrons would oppose me. I proposed that a commission be established—including representation from the SESI clubs, the leadership of the nucleus, and representatives of the divisions—to implement a service-related cost, with the exception of the educational services. For example, the commission would establish the cost for a movie ticket, a medical visit, a chest x-ray, a urine exam, a filling, a tooth extraction, and so on. These costs were modest and considerably less than what was normally charged for shows and dances.

The proposal meant that the clubs would keep 50 percent of the money generated by the charges for medical, dental, and legal services.

The other 50 percent would go to the regional division to be distributed to the services. All the money generated by dances, feasts, and shows would belong to the SESI clubs while the regional division would cease to support these types of club festivities. The clubs would resume responsibility for their own affairs. They would develop their independence and then, as independent organizations, they could borrow from the regional division.

The decision on which services to provide would be relegated to the leadership of the clubs and their board of directors. Decisions included, for example, the type and duration of unemployment benefits.

The meeting at Vasco da Gama was the point of departure for a discussion that became more profound in subsequent meetings regarding the polemical thesis of charging for services rendered by SESI and the autonomy or dependence of the SESI clubs.

During the first discussion, a leader of one of the SESI clubs stated that I was working for capitalists and against the workers. He added that what I had proposed represented a step backward and worked against the interests of workers. Ironically, a few days after the meeting at Vasco da Gama, I was approached by a young industrialist who was a member of the SESI board of directors. He told me without mincing words that my politics were antimanagement. He added that the correct politics, from the corporations' point of view, would be to reinforce free services while highlighting the charitable generosity of those in power.

Feeling attacked by both sides, I was forced to learn how to structure my arguments to defend my point of view.

Even though I had not anticipated it, in a very short time the SESI meetings were transformed into rigorous seminars, informed by serious study, in which no one could overpower another or impose knowledge on the rest.

I also learned in these meetings how to respond to criticism leveled against me. I learned that I should always use the same tone of voice and the same passion. I did not have to be agreeable toward those who were abrupt with me. By the same token, I did not have to be rude toward those who treated me politely. What became very clear to me was that I had no right to lie, to be incoherent, or to be fearful of agreeing with my opponent, particularly if he or she had convinced me with his or her arguments. I was certain that if I was defeated by majority vote I should not use my power as superintendent to invalidate the vote.

My proposal to grant the clubs greater autonomy was unanimously defeated. An amendment was attached to the vote, however, that each SESI club could study the proposal with its board members and, if they approved the proposal, they could individually adopt it.

It is worth saying that the unanimous defeat of my proposal that day did not mean its death. The proposal could reappear in a given SESI club and, after being tested in practice, return to the general assembly for a vote based on the proven power of experience.

At the end of the meeting, the leaders chose the nucleus where the next meeting was to be held. They also chose the theme for the debate. The leaders agreed that the SESI leadership would meet at each site with the workers from each nucleus to give them information regarding what had transpired at the previous general meeting and to inform them of the selected theme for the next meeting.

Another duty of the SESI leadership was to call general assemblies, at which they would give updates on all the work and activities that had taken place at each nucleus. For example, the number of assistants increased because of this need established by the advisory council. Heloisa and I benefited from having new assistants, as did the workers' director's office. The new assistants also took part in the general meetings. They participated in debates and had the right to vote on issues.

Once the meeting had ended, I received the officers of all of the SESI clubs who were requesting schedules for coming events and inquiring about the approved budget. I signed off on all of the requested budgets while indicating that I disagreed with some items. To point out my disagreement with their budget requests was a political-pedagogical act that I could not ignore. At the same time, to have rejected their entire budgets because they had not approved my proposal would have constituted a grave error. It would have been a disgrace.

The second meeting took place at my house.

Heloisa, as the representative of the office of the superintendent, began to meet with the directors of each SESI nucleus and other agencies located in the rural areas of Recife. In the meetings, she would discuss the progress of each project. Our objective, which had support from the club's general assemblies, was to incorporate the rural agencies into the citywide SESI network. This task was accomplished in two meetings by bringing together the directors of the sites to discuss their work plan. A meeting took place in Caruaru at which the directors of Agreste were all present, the second meeting took place in Ribeirão at which the directors of Zona da Mata were present. The meetings made it possible to bring to Recife the voices, the criticisms, the restlessness, and the suggestions of the rural centers.

One of the staunch opponents of the fee for services had excellent relations with the office of the superintendent. He was, in fact, a friend of mine. His name was Severino. He was a textile worker and the president of the SESI club in President Dutra's nucleus, at Vasco da Gama in Casa Amarela. Our camaraderie was cemented during the first debates in the parent-teacher circles, which he strongly supported. Our relationship was not going to suffer just because he took a contrary position on my proposal.

Among the leaders, another director was just as serious as Severino but had less power. From the first moments of the discussion concerning the service charge he revealed himself as a strong supporter of the program. He had sponsored the amendment enabling the general assemblies of each social nucleus to decide how to spend the money generated by the service charges.

At one of the club's meetings, I think it was either the sixth or seventh, he announced that his general assembly had approved the service charge for various services. He added that his club was harmoniously working with the nucleus' leadership to determine the costs for services.

He always signed up to speak at the very beginning of each meeting so he could give a detailed account of the progress of the work at his site. After three months of activities, his club had already deposited a substantial amount of money in their bank account and had stopped asking the regional division for money.

These positive results began to shake Severino's resistance. Although he was seriously ill, he invited some friends over to share his radical shift of position concerning service charges. "If I still had the strength," he said, "I would reintroduce the issue of service charges in the next meeting so I could fight to implement it."

Severino died without having the chance to speak in favor of service charges at a meeting with his peers. The issue of service charges was reintroduced, however.

After one year or so, all of the SESI clubs managed their own accounts, had expanded their service activities, and covered the cost of lunch for all the assembly's participants in the meetings between the clubs and the office of the superintendent. The rural clubs began to absorb the cost of transportation to Recife as well as the hotel bill for representatives' one-night stay. The clubs had also developed a better relationship with their respective general assemblies, which oversaw their expenses and budgets.

Some clubs also implemented forms of unemployment assistance. They would lend to the unemployed worker a predetermined amount of money without interest. This sum would be paid off in small installments when the person returned to work.

Some of the SESI officers resisted the critical posture being adopted by the SESI clubs, which were necessarily expanding their democratic space and the chance for workers to speak. Although these officers were not in the majority, they continued to believe that all of those in need of the SESI services were mere recipients of the charity of the organization. Thus, they began to feel disrespected by the recipients, who no longer were docile and submissive. The recipients, in turn, became vigilant about the punctuality of doctors, dentists, teachers, and so on.

Once more one could detect the presence of the dominant ideology in these officers' views, an ideology with authoritarian, antidemocratic, racist, and elitist characteristics. On many occasions these regressive voices filtered through the back alleys and hallways to the office of the president Holanda Cavalcanti, who always refused to listen to them.

Upon reevaluating these episodes today, I ask myself if these lived experiences and knowledge, produced by all those who participated in the meetings, make sense. In my case, they undoubtedly make a lot of sense. They represent a precursor of the things that I did many years later and are part of the indispensable learning process that informs my practice today.

My work in SESI with various professionals from different levels and my experience with workers, whom I challenged to assume the attitudes of subjects and to learn about democracy by practicing it, ended up teaching me many indispensable things that changed my reality. For example, I learned a great deal about the importance of information and education; in other words, information that through process becomes educational.

I did many things—sometimes I thought beforehand and other times I thought after—which possibly touched me more than the other participants. I remember, for example, the time that an administrative director came to my office to tell me that he had decided to standardize the janitors' hats at SESI in Pernambuco. He had already signed an order to purchase the hats.

"Look sir, my dear Travassos," I said. "I would prefer that you bring together all of the janitors, show them a hat, ask them what they think of the size, and if they want a hat or not. The fact is that a hat alters a person's face and we don't have the right to change anybody's face without his or her consent. If we were suggesting hard hats to protect the workers from accidents, then the hat could be part of their work equipment. In that case, you wouldn't have to consult them since there would be a rationale for the hat."

The director agreed with me. A meeting took place the next week. The suggestion of the hat was defeated. It is possible that after so many years the case of the hat has disappeared from the memory of those participants who are still alive but not marked by what occurred at that meeting. The hat incident never left my memory, and it was with great joy that, in the beginning of 1993, I heard the hat story once again from an old friend of mine, Professor Paulo Rosas, who was a comrade in struggle in Recife.

The hat incident became an exemplary case for me. How many hats have been imposed on us without our consent and in the name of our self-interest and welfare?

Today, new technology—fax machines, video recorders, and computers—aids in the acquisition of in-depth mutual knowledge between the clubs and the social service centers. I think about the incredible speed with which we can disseminate information and conduct research in our effort to educate.

I want to end this letter by repeating the statement I have often made before: "Practice needs theory and theory needs practice just like fish needs clean water."

Practice apart from critical reflection, which illuminates the theory embedded in practice, cannot help our understanding. Revealing the theory embedded in practice undoubtedly helps the subject of practice to understand practice by reflecting and improving on it. Even without engaging in rigorous critical analysis—which would enable the subject of practice to obtain knowledge beyond "common sense"—practice does offer a type of operative knowledge. This, however, does not justify failing to search for more in-depth knowledge.

It was by searching for the reason behind the knowledge I was acquiring through practice that I shaped my years at SESI.

Hence we must always engage in an investigation of practice, even if the first results are not satisfactory. We must submit practice to strict, methodological, and rigorous questioning. My practice led me to many of the readings I did at that time.

These readings helped me to understand what I was doing. Sometimes these readings confirmed my practice and other times they helped me improve my practice. These readings also lead me to other readings in the areas of the social sciences, linguistics, philosophy, the theory of knowledge, pedagogy, history, and Brazil's educational history.

My reading of these texts simultaneously equipped me with the necessary tools to continue to read context, and enabled me to intervene in that context. Through my time at SESI, I learned something that I will never forget. That is, how to deal with the tense relationship between practice and theory.

Twelfth Letter

~

> It is in this context that a progressive, who works and thinks dialecti-
> cally, is often the target of attacks. The attacks come from those who,
> while thinking of themselves as progressive, engage in authoritarian
> "reactionarism," a sort of "original sin" of the mechanists. Attacks also
> come from the right wing, which is no less authoritarian.

I FEEL THAT I CANNOT GO ON TO THE REST of these letters, in which I discuss a number of political-pedagogical problems and topics, without considering some defining moments in Recife and since Recife—before the great challenge of exile—that I have mentioned in previous writings.

They are my involvement with the Movement for Popular Culture (MCP), the Cultural Extension Service (SEC) at the Federal University of Pernambuco, and adult literacy in Angicos, Rio Grande do Norte.

Up front, however, I would like to make it clear that it is not my intention to make up a story about those times. By saying something about them and my presence in them, I hope to contribute to their history.

I must also say that my intensive and extensive practice at SESI, on which I have reflected so much, provided me with the knowledge that would become essential for all I realized at MCP and SEC and for my pedagogical development. Understanding and practicing adult literacy was an indisputable dimension of that development.

At MCP
The MCP[1] was born of the political will of Miguel Arraes, who had recently been inaugurated mayor of Recife, and the equally strong political will of a group of workers' leaders, artists, and other intellectuals. I was

part of that group, which the mayor had invited to meet in his office. At the meeting, he spoke about his dream, that of making it possible for an agency or service, pedagogical in nature, which would be moved by the desire to work with the popular classes and not above them, to work with them and for them.

He went on to say that the city had no funds for salaries, but that it would provide some help to the organization to be created.

It was up to a young teacher, Germano Coelho, to present a plan for the creation of the institution at the next meeting.

Germano had recently arrived from Paris, where he had been conducting graduate studies at the Sorbonne. It was there that he met Joffre Dumazidier, the renowned French sociologist, who was then the president of the Movement Peuple et Culture and whose work influenced Germano. Peuple et Culture inspired the creation of MCP, which still maintained its radically Northeast Brazilian identity.

Germano Coelho's proposal, which was accepted with minor corrections, called for the creation of a movement instead of an institute or organization of popular education and culture. The idea of a movement suggested a process of coming to be, of change, and of mobility.

The men and women who came to be involved with the movement were partners, companions in the same adventure, the same project, and not just technicians or specialists.

Even though it was never imposed on anyone who joined the movement, there was a condition for anyone who intended to remain a member: to dream about the transformation of Brazilian society and to fight for that dream. It was not possible to stay in MCP without betting on utopia. I don't mean utopia as something unattainable, but utopia as a possible dream. It wasn't as if MCP would expel anyone who did not comply, but rather that those who did not believe in utopia would feel uncomfortable in the movement. On the other hand, the MCP style of operation, focused on the development of projects as opposed to the creation of departments, indicated the movement's nonbureaucratic spirit, which never declined into a random or permissive character. We had, then, as many projects as we were able to develop and implement. That is why every project depended on approval by the council, which was made up of founding members in charge of project coordination.

Another part of the movement's nature was a critical understanding of the role of culture in the educational process, as well as in the political struggle for the change that Brazilian society needed then and still needs today; change in culture in general, in popular culture in particular, and to the progressive education of children and adults.

A dialectic view of the role of culture in the historical process aligned the movement, or more precisely, some of us within it, with an antimechanist, antideterminist position, but never with an idealistic one.

In a mechanistic conception of history, in which the deproblematized future is already known, the role of education is to transfer packages of knowledge anticipated to be useful in a future already known.

In a dialectic, nonmechanistic conception of history, the future evolves from the transformation of the present as it occurs. Thus, the future takes on a problematic and undetermined character. The future is not what it needs to be, but whatever we make of it in the present.

The mechanist understanding of history throws education and culture into mechanist boredom, the fundamental root of authoritarianism. Necessarily absent from this understanding of history is any important role for consciousness and subjectivity.

The power incorrectly attributed to consciousness by idealistic subjectivism winds up resulting in its equally erroneous opposite: nullifying subjectivity into a determinist mechanism.

It is in this context that a progressive, who works and thinks dialectically, is often the target of attacks. The attacks come from those who, while thinking of themselves as progressive, engage in authoritarian "reactionarism," a sort of "original sin" of the mechanists. Attacks also come from the right wing, which is no less authoritarian.

To the extent that a dialectic understanding of history as possibility defeats determinist understandings, overcoming the notion of the inexorable future and problematizing it, men and women are faced with the issue of responsibility in history. They are faced with decision, belief, valuation, ethics, and aesthetics. And such issues necessarily imply certain concrete historical, cultural realities at which the generations arrive. This concreteness is the base from which men and women dream, choose, value, and fight for their dreams, becoming subjects rather than just the objects of history. However, it is also a reality that the large popular majorities are disempowered and silenced by the dominant minorities. To focus just on our own reality for a moment, the central question to be posed is how long the thirty-two million hungry will quietly and patiently bear the situation imposed on them as if by fate or destiny. In fact, reactions are already occurring and increasing as seen in the demonstrations of the "class war" we presently experience.

With rare exceptions, Brazil's dominant class does not yet realize the hunger that haunts a significant part of our population. For the most part, the Brazilian elite lacks a minimum of sensitivity to see, if nothing else, the danger to which they expose themselves and the nation by allowing the misery of so many brothers and sisters, let alone being offended as human beings.

What the sociologist Herbert de Souza, whom I call Betinho, has been doing, assistance not assistantialism, is an act of wisdom and hope. Giving assistance so as to create a stimulus, a challenge capable of transforming the assisted individual of today into the subject of tomorrow, who will take history in hand and remake it, in justice, decency, and beauty is an act of wisdom and hope. Betinho is not a subjectivist, nor is he a mechanist. He knows that we can change the world, but he also knows that without the practice of transformation we will not achieve world intervention. Transformation is a process in which we are both subjects and objects; it is not something that takes place inexorably.

In a mechanistic and authoritarian understanding in which the future, nonproblematized, is already known, already certain, education is reduced to the transfer of recipes, packages. In a dialectic understanding, just for starters, there isn't only one future, but multiple hypotheses for the future. Men and women are programmed and conditioned beings, but not determined ones. Besides being conditioned, they are aware of their conditioning and become able to intervene. We could not talk about liberation if its occurrence were predetermined. Liberation is a possibility only because domination may prevail in its place. That is why, in a dialectic, nondeterminist perspective education should become more and more identified with the experience of decision, rupture, right thinking, and critical knowledge. It should be a hopeful experience, not a hopeless one in which the future is a given fact, a burden. That is why education should also demand a high sense of responsibility from its subjects. After all, there is no historical experience without responsibility. In other words, the fulfillment of obligations and the struggle for rights are in the very nature of historical experience. That is why popular education, democratic education, as we see it today and as we announced it yesterday, rejects distorting dichotomies and should seek to understand the complexity of their relationships.

A necessary implication of such critical education is the need for information. Information per se, however, isn't of much interest to us, nor is education itself, but the relationship between the two is, so that we can reach that critical moment when information is transformed into education. That is the moment when the "patient" gradually becomes a subject, in relation to the informing subject.

On the other hand, in a process committed to the democratic future, education cannot be reduced to isolation. First of all, science and technology cannot escape the political and ideological implications with which they are conceived and with which they are used. Furthermore, science and technology are not "asexual" or neutral endeavors. Yesterday and today, technoscientific education could not and cannot be reduced to purely technical training or to the simple memorization of scientific principles, which is no less mechanical. Technoscientific education involves technical ability and a grasp of technology's reason for being. Furthermore, technoscientific education must not lack, at the risk of becoming mutilated or mutilating, the incessant search to learn right thinking and critical thinking. Thinking and knowing, which cannot be satisfied with the "phonology" and "morphology" of technology, will get to their own "syntax."

The better a plumber is, the more competently he or she operates tools and the more lucidly he or she can move about the world. In other words, the plumber is a better worker, in a democratic perspective, if he or she has been educated and can assert himself or herself as a citizen. Citizenship is a social invention that demands a certain political knowledge, a knowledge born of the struggle for and the reflection on citizenship itself. The struggle for citizenship generates a knowledge indispensable to its invention. Some, or even many, of the foundations of citizenship and its invention can and should be the object of the epistemological curiosity of those who are trained as plumbers. What I mean to say is this:

the education of a plumber should not be strictly technical, nor should it be exclusively political. A plumber who cannot operate the tools of his or her trade is no longer a plumber. Likewise, the competent plumber who is not involved in the struggle for citizenship—which requires critical knowledge about our presence in the world, about production, and about creation in general—is no longer a citizen. The struggle for citizenship requires some political wisdom.

Yesterday, the Right, while strongly opposing progressive educational practice, accused us of being subversive and irresponsible because we proposed an education committed to transforming the world, aimed at overcoming social injustice.

Today, the resistance to progressive pedagogy is manifested, above all, in neoliberal discourse, which speaks of a new history without classes, without struggle, without ideologies, without left, and without right. And in this discourse, many of those who were aligned with the Left yesterday join in to say, awestricken by the fall of the Berlin wall, that in this new time our struggle is for democracy. If things change, we will see then what we can do for socialism. We should not, then, speak about dreams or utopia, but rather pragmatically commit ourselves to the technoprofessional education of the working class. Education for production.

When yesterday's progressives, today's pragmatics, say that now our struggle is for democracy, they continue to set socialism and democracy against each other, repeating, thus, an old mistake: the mistake of assuming that democracy is the exclusive possession of the bourgeoisie. They demonstrate a profoundly mechanistic understanding of democracy, so mechanistic that it does not call for questions about the world of values, beliefs, freedom, and being or not being.

Not only do I refuse this type of discourse, I say it will be short-lived. It may not even endure one decade.

To state that this new time is that of democracy is to conceive of democracy as a game of tactics. I do not identify myself today as democratic just because socialism cannot offer current historical opportunities. While I am a radical and substantive democrat, I am a socialist. There is no way of countering the one with the other. To do so is one of the tragic errors of so-called realist socialism.

On the other hand, while "programmed to learn," and thus to teach and know, men and women will always be at their most authentic when they develop the curiosity that I have been calling epistemological. It is while epistemologically curious that we get to know, in the sense that we produce knowledge and don't just store it mechanically in our memories.

The exercise of curiosity is accomplished not by dichotomizing the undichotomizable, but through a dialectic understanding of reality. In the education and training of a plumber, I cannot separate, except for didactic purposes, the technical knowledge one needs to be a good plumber and the political knowledge one needs to be a part of the polis, the political knowledge that raises issues of power and clarifies the contradictory relationships among social classes in the city.

I dream of a time and a society in which one's learning nature and epistemological curiosity will not be satisfied, say while a carpenter, with just the technical knowledge of operating a saw or working the wood to make a window, table, or door. In consonance with my evolving social and historical nature, I should go beyond the fundamental questions about what I do, how I do it, and what I do it with. I should challenge myself with other indispensable questions: who do I serve doing what I do, against whom or in favor of whom, and why do I do what I do?

These were some of the questions we gained a greater intimacy with on the MCP projects: philosophical, epistemological, aesthetic, ideological, political, methodological, and pedagogical problems. Our choice, while progressive activists, was to empower the popular classes, a task that can only be accomplished through the political, social, and economic transformation of society.

If the ruling class in this country today continues to dodge Luíz Inacio Lula da Silva (president of the Brazilian Workers Party) as the devil dodges the cross; if one of the most important representatives of that class continues to announce, as in the last presidential race, that a massive exodus of industrialists from the country will result if Lula wins; if it continues to be said, with total conviction, that Lula's victory will mean the end of all private education in Brazil; if the end of private property continues to be feared as a result of Lula's heading the government—can you imagine how this same ruling class reacted, back in the 1960s, to the MCP popular policy? Unfortunately, the reaction wasn't weakened by the MCP association with Miguel Arraes, a kind of demon in human form.

It was even said, after the coup d'état of 1964, that large quantities of guerrilla uniforms and weapons had been found in our headquarters, readied for the armed movement we were supposedly planning. When this accusation was made informally at one of the military headquarters to which I had been brought when I was arrested, I could not help but laugh at the idea of myself, Professor Paulo Rosas, Professor Germano Coelho, Professor Anita Paes Barreto, and the sculptor Abelardo da Hora in commander's uniforms, and with commander's hats on our heads, training young guerrillas. Some people in our circle of friends whom we considered serious and sane still publicized this lie, this hallucination. They did so, as do victims of hallucinations, absolutely certain of the facts, objects of their insane fantasy.

While I was exiled in Paris, a great friend of mine—who had worked with me when little more than an adolescent on one of the projects that I coordinated—told me that she had participated in a meeting after the 1964 coup d'état in Recife at which a certain intellectual who was considered sensible angrily asserted the veracity of that insanity. And, giving himself airs of a defender of justice, he stated that one way or another we were to pay for our craziness: whether in exile, in jail, or away from our academic activities.

How much can political passion, at the service of class interests, lead us into distorting the truth of the facts; how much can it blind us and make us irrational!

The only weapons we had at MCP were our certainty about the deep injustice of Brazilian society, the commitment with which we embraced the democratic struggle in defense of human rights, and our confidence in progressive education, which was not generally seen as a lever for social transformation nor understood as a consequence of it. It was our understanding of the role of culture in general, and popular culture in particular, in transformation that led us, some more than others, to be criticized and deemed "idealistic bourgeois" by ardent mechanists both within MCP and, with more vehemence, on the Left, outside the movement.

Unknowingly, we were following in the footsteps of Antonio Gramsci and Amílcar Cabral and their dialectic understanding of culture and its role in the liberation of the oppressed.

It is no accident that the words *culture* and *popular* were so frequently present in the movement's vocabulary. Popular Culture Movement. Cultural centers. Cultural circles. Cultural squares. Popular theater. Popular education. Popular medicine. Popular poetry. Popular music. Popular festivals. Popular mobilization. Popular organization. Popular art. Popular literature.

One of the stated objectives of the movement was the preservation of popular culture traditions: the people's festivals, their stories, their mythic figures, and their religiousness. In all this we found not only the resigned expression of the oppressed but also their possible methods of resistance. All the June festivities, the *maracatus*, the *bumba-meu-boi*, the *caboclinhos*, the *mamulengo*, the fandango, the *carpideiras*, the *cordel* literature, the handicrafts, the excellent ceramic sculptures—none of these ever escaped the movement's notice.[2]

As I write, a memory comes to my mind of the sculptor Abelardo da Hora working in the shade of the trees at the Trindade Ranch, the MCP headquarters. His thin figure and strong gaze, his work in an improvised studio with the popular youth, these are very vivid memories. One of his theories was that drawing the world, depicting things, using other languages, was not the exclusive privilege of a few. All people can make art, he felt, which did not mean that all people could be remarkable artists.

In general, it is school that inhibits us, making us copy models or color in drawings we have not made ourselves, when school should do the opposite and challenge us to take risks with aesthetic experiments. After all, aesthetics is the very nature of educational practice, meaning we must not be alien to beauty. Abelardo da Hora's work in MCP was a testimony to our confidence in human creativity and its ability to transform the world.

One of the mistakes made by the mechanists is their failure to realize that not all that results from the relationship between the oppressed and the oppressor is an expression of the inherent limits of the latter. To say that all creation by the oppressed is solely an expression of inherent limitation is merely to duplicate the oppressor's model. Things are not exactly like that. Were that the case, the contextual phenomena involved in the relationship would be clear and simple. It is true that in oppressor-oppressed relationships, the oppressed often become ambiguous and dualistic as they internalize the oppressor, who becomes almost like a shadow inhabiting the oppressed. They lose their authenticity. They become the oppressor. However, the part of themselves that is not the oppressor internalized prevents them, in spite of their ambiguity, from being reduced to the oppressor. It is this almost tenuous trace of themselves that makes their creation, their language, and their culture something more than just a copy, makes it a kind of muffled cry of resistance, of the rebel in them.

In truly democratic educational practice, nonmechanistic and also radically progressive, the educator must not suppress this rebellious nature. On the contrary, while teaching the indispensable content, he or she should bring this rebelliousness into focus and analyze it as a position to be overcome and replaced by another, more critical, more consciously political, and more methodologically rigorous position.

The ideal is to promote the transformation of rebellious consciousness into revolutionary consciousness. To be radical without becoming sectarian. To be strategic without becoming cynical. To be skillful without becoming opportunistic. To be ethical without becoming puritanical. This is an ideal whose promotion, despite its undeniable importance, is often blocked. The rebellious consciousness of the popular urban masses is terrified, cornered up on the *morros* or slums, in the *favelas* or ghettos; the masses face an infection to which they are exposed by the evil of outlaws and police, equally outside the law, who fight for control of the drug traffic.

The state crumbles before our very eyes. Lack of shame is both a symptom and a cause of the crumbling. Criminals of popular origin are encouraged by the shamelessness of criminals from the dominant class.

Paulo Farias, for example, the strategist behind his own escape from Brazil, gave interviews while in hiding telling how easy it had been to get out of the country. Fernando Collor[3] currently threatens us with his possible election to Congress! Thousands of tons of food are being buried or burned because of deterioration due to the irresponsibility or incompetence of personnel who never admit errors. International corporations rule us as if we were their objects. Judges are involved in corruption schemes. Congress members switch parties for dollars. A state governor is suspected of having ordered the murder of a senator who, in turn, was involved in drug trafficking. Scandals in Congress. Representatives, senators, ministers, and governors involved in a corruption scheme for distributing funds in the federal budget. A congress member speaks smoothly, giving himself the air of a saint, while explaining that he won the lottery two hundred times over a short period because he was protected by Christ, who cares a great deal for him and always helps.

The ideal is to promote revolutionary consciousness, which despite being more difficult to attain, continues to be essential and possible. This process of promoting revolutionary consciousness has been proven to be possible. Just look at the advancement of popular movements throughout the 1980s and into the 1990s, a decade seen as lost by many.

Look at the advances made by the landless; their victories in claiming land rights, cooperatively developing the land, and creating settlements. Look at the homeless and the schoolless. Victories exist side by side with the sacrifice of lives, paid by "the peoples of the jungle." Look at the community schools.

About three or four years ago, I had the opportunity to teach a final class to a group of young popular educators on a farm in Rio Grande do Sul.[4] The farm had recently been successfully claimed by the landless movement. The following day, the educators were to split up and leave for the different settlements into which the farm had been divided.

At one point, a young man who was a literacy educator active in the movement spoke. In his speech, after a small pause to organize his thoughts, he said, "During one of the early moments of our struggle, we had to cut, with the strength we gained from our union, the barbed wire surrounding the farm. We cut it and entered. But when we got in, we realized that the hardest fences to cut were within ourselves. The fences of illiteracy, ignorance, and fatalism. Our ignorance makes for the happiness of the land owners, just as our learning, reading, improving memory, and advancing culture makes them tremble in fear. That is why we have to transform what was a huge latifundio into a great cultural center."

The speech of that country leader in the south of the country took me back almost thirty years, back to our discussions about culture, its importance in the democratic struggle, and the role of critical education. These animated discussions, at times private discussions, were held at my house, at Argentina and Paulo Rosas's, at Norma and Germano Coelho's, and at Anita Paes Barreto's.

As the young country leader spoke, I kept saying to myself: there is no need to recreate MCP. It is alive without that name and without its organization, in the struggle and spirit of the popular movements of today. Wherever educators learn from popular movements and teach them, the MCP of the 1960s in Recife is still alive. Something, however, scares me today, and the more it scares me the more it moves me to speak, in fact to shout to express my concern. It scares me that the disillusionment of millions of Brazilians—caused by cynicism, dissimulation, the democratization of shamelessness, which covers up everything and leaves for tomorrow the necessary but never applied punishment—may end up leading Brazilians to defend the dictatorship that emerges from democracy's drowning in corruption.

The path to our reinvention does not proceed through dictatorship, through shutting down Congress, or through denying freedom. The discourse that levels all politicians, deeming them all birds of a feather, is false and unfair. There is no unanimity, either in virtue or in error.

Closing Congress will not eradicate the problems of our society, nor will the restriction of freedom of expression. We have to remake Congress.

If, however, you the reader ask me whether I have a solution, I will tell you that I do not, that no one has. But one thing I know and can tell you—based on the teachings of history, our own history as well as that of others—the way to go is not antidemocratic, it is not the path of authoritarianism, or of sectarianism, either by the Left or by the Right. The way to go is the democratic struggle for the possible dream of a fair society, one more human, more decent, and more beautiful for those reasons.

I brought to MCP everything I had learned in my rich experience at SESI, which I spoke about in my previous letter. To my practice during the final stages of family and school as well as the parent/teacher circles was added the no less rich experiment with the direction of the SESI clubs, encouraging them to take charge of themselves, challenging them to overcome the SESI assistantialism. In those democratic practices, the process of discovery was lived dialogically, down to the choice of the word *cognition*, in which to know is not simply to receive knowledge but also to produce it.

Concerned, in my informal educational practice, with the authoritarianism and mechanism of the traditional school, I dreamed of the creation of an open, living, curious institution, one where the educator would, while teaching, expose himself or herself to learning and where the learner learned that only those who produce understanding or intellectualize what is taught can truly learn. In other words, only those who comprehend and reformulate what is taught can truly learn. That is why mechanical memorization of the profile of a concept creates no knowledge.

Thus, as an offshoot of the adult education project I coordinated in the movement, the cultural circles and the cultural centers were born. The latter were large spaces that housed cultural circles, rotating libraries, theatrical presentations, recreational activities, and sports events. The cultural circles were spaces where teaching and learning took place in a dialogic fashion. They were spaces for knowledge, for knowing, not for knowledge transference; places where knowledge was produced, not simply presented to or imposed on the learner. They were spaces where new hypotheses for reading the world were created.

The educators we had were young university students who came to the movement as volunteers. After being briefed on the different projects in progress within the movement, they would choose, according to their personal preferences, where they wanted to make their contribution. After a learning stage, which was never considered complete—learning is permanent—the candidates began to work under the supervision of the team coordinating the project.

The first cultural circles were held in popular locations throughout Recife.

Circles formed in philanthropic organizations, soccer clubs, neighborhood associations, and churches. The educators were in charge of preparing these sites for the circles. They would visit the club, church, or neighborhood association and talk about the possibility of pedagogical work. If the proposal was accepted, we promoted the activities using popular resources. We took advantage of word-of-mouth promotion through neighborhood bars, barber shops, clubs, and churches.

Once two or three circles had formed, the educators would conduct a thematic assessment among the participants. As a team, at the movement headquarters, we would analyze the assessment. Once addressed, we developed the themes and organized a program to be discussed with the participants of the circle. The number of meetings varied from circle to circle as a function of the different possibilities and the interests of circle members. We prepared materials for sessions on the basis of what we had available: blackboards, chalk, slide projectors, felt boards, tape recorders, and so on. I wonder sometimes about how much we would have been able to do today with the technological resources available.

After a few of these thematic assessments, I developed a sense for the fundamental topics that research would raise.

Nationalism, democracy, development, imperialism, voting by illiterates, agrarian reform, money transfers from abroad, illiteracy, and exclusion from education were some of the themes that made up the universe of curiosity in popular areas around Recife in the 1960s.

The effectiveness of this work, the interest it generated, the liveliness of the discussions, the critical curiosity and learning ability that the groups demonstrated made us think about developing something similar focusing on adult literacy.

The results of the cultural circle activities within MCP repeated the methodological success of dialogic activities developed at SESI.

When I started to teach about paths to adult literacy, I was already convinced of the validity of certain principles. I just got to go more deeply into them and understand better, in the light of practice, how I became involved with the theoretical reflection that I always embraced.

As I write today about that time, I am not just what I was yesterday, but also what I am today. I speak of what I thought yesterday and today in a continuum, which really exists.

If one thinks about my time at SESI—the political-pedagogical practice about which there was never a lack of critical reflection and always an intensive reading of extensive literature—one realizes how the MCP principles and dreams were the same as mine. They were handed to me, an excellent field of activity. Activity that was an expansion of other activities lived out in a different place at a different time, the SESI time and space. One difference, though, was that at SESI I was a possible contradiction while at MCP I was a fortunate coincidence.

Let us then look at some of the principles from which I started and about which I will not speak at length, for I have developed them, at times to exhaustion, in previous studies.

Perhaps the best way to talk about them is to take educational practice—given an educational situation—as the object of our curiosity and to seek, by unveiling it critically, to detect its necessarily constructed elements.

Let us engage in an exercise. Maria is a teacher. As a teacher, she feels and knows herself to be an educator. She works three times a week with a class of thirty students to whom she teaches Brazilian history.

The first observation is that education takes place in a given space, to which, customarily, little or no attention is paid. In reality, the space in which the educational experience is lived is just as important for educators and learners as is my house or place of work. For me, this would be the space where I write or read. The apparent lack of order on my writing desk might become real disorder if anyone other than myself tried to organize it. After all, the setup in the room or on the desk has to do with what I do and what I do it for—it has to do with my own self. It has to do with my taste, or lack thereof, which I may not have worked on to turn into good taste. We need to associate our work space with certain qualities that are extensions of ourselves. We make a space that will either remake us or will help us accomplish our tasks. It is in this sense that what may seem circumstantial, mere accessory in the educational space, ends up becoming as essential as the space itself. Beauty and care for the space is necessary to connect with the frame of mind needed for the exercise of curiosity. A good starting point for the school year may be a discussion among educators and learners about their space and how to make it or maintain it as a happy and pleasant place. There is a necessary relationship between the educator's body, the learner's body, and the space in which they work. No living body fails to experience its space. Care for space reveals a willingness to fight for it and an understanding of its importance. It also reveals that a conscious body refuses and resists fatalist indifference, the idea that nothing can be done.

It is for a reason that animals always mark their space, in defense of which they will fight to the end. It is for a reason that, while sitting on a park bench, we react if a stranger sits too close. I am convinced that the lack of interest in space denotes a certain "mental bureaucratism" about the task to be accomplished in the space. It does not seem to me that care for what we do can coexist with indifference or disregard for the space in which we operate. Besides, showing respect for the work space is an excellent way for the educator to give learners an example of discipline and to help learners recognize the importance of space for good practice. The same can be said about the space in which children live and play. How will they respect the classroom tomorrow if they disrespect the living room in their houses today in the name of being free? How will they respect the world out there, the trees, animals, and water, if they mistreat the furniture in their house, their pets, and the plants in their backyards?

On my excursions through the popular areas of Recife, I was impressed with the healthy and legitimate vanity with which truly poor housewives presented their living rooms—the "pressed ground" floors absolutely clean;[5] their stools varnished; and, once in a while, a chair sporting an artistically embroidered, immaculate white doily. The walls were sometimes covered with family pictures.

A house like that could not coexist with fatalism.

Jonathan Kozol, one of the most important U.S. educators today and author of the best-seller *Death at an Early Age: The Destruction of the Hearts and Minds of Negro Children* tells of his experiences as a teacher in the Boston public schools, where racial discrimination lead to the most absurd disregard for the pedagogical space of the oppressed.

As I say in the preface to its Brazilian edition, *Death at an Early Age* is a phenomenal book, unfortunately little read, and one of the first books in which I found myself. During one of my almost daily pilgrimages to the excellent bookstores in Cambridge, Massachusetts, back in early 1969, I took this book off the shelf and flipped through the pages—a universal gesture well known to those who lose themselves in walking the "streets" of large bookstores. I had already been introduced to the book. Someone in New York had told me enthusiastically about it weeks before.

Still, in the bookstore, I read Robert Coles's preface to the book and it propelled—this is exactly the verb—me home to read Kozol's excellent book, which I did in almost one sitting.

As I read, everything in the book touched me strongly, demanding my total focus, not letting me put it down. His smooth but not sweet style, his strict but not arrogant tone, the accuracy of his words, his clear depiction of oppressed children's suffering, his ability to be with them and be close to them without doing them any favors, all added to his courage not to take the path of least resistance: settling into the discriminatory game with the false air of a children's rights advocate. Kozol would never hesitate to chose between the silence of those who condone the "death at an early age" of unloved children and the practice and gestures that would expose that death. He exposed problems and was removed from his substitute teacher position in a public school of Boston's "Third World." It is not an accident that his book remains current in the United States, published year after year, or that it had six printings within the first month of its launching.

The book's title describes its content, which Kozol approaches passionately. That is how he always writes. Kozol does not write books just to meet bureaucratic demands. Kozol gestates his books in the love and passion that rise from the battles he wages and the reality he engages.

One month after I had read and reread *Death at an Early Age*, I went to coordinate a program in Cuernavaca, Mexico, at the center Ivan Illich kept dynamic and open, and which attracted a countless number of Latin American, European, and U.S. intellectuals—including at that time Kozol.

In the circular courtyard filled with ferns at the pleasant house in which the center was based, Illich gathered the intellectuals who, for one reason or another, were there—some doing research, with the wealth of documents available at the center, others coordinating programs, sometimes permanently like Francisco Julião,[6] who lived in Cuernavaca Northeast Brazilian style.

Once we returned home, I to Cambridge and Kozol to Boston, we never stopped filling our Saturday afternoons with friendly conversation.

"After the window had collapsed," Kozol wrote in *Death at an Early Age*, "the janitor showed up to nail it down so it would no longer fall open. It took a month to obtain the glass pane that was missing. The children near the window shivered. The principal passed our room frequently and could have noticed the situation, as could the school supervisors." What to do, from a pedagogical and human point of view, in a space disregarded to such an extent!

What to do with the most impoverished spaces of Brazilian schools, mostly in popular areas that are forgotten and discriminated against? Brazilian educators' struggle must begin with a radical demand for decent salaries that respect teachers' personal and professional dignity, and then defend pedagogical space, permanent professional development, and paid study time.

We need to arrive at the moment when no man or woman can say, in his or her own defense, "Teachers are right, they do not get paid enough, but I don't have the funds to pay what they are asking."

Those who govern must develop in themselves what they seem to be lacking, with rare exceptions: the political will not just to campaign on health and education as priorities, but also to prove that they are priorities once elected.

For health and education to become priorities, funds are indispensable: concretely, prioritizing them must translate into money for personnel, research materials, and for the permanent development of personnel.

What seems immoral to me is the accentuated gap between salary levels. Some have so much while others have nothing, as is the case with educators.

We must, for that reason, not only collect taxes from those who do not pay but also redirect policy on public spending. We must eradicate unnecessary expenses and make the distribution and use of funds more honest. We must punish those who in their practice as elected officials do nothing in favor of education, despite their campaign discourse, by denying them our future votes. In reality, whenever a new government steps into power, it inherits five hundred years of disregarding public education. They always claim that during their administration they granted salary adjustments that went beyond the inflation rate, but they must do more: overcome the marginalization to which educators have been subjected. It is not possible for us to keep up with the times in schools that are mistreated and underequipped, or to have competent and good-humored teachers with the current salaries.

We must exhort, almost preach to, our society and wake the nation's conscience about what education really represents. An awakening of conscience is needed to accept the profound significance of educational practice and certain necessary sacrifices.

That is why whenever teachers in a public school system go on strike, defending or demanding decent salaries, they are exercising a legitimate, democratic right and testifying to children and teenagers about the struggle to advance society.

Instead of criticizing teachers, the families of students should fight against the state, which, historically, has failed in its duty to offer quality and quantity education to its population. It is not with make-believe salaries that we can achieve quality education. The struggle of teachers is fair, and it will be all the more beautiful the less it hurts ethics in the course of its implementation.

If the first basic principle of educational practice is the importance of pedagogical space, the second basic principle is the existence of subjects, educators and learners, which does not mean they are equal to each other. The fact that both are subjects of the practice does not nullify the specific role of each one. The former are subjects of the act of teaching; the latter are subjects of the act of learning. The former learn as they teach; the latter teach as they learn. They are all subjects of the knowing process, which involves teaching and learning.

A third principle is the importance of content or the object of cognition; given that practice is cognitive by nature, it cannot exist without the object of knowledge, which must be taught by the teacher and learned by students.

On the other hand, and now I speak about the fourth principle, there can be no educational practice that is not directed toward a certain objective, which does not involve a certain dream, an idea of utopia. The direction of educational practice explains its political nature, and this is the fifth principle: the impossibility of an "asexual," neutral endeavor.

That educational practice cannot be neutral, however, must not lead educators to impose, subliminally or not, their taste on learners, whatever those tastes may be. This is the ethical dimension of educational practice, the sixth principle.

Finally, a fundamental starting point is respect for the learner's cultural identity and the aspects of class that mark this identity: the learner's language, syntax, prosody, semantics, and informal knowledge, realized through the experiences the learner brings to school.

For all these reasons, I based my adult literacy practice—following research and experiments (anchored in a critical understanding of education that started in the founding days of SESI) I carried out at MCP—on the following points:

1. Literacy education is an act of knowing, an act of creating, and not the act of mechanically memorizing letters and syllables.

2. Literacy education must challenge learners to take on the role of subjects in learning both reading and writing.

3. Literacy education must originate from research about the vocabulary universe of the learners, which also gives us their thematic universe. The first codifications to be "read," decodified, by the learners offer possibilities to discuss the concept of culture. To understand culture as a human creation, an extension of the world by men and women through their work, helps to overcome the politically tragic experience of immobility caused by fatalism. If men and women can change, through action and technology (whether incipient or sophisticated), the physical world, which they did not create, why can't they change the world of history—social, economic, and political—which they did create?

4. Literacy education must be characterized by dialogue as a path to knowledge, which does not invalidate informative discourse, without which there is no knowledge.

5. Literacy education must codify and "read" generative words, allowing for the creation of a number of sentences with the words. Only after long experimentation with sentence creation, using generative words in different positions and functions, can the work of decodifying words into syllables begin, followed by combining syllables into new words, and from there to new sentences.

6. Literacy education must not dichotomize reading and writing. One does not exist without the other, and it is fundamental to exercise both systematically. Moreover, learning to write and read must also help improve oral expression, thus the need for exercising both.

7. Literacy education must be premised on remembering what it means for thirty- or forty-year-old adults, used to the weight of work instruments, to manipulate pencils. At the beginning of this new experience, there may be some discrepancy between the strength exerted and the strength of the pencil. Adults must become reconditioned, little by little, through repeated practice.

8. Literacy education must also be premised on remembering the

insecurity of illiterate adults, who will become upset if they feel they are being treated like children. There is no more effective way to respect them than to accept their experiential knowledge for the purpose of going beyond it. Working with learners to create a climate of confidence in which they feel secure is beneficial to the learning process.

For instance, discussing the statements that "nobody knows it all" and "nobody misunderstands it all," if enriched with concrete examples, may contribute to learners taking a more critical position, which in turn reinforces the previous discovery about culture.

Considering the political-pedagogical principles on which I based my work, as well as certain epistemological principles I have addressed in other texts, I have no reason to disavow my propositions. They remain as valid today as they were yesterday, from a progressive perspective. From a literacy point of view, however, the present studies in sociolinguistics and psycholinguistics as well as the contributions of Piaget, Vygotsky, Luria, Emília Ferrero, Madalena Weffort, and Magda Soares, can, if well applied, rectify and improve some of my propositions.

Although my intent in writing about MCP was to talk about my passage through it, I am not satisfied with talking just about the processes in which I was involved. A special importance is attached to everything (or almost everything) that was done in the short time the movement existed. I have mentioned, for example, the value given to popular festivals, which filled the Bom Jesus Village (or Trindade Ranch, as it also is known) with simple people singing, dancing, playing, and being. I have also mentioned the artistic experiments of Abelardo da Hora, who believed that the taste for beauty must be challenged, worked, and was not the property of a few.

Along these lines, I would like to emphasize the cultural square, a project coordinated by Professor Paulo Rosas; the popular education of children and adolescents under the responsibility of Anita Paes Barreto, a remarkable psychologist who expanded herself into a no less remarkable educator; the popular theater, coordinated by Luíz Mendonça and which trained Ariano Suassuna; and the reader for adults, created by Norma Coelho and Josina Godói, which Anísio Teixeira, then head of the National Institute for Pedagogical Studies (INEP), favorably reviewed.[7]

The research project—in which I participated, but which had in Paulo Rosas and his collaborators its most remarkable participants—played an important role in the movement.

Now, relying exclusively on memory, I recall some instances when Anita Paes Barreto, Paulo Rosas, and myself debated, before the audience at a theatrical play, the implications of MCP.

The popular theater project created a mobile circus that went from neighborhood to neighborhood offering theatrical presentations and movies. The tickets were priced at the same level as the least expensive movie theater in the neighborhood. Before the show, they announced that after the presentation three educators would come on stage to discuss, with whoever had the interest to remain, what everyone had to say. Few left, such was the interest in discussions during the sixties. We discussed political, social, economic, cultural, and historic issues. Immersed in the historical process, the popular classes experimented with their curiosity as if measuring the limit of their rights. Populist politics, ambivalent by nature, allowed for more popular participation, while simultaneously restricting it. People came to the debates, to the meetings, sometimes because they were motivated to know more and to intervene, other times because they needed to know how far they could push their right to participate, which they had heard so much about.

MCP subscribed to the school of thought that political-educational practice and educational-political action were unveiling, enlightening practices that sought the maximum of critical consciousness. With this, the popular classes could engage in the effort to transform Brazilian society, from a perverse, unfair, authoritarian society into a less perverse, less unfair, more open society.

This is the necessary utopia—as timely and essential today as it was yesterday—with which I oppose the pragmatists' antidream "dream." Pragmatists decree the death of utopia, ideologies, social classes and conflicts, and the death of history.

Today there is a generative theme that concerns both the powerful and the disempowered alike. It is the theme of knowledge, of the production of knowledge and its instrumentality. Knowledge that, in practical terms, constitutes the preparation of men and women for the production process.

The viability of human groups depends more and more on technical and scientific knowledge.

The neoliberal answer to this challenge is to reduce technoscientific education to training, in which the trainee is not allowed to be concerned about our reason for being or facts that demand any explanation beyond strictly practical techniques.

The progressive answer, whose ideal I have referred to many times in these letters, does not separate technical ability from philosophical reason, manual skill from mental exercise, practice from theory, economic production from political production.

I will not have betrayed the truth if I say that this was the spirit that underlay the work of MCP in Recife.

I believe also that MCP still awaits objective study—which cannot be done by denying the subjectivity of whomever does it—and historical analysis that goes further than essays like this one, which is eminently impressionist.

From MCP to SEC at the Federal University of Pernambuco

The Cultural Extension Service (SEC) of what was then called the University of Recife was born of a dream of President Dr. João Alfredo Gonçalves da Costa Lima's and mine.

I first met him at SESI when he headed the Division of Health and I headed the Division of Education and Culture. Long before he became president, when he was still vice-president, we talked about the possibility of breaking through the university's walls and extending its presence into nonacademic areas among such schooled populations as pre-college students and public school teachers; and extending it to potential clientele in popular areas—for example, offering educational programs with union leaders or (why not?) facing challenges like illiteracy. The importance of the Federal University of Pernambuco in Northeast Brazil contributing to the permanent development of elementary and secondary teachers in the state (or at least in the surrounding towns of the so-called Greater Recife), as well as participating in popular education (beginning with literacy itself) was something that we believed was the essence of a university's mission and did not undermine its rigor in teaching or research.

When we thought in critical terms about the university and popular areas, people, and popular classes, by no means were we suggesting that the university should become indifferent to research and teaching. Lack of rigor or incompetence are not part of the nature of the university's relationship with and commitment to the popular classes. On the contrary, a university that does not fight for more rigor, for more serious-ness in its teaching and research (always inseparable) is a university that does not seriously approach popular classes, nor commit to them.

Discourse that undervalues academia, theory, and reflection in favor of pure practice is false, as false as that which exalts theoretical reflection and denies the importance of practice.

A university, as I have said in previous works but can and should repeat, must orbit two fundamental concerns from which others derive and which relate to the cycle of knowledge. This cycle has only two moments, which are in permanent relation: one is the moment when we learn about existing knowledge; the other is the moment when we produce new knowledge. Even though I insist that it is impossible to separate one moment from the other, even though I emphasize that they are moments of the same cycle, I must highlight that the moment when we learn about existing knowledge is predominantly that of teaching and learning, and that, the moment when we produce new knowledge is predominantly that of research. In fact, however, all teaching implies research and all research implies teaching. There is no real teaching in which one does not find research, as questioning, inquiry, curiosity, and creativity; just as there is no research in which one does not learn why one knows.

What seems so tragic to me is that, most of the time, our universities cannot dedicate themselves to research while producing knowledge. At times, this is due to lack of funds or lack of competent staff; at times, for both reasons. Also, our universities do not assert themselves as centers where learning existing knowledge, the act of teaching, takes place in a rigorous and serious fashion. In fact, such learning is the only way to produce personnel capable of high-level research. The role of the university, be it progressive or conservative, is to live the moments of this cycle seriously. It is to teach, educate, and do research. What distinguish-es a conservative university from a progressive one should not be that one researches and teaches and the other does nothing. I insist that we not, in the name of the university's redemocratization, lessen its seriousness about any of the moments in the knowledge cycle. No progressive educator should ever reduce the democratization of the university to simplifying the treatment of knowledge. This is not what is intended. Rather the distance between the university (or what is done in it) and the popular classes should be shortened without losing rigor and seriousness, without neglecting the duty of teaching and researching.

In order for that to happen, the university must, if it hasn't yet, increasingly become a creation of the city and expand its influence over the whole city. A university foreign to its city, superimposed on it, is a mind-narrowing fiction. I do not mean to say that the university should be the sole expression of its environment, but that the university must start to be identified with its environment in order to move it and not just reproduce it. An individual educator must, in order to go beyond the learner's level of knowledge, set out from that level. Just so must the university have its original context as the starting point of action. Or, in other words, the university must speak its own context in order to be able to unspeak it. To speak your context is to recognize it as your own expression; to unspeak it is a condition of being able to intervene in it, to promote it. That is why nobody unspeaks without having spoken or simultaneously speaking.

The university that is foreign to its context does not speak it, does not pronounce it. It speaks a distant context, alien, thus it cannot unspeak one or the other.

It is unfair and blind for a university to serve only the elite of its context, to offer it excellence, while doing nothing to improve the standards of basic education in its context. Yet, almost always, the university avoids its role by stating that a university is not a high school.

In a democratic and nonelitist university, epistemological demands are different—deeper and wider—but we also know that university studies are a moment of the knowing process in which we participate. For that very reason, universities require appropriate primary and secondary education, indispensable preparation for moving effectively within the university and with good results.

No context can grow if we only touch it partially. The development of a region demands the critical and intellectual education of its majorities, not only a selfish and self-centered elite.

The university that suffers a weak local and regional context, with the largest deficiencies in basic education—a surprising number of lay teachers, underprepared and disrespected with starvation wages—should have, in its departments of education, areas seriously devoted to the permanent development of educators.

These universities should cooperate with the state, towns, popular movements, production cooperatives, social clubs, neighborhood associations, and churches. Through such cooperation, the university could intensify its educating action.

To unspeak your context is to contradict it in order to modify it. If the university context is high rates of illiteracy, with underprepared basic education teachers, the university cannot refuse to improve the situation. For exactly that reason, from June 1963 until April 1964, when a coup d'état was staged against us, the SEC of the University of Recife participated directly in the work carried out by the National Literacy Program (PNA), under the responsibility of the Ministry for Education and Culture. Due to lack of time, we didn't get to initiate any efforts in educating public basic education teachers. The SEC had a very short-lived existence, less than two years, and the directors who followed us had no reason to share our dreams or our understanding of the university's role.

We did start, however, several projects that allowed SEC to speak its context: the agreement with the state government in Rio Grande do Norte that made possible the experience in Angicos; the cooperation with the Ministry for Education and Culture to educate teams responsible for literacy programs all over the country; the extension programs for high school students from private schools in Recife; the courses in debating education and contemporary Brazilian issues with students from normal schools in Recife; the courses on the Brazilian reality and popular education offered to various groups involved in popular education programs; and the beginning of a directory of professors at the University of Recife created to inform them about the communication we maintained with foreign universities.

We also published a newsletter that talked about what we were doing and what we intended to do. In addition, we created the university radio station, with excellent and varied programming. We were in the process of obtaining authorization to develop projects geared toward Africa when we were stopped by the 1964 coup d'état. The coup d'état also frustrated our dialogue with union leaders to make the time and space to grow together by debating our reality.

Concerned about being able to speak our context in order to unspeak it, the carefully and seriously constituted SEC directing team and I visited the most important institutions, universities and otherwise, in the Recife area. These institutions were devoted to research, education, and reality intervention; with their directors we discussed what we intended and opened ourselves to suggestion. That was how we contacted all schools and research institutes within the university; agencies like Superintendent of the Development of the Northeast (SUDENE), headed then by the economist Celso Furtado; and the Rural Social Service, under the direction of Professor Lauro Borba.[8]

It is interesting, and my duty, to mention the excellent team with whom I was able to create SEC at the University of Recife. The team shared duties in developing and coordinating different projects. They were all very young then, and today they are all well-established intellectuals in this or that area: Luíz Costa Lima, José Laurênco de Melo, Juracy Andrade, Sebastião Uchoa Leite, Orlando Aguiar da Costa Ferreira, Jarbas Maciel, Jomard Muniz de Brito, Roberto Cavalcanti de Albuquerque, and Francisco Bandeira de Mello. To them was added later a good group of educators invested in understanding the practice of popular education.

In addition to the fundamental contribution that Luíz Costa Lima made in SEC—coordinating programs in literary theory and Brazilian literature that were offered to young college or precollege students—he also directed the *Cultural Journal of the University of Recife, University Studies*, of which he was executive secretary.

Another project that I want to mention here (only because it has insisted, almost as if it were a person, on being mentioned ever since I started to organize my notes about my remarkable experience with SEC), is that of joining efforts with MCP through an MCP–SEC cooperation agreement. I am talking about the cultural circles already up and working in popular areas around Recife. The project, equally frustrated by the coup d'état, called for the circles' expansion and reinforcement, transforming them, little by little, into Popular Institutes of Brazilian Studies (ISEB).[9] They would then be popular, nonpopulist versions of the circles. This project, and the very idea of SEC and MCP, really made clear that we bet on the popular classes' ability to mobilize, organize, empower themselves, and know; and not only that we bet on them because this was our choice, our political utopia, and we were moved by an impossible dream, but that we saw as one of the conditions of life itself the necessity of never becoming immobile. Picture yourself at this level of human existence.

The permanent process of learning, and thus of teaching and knowing, makes immobility impossible. The human presence in the city, translated into transforming social practice, brings about more knowing, more teaching, more learning. What changes from human culture to human culture is the speed with which each transforms itself within history.

The popular classes learn and know, in spite of the obstacles imposed on them. Our political-pedagogical thesis was to provide the popular classes with opportunities to uncover hidden truths. To this uncovering of truths, we added the acquisition of technical and scientific knowledge.

Our political-pedagogical thesis, then, had an ethical, scientific, and philosophical foundation.

Yesterday, as much as today, paralyzing reactionary forces were and are against the lucidity of the popular classes.

Yesterday, conscientization was seen as a devilish instrument, and I was seen as the devil himself, threatening the suffering souls of so many innocents with destruction.

Today, conscientization, dreams, utopias, none are valid to the immobilists. Only what is practical, they say, is valid, and only scientific and technical effectiveness is practical.

Today, given the circumstances of our time, neoliberal, pragmatic discourse has been less and less capable of vindicating what endured the "threat" of communism.

The proclaimed triumph of capitalism and death of socialism actually just underlines the perversity of capitalism on the one hand and the enduring socialist dream on the other, if it is purified, with sacrifice and pain, from authoritarian distortion. Thus, the necessary dependence between socialism and democracy has been affirmed, in light of the failure of authoritarian socialism and the intrinsic evil of capitalism, which is insensitive to the pain of the exploited majorities. If the dream of the emerging bourgeoisie was capitalism as the mark of bourgeois democracy, so the dream of the popular majorities today is socialism as the mark of popular democracy. The fundamental point is not to end democracy, but to perfect it and have not capitalism but socialism as its filling. Those who are devoted to this dream must not give into the mechanistic view of history, already so criticized in these letters, according to which the future is a given fact, not a changing reality that we shape through struggle. One should not believe that it was enough for the bourgeoisie simply to dream of uniting capitalism and democracy for it to happen. The bourgeoisie had to fight the aristocracy and anticapitalist forces to gain that unity.

Forging the unity between democracy and socialism is the challenge that inspires us, clearly, at the end of the century and the beginning of the millennium. It is a challenge and not certain destiny, hope of utopia and not fate. The future is a problem, a possibility, and not inexorable.

The SEC of the Federal University of Recife and the Adult Literacy Experience in Angicos, Rio Grande do Norte

On a Sunday afternoon, I forget in what month of 1963, I arrived home with my first wife, Elza, and daughters and sons from our regular walk. Calazans Fernandes, a young but already well-known journalist, then secretary of education for the state of Rio Grande do Norte, was waiting for me. Fernandes had written an excellent report on Angola in which he denounced colonialist evil but he had not found a place to publish it. Luíz Costa Lima offered him space in the *Cultural Journal of the University of Recife, University Studies,* which did well by lovers of freedom and the people's autonomy, but certainly created some diplomatic and political problems for the university's President João Alfredo.

It was worth it.

Fernandes had come from Natal to hold a preliminary conversation with me about my research on literacy work.

Not long before, Odilon Ribeiro Coutinho, an old and close friend, and I had had one of the long conversations we used to have, and which I miss today, touching on many topics, some raised by others and expanding into unexpected themes. One of my conversations with Odilon had been exactly on the topic of my literacy research. I had told him about the experiment I conducted at Poço da Panela—the old house deemed a national historic treasure and which belonged to Olegário Mariano's family. I had told Odilon about the emotion I felt when a literacy student named Joaquim (my father's name and one of my sons' name) wrote his first word, "NINA," and exploded into nervous uncontrolled laughter. I, involved in the emotion of the moment, asked him, although I guessed the answer, "What's the matter, why do you laugh so much?"

"Nina, Nina," he said, not laughing anymore, as if he was certain he had reinvented a person. "Nina is my wife's name. It's my wife."

That moment, rich in humanity, I lived intensely in my practice as an educator. I shared the happiness of someone who wrote, for the first time, his wife's name.

I had told Odilon about the surprise, almost disbelief, with which one of my students at the philosophy school—who had accompanied me to Poço da Panela to meet Joaquim—greeted Joaquim's reading of a page from a book I had assigned, a book by Machado de Assis. Joaquim read with no hesitation, and my student could not believe that not too long before it would have been impossible for him to read it. Odilon had repeated these comments to the governor, who in turn had passed them on to Fernandes and asked that he contact me.

That was why Fernandes was there, on my porch, sitting in front of me on a Sunday afternoon one month in 1963. He wanted to inquire about obtaining my assistance in the area of adult literacy in the state of Rio Grande do Norte.

"What can we do," said Fernandes, "to get you to help us lower illiteracy in Rio Grande do Norte? We have funds from the Alliance for Progress earmarked for education."

My cooperation, I said, depended only on the state's acceptance of a few conditions:

1. a cooperation agreement between Rio Grande do Norte's state government and the University of Recife be written up;

2. the agreement should specify that the state's Department of Education be responsible for the expenses of transportation, meals, and accommodations incurred by the team accompanying me to Natal each time, and for honorariums to be stipulated;

3. the state government pay only for my transportation, meals, and accommodations; I was already paid by the university to work full time;

4. my cooperating with the state government not prevent me from also cooperating with the city of Natal, whose education secretary, Moacir de Gois, was and continues to be a close friend;

5. no conflict between the political positions of Major Djalma Maranhão, a man of the Left, and Governor Aluízio Alves, a man of the center;

6. the coordination of the project be left to the university leadership, in close cooperation with the secretary of education;

7. the state governor refrain from paying any visits to the centers or culture circles during work, to avoid their political exploitation.

I also remember that Fernandes humorously mentioned the Alliance for Progress and asked whether my relationship with it might hurt me politically.

"First of all," I answered, "my relationship will be with the state government of Rio Grande do Norte, through its education department; second, what matters most to me is the autonomy that the university leadership and I will have to make decisions, as well as your seriousness and the state's acceptance of my requests. Where the money is coming from does not matter if I can work independently for the political dream to which I am committed. I am certain that if the Alliance for Progress intends to corrupt us, it will soon give up due to the impossibility of succeeding."

In 1970, when I was still in Cambridge, I bought a book written by Jerome Levinson and Juan de On, called *The Alliance that Lost Its Way*, which said—and now please allow me the long quote—that:

> Paulo Freire's program was naturally subversive in its deliberate
> provocation and in its purpose of developing a critical conscious-

ness, creating a sense of moral duty in the individual to change his or her own life and the world around him or her. In a paternalistic and hierarchical society, where the colonel's word was law, this emphasis on critical thinking and on individual and community action was destructive of traditional values. Freire's program was revolutionary in the deepest sense of the word.

In January 1964, dissatisfaction with Freire's pedagogical technique and uneasiness around the political content of the program led the alliance to stop its financial support of the program (exactly three months before the coup d'état against President Goulart).

I never stated it better. The point was objectively proven, later, by the facts when I went to Angicos.

Let's return, though, to the conversation with Fernandes. After hearing me and taking notes, he told me that he would brief Governor Aluízio Alves on our conversation and then would get in touch. A few days later I received a telegram suggesting three possible dates for me to go to Natal to meet with the governor and, if he and the secretary of education accepted my conditions about university leadership, to form a team and set the agenda for our cooperative work.

I chose a date, received tickets, and traveled to Natal. I had a long conversation with the governor, who accepted my conditions without any difficulty. He did manifest an interest, however, in choosing Angicos as the city for the experiment. Angicos was his hometown, and it was up to him as governor to choose the city from which to start the project.

Before leaving Natal, I had a meeting with the university leadership and Secretary Calazans Fernandes during which we set two dates in our calendars: one for the leadership to take a work trip to Recife, where we would discuss the program to be presented by the SEC team and its beginning; the second to discuss the program's length and content.

The university leadership's responsibility would be to select the twenty candidates who would participate in the educational program, which would be followed by field activities.

Ideally, the study of Angicos's urban environment, its rural surroundings, and its vocabulary would give us our theme. The choice of generative words and the creation of codifications would constitute the first stage of the educational program. That way, the future educators would have learned by doing, freeing themselves from the practice of their theory.

We had three hundred learners in Angicos, literacy learners distributed among fifteen cultural circles set up in rooms in schools or houses around the city.

Recently, I went back to Angicos: it had been thirty years since I had lived—strongly, intensely, and happily—the experiment in which three hundred people of different ages learned how to read and write by debating local, regional, and national problems. One in which three hundred people realized how they previously had read the world and began, as they learned to read and write, to read it more critically. I was in Angicos with Ana Maria Nita; Professor Moacir Gadotti, from the University of São Paulo; and Professor Carlos Torres, from the University of California in Los Angeles. We met with ten of the literacy educators and twelve of the former literacy learners. We talked and reminisced about memorable moments like, for example, the request that ten convicted recent literates receive amnesty, a request made by Marcos Guerra, leader of the group and today secretary of education for Rio Grande do Norte. We discussed President Goulart's decision to concede after regular hearings. Marcos told the story about the first strike to take place in the city, in the construction business. Workers from neighboring towns had been brought in to weaken the local movement, most of whom were participants in our program. There was a meeting held between the locals and those coming in. After some dialogue, it was agreed that those coming would go back and that the locals would continue in the struggle for their rights. Angicos was a progressive place.

While we were talking and listening, former participants testified about how much they missed that time and their teachers and about their experiences learning to read and write.[10] One speech writer gave us a lot to talk about during the program's closing reception with President Goulart, in which the writer stated that program participants not only learned how to read Brazil's ABCs and its constitution, but also how to rewrite it. During the conversations, I remembered the Alliance for Progress's decision to interrupt its support to the program, three months before the coup d'état of 1964.

How right I was to make a contribution to that program. How wrong were those who criticized me for it.

During the ceremony in which the Municipal House of Representatives officially granted me the title of honorary citizen of Angicos, a young woman interviewed by Nita told Nita that she had been taught literacy side by side with her parents, who had to bring her to class because she could not be left at home alone. She must have been six then.

"I took such a liking to reading and writing that I became a teacher. On the last day of the program, I approached President Goulart and told him that I could read and write too. Laughing, he asked one of his assistants to give me a newspaper so I could read. I had no problem and read a good part of the news on the front page. Then he asked me, 'What would you like as a gift?' 'A scholarship,' I said."

"If a president asked you that question today, what would you say?" Nita asked.

"Today, I would ask the president for respect toward the teachers of this country, decent salaries, and a serious education for all Brazilian children."

Thirteenth Letter

~

Dear Cristina:

Now I get to the end of the first batch of these letters to you. This is a transition letter after those in which, in response to your initial request, I talked primarily about myself: myself as a boy, as a youth, and as a man; myself and how I think, how I always subject my practice to theoretical reflection, how, without martyring or punishing myself, I consistently try to shorten the distance between what I say and what I do. This is a transition letter between the first batch, in which I talked about happiness, pain, suffering, and personal experiences, and the second batch, in which, although talking some about myself, I focus on the spectrum of topics that have been suggested to me inside and outside of Brazil in seminars, interviews, and newspaper and magazine articles.

I hope, however, that there will be some harmony, from the point of view of language or style, between the first and the second batches as there is between the letters themselves. In fact, rare is the letter in the first batch in which, while talking about my father, my mother, or myself, I did not devote some time to analysis, at times careful analysis, of a concept or topic. Rare is the letter in which, while discussing a problem, I do not expand into another, without losing, however, the focus of the discussion. But, above all, I hope not to disappoint readers who, by chance, may have enjoyed the first batch of these letters.

Uncle Paulo

Fourteenth Letter

~

It is not possible to act in favor of equality, respecting others, the right to a voice, participation, and reinventing the world in a regime that denies the freedom to work, eat, speak, criticize, read, disagree, come and go; in short, the freedom to be.

ONE OF THE NEGATIVES OF THESE LETTERS winds up becoming a positive in terms of the greater challenge that writing them represents to me. I am referring to my not quoting much outside support for the analyses that I make of this or that topic in my discussion. The quick spirit of the letters has led me to adopt a simple language, accessible and personal. I want to make it clear that avoiding the anguish of nervously searching for texts or statements that might lend weight to mine does not imply the arrogance or self-sufficiency of someone who, full of himself, does not need the support of anybody. On the contrary, I do require the support and help of others, and I do not find it demeaning to receive it.

For example, if I talk, as I have and will continue to do, about education and democracy (in the context of these letters and in the style in which I write them), I am satisfied just to describe how I see and understand the problem.

As I center education and democracy as the focus of my curiosity, I should first pose a question: what do we mean by education and democracy? What does my approach to the words, in search of an understanding, lead me to? Undeniably, there is in my approach an intention to establish relationships between education and democracy.

Education for democracy, education and democratic experience, democracy through education. There is no doubt that the words suggest further questioning: Is it possible to teach democracy? What does it mean to educate for democracy? What do we do as educators if our society has a strong democratic tradition? What do we do if it does not but the educator still has progressive beliefs? What does it mean to be a democratic society?

Another aspect to think about, as we question ourselves about education and democracy, is centered in the contradictory, dialectic relationship between authority and freedom. Relationships that, in turn, cannot be separated from their ethical nature.

I have insisted, throughout my educational practice, which has never lacked philosophical reflection, that finite, unfinished beings, men and women, be socialized into being more. Thus, I have always stated that humanization, while an orientation, has in dehumanization its distortion. This orientation is part of the nature of human beings, their historical nature, socially constituted, and its distortion has always been a historical possibility.

No reflection about education and democracy can exclude issues of power, economic, equality, justice and its application, and ethics.

I would not hesitate to state that since the ontological orientation of men and women has evolved toward being more, democracy will be the form of struggle they chose as the most appropriate to realize this orientation. There is, then, an ontological and historical foundation for the political struggle around democracy and its permanent improvement. It is not possible to act in favor of equality, respecting others, the right to a voice, participation, and reinventing the world in a regime that denies the freedom to work, eat, speak, criticize, read, disagree, come and go; in short, the freedom to be.

The democracy that is solely political denies itself. In it, the only right that is offered to the masses is that of the vote. Under the perverse circumstances of misery in which the masses survive, the vote is insulted and degraded. In these societies, democracy ensures the miserable and the poor only the right to die from hunger and pain. This is the case in Brazil: thirty-three million Marias and Josefas, Pedros and Antónios suffer from hunger and pain day in, day out. A solely formal democracy does very little, almost nothing, for the liberation of the oppressed except for providing political spaces, the existence of which merely formal democracy cannot disallow. These are spaces that should be used by progressives in their struggle to transform society. At the same time, the democracy that calls itself economic—whose dream is in part to overcome the injustices brought about by the capitalist system, but whose ideals of justice, equality, and respect have been subjected to an authoritarian framework—perverts itself.

I do not believe in any struggle for equal rights, for overcoming injustice, which is not blended with an orientation toward humanization, toward being more about men and women.

As I have always insisted, this orientation is not the expression of an idealistic dream, but instead a quality that human beings have incorporated into their nature historically and socially. It is in this sense that class, gender, and race discrimination, to which may be added any disrespect or diminution of another human being, denies democracy by denying that orientation.

No society can reach democratic plenitude if it is not legally structured to defend itself, vigorously, from such attempts. Even more so, if its antidiscrimination laws are not put into practice or applied improperly. Thus, the existence of laws is not enough; it is indispensable that they be applied regardless of who the individuals involved may be.

Even when good results only sometimes are achieved through critical discourse—results well articulated and supported by human nature and that underline contradictions between discriminatory practices and men and women's orientation toward humanization—it is necessary to pursue critical discourse. It is necessary to insist on unveiling or uncovering the power of those who discriminate while calling themselves Christians, or those who call themselves progressive and discriminate. It is absolutely necessary that they perceive themselves as contradictory and incoherent so that they can work on their lack of synchrony.

We must not give those who discriminate any rest, which only enables them to attempt to solve their problems through the sleazy game of false explanations.

The discriminatory process generates in those who discriminate a defense mechanism that makes them resistant, almost as if they were made of stone. Sometimes, it even seems like they have been convinced, but they have not been. Intellectually, they accept that they have contradicted themselves, but at the gut level they do not feel it. For them, the Christian discourse of "loving thy neighbor as thyself" is reconcilable with racist practices. For the racist, those discriminated against are not equal to others but are just objects. The practice of discrimination belittles as much as it brutalizes people.

Discrimination, regardless of what it is based upon, directly damages democracy, which has tolerance as its foundation. Tolerance is the virtue that teaches us to live with difference and learn from it, to live with those who are different without considering ourselves superior or inferior.

Tolerance is not a favor that "superior people" do for "inferior people." It is the duty of all of us in our dealings with others, the duty of respecting the right of others to be different. Tolerance does not oblige me, however, to agree with others if I am opposed to their opinions.

It does not oblige me, once I have used up all my arguments against the other's position, to continue, in the name of dialogue, a boring and repetitive conversation, ineffective and taxing on both. It does oblige me to respect thinking that contradicts mine and the subject who thinks it. Being tolerant does not mean denying a conflict or trying to escape from it. The tolerant are all the more authentic when they defend their positions, convinced of their correctness. The picture of a tolerant person, then, is not a pale or amorphous one of someone who has to apologize every time there is disagreement. The tolerant know disagreement that is based on respect for those with whom they disagree is not only a right but also a means to grow and develop knowledge. However, as much as disagreement has an important role in social relations, it places a profound ethical demand on those who disagree or criticize: the duty not to lie. Tolerance, after all, is a virtue and not a flaw. Without it, there is no democracy. Teaching tolerance and democracy requires the coherent testimony of parents and teachers. How can we teach tolerance to our children and students if we deny them the right to be different from us, if we refuse to discuss their positions, their reading of the world, if we refuse to see that their world places demands and challenges on them that ours did not?

How can we teach tolerance to our children and students if we teach them that demanding their rights, fighting against untruths, and resorting to the law are authoritarian, as if democracy were loose or lax?

Recently, the mayor of São Paulo, in an interview with a newspaper from the state capital, referred to what he called the distorted use of a photograph of himself next to another politician. He said that he had not taken legal action against the newspaper because he was in favor of democracy and not an authoritarian. No! The mayor did not take any legal action for some other reason, which he has the right not to explain, but not because he is for democracy. Democracy guarantees him the right to seek legal compensation for any damage he suffered.

Freedom of press does not mean an unrestricted press. Only the press that does not lie is free, the press that does not distort, misrepresent, or omit, the press that respects the views of those interviewed by not changing their words. The real defender of democracy believes in freedom of press and knows that legal disputes, from which ethical learning results, are part of the struggle to defend a free press.

To defend our rights is not a demonstration of authoritarianism; it indicates love for freedom, democracy, and justice.

In any case, it is interesting to observe how our strong historical-cultural traditions, authoritarian in nature, almost always put us in ambiguous positions before the contradictory relationship between freedom and authority. Relationships are dialectic and not mechanical. Sometimes, although we are just using our necessary authority, we judge ourselves as authoritarian. Sometimes, afraid of becoming authoritarian, we end up becoming permissive.

Neither one of these positions, authoritarian or permissive, works in favor of democracy. Living the tension between freedom and authority, both at home and in school, is of the greatest importance. It is through these relationships between freedom and authority that, little by little, we learn to define limits for freedom and authority, without which both positions deteriorate and democracy is denied.

One of the mistakes made by family or school authorities is to think that freedom can be limited through fear, coercion, reward, and punishment. By experimenting, a moral individual realizes, little by little, the necessary limits to freedom, but not because he or she is coerced, threatened, or afraid of the reaction of the powers that may violate freedom by not limiting their authority. The authoritarian individual is not concerned about the moral impact on the behavior of the free individual against whom his or her transgression is aimed. To the authoritarian, his or her voice of command is all that matters. It does not matter if the obedience achieved is the result of adhering to a freedom that ethically validates the command. Authoritarianism is immoral: it denies not only the freedom of others but also its own, turning freedom into the immorality of crushing other freedoms.

There is no real limit without the free individual accepting the moral reasons for limits. External limits are only authentic when they become internalized. External authority needs to be internalized, becoming internal authority.

I do not mean to say that authority, when confronted with a freedom that refuses to adhere to limits, should wash its hands and leave things as they are. This kind of authority is permissive, nullifying itself as an authority, and contributes nothing to the authenticity of freedom. The democratic exercise is sacrificed in this distortion of the relationship between authority and freedom. As much as freedom needs to accept limitations to itself as a necessity, authority needs to make itself respected. Disrespect to both makes democracy not viable whether in school, at home, or in the politically organized society.

The freedom that accepts its necessary limits is the one that fights fiercely against the hypertrophy of authority. How wrong are those parents who allow their sons and daughters everything because they had difficult childhoods or because they believe children should be free. This way children regress, instead of grow, and, unaware of limits, tend to lose themselves in the irresponsibility of thinking anything goes.

I believe that a fundamental aspect of the practice of authority, in relation to freedom, is a clear understanding that no authority is solely an authority and no freedom is solely a freedom.

As a father, I am not only paternal authority but also filial freedom and citizen freedom. If I cannot, for different reasons, carry out my duties as a father or as a citizen, I am a paternal authority out of sync and a citizen freedom that is incompetent.

The freedom that frees itself from authority denies democracy as much as the authority that muffles its freedom and that of others.

In the final analysis, authority is an invention of freedom so that freedom may continue to be. Parental authority did not create the freedom of children; the children's need for freedom generated the authority of parents. Authority, then, makes no sense and is not justifiable if it loses its principal task: to assure freedom the possibility of being. Authoritarianism and permissiveness, expressions on the one hand of abuse and on the other of the emptying of real authority, impede real democracy.

For that reason, a progressive educational practice must instill in educators and learners alike the unrestrained taste for freedom. The young should sing, scream, paint their faces,[1] go out into the streets, fill the squares, and demonstrate against lies, deceit, and shamelessness. The young should—while accepting the indispensable limits to freedom, the only way in which their freedom will be real—fight against the abuse of power. The argument that the young should just study is a fallacy. Defense of freedom and alertness to its betrayal are democratic duties that we cannot neglect whether we are young or not. Moreover, protesting against the ethical slips of morally incompetent authorities is not only a way of studying and learning, but also a way of producing knowledge and deepening and strengthening the roots of democracy.

The taste for freedom disappears if its practice becomes scarce, even though it may return in libertarian expressions. The taste for freedom is part of the very nature of men and women, it is part of their orientation toward being more. That is why we talk about the dream of freedom, about the possibility of the taste for freedom when necessity overcomes freedom. Freedom, a sine qua non of being more, is not the finish line but the starting point.

On the other hand, the orientation toward being more is conditioned by the concrete reality of context. It is conditioned by the historical, economic, social, political, and cultural reality.

Freedom of press has different significance for the famished, miserable populations of our country and for those from the popular classes who at least can eat, dress, and sleep somewhere.

What is tragic is that freedom of press is fundamental for all, whether they eat or not. Of course, in miserable conditions, objectively speaking, not everything felt is perceived as abuse. Abuse has been or is being understood along with all its reasons for being. A famished and illiterate population, even if occasionally touched by radio, hardly reaches an understanding of the value of a free press before eating, a press that they

[151]

cannot even see. If, however, such a population is able to start eating, over time their understanding of freedom changes and unveils the value of a free press. Once the basic right of eating is exercised, the denial of other rights becomes emphasized. This is one of the central aspects of the extraordinary work of sociologist Herbert de Souza, whom I prefer to call Betinho.

Perhaps someone may ask: And where does that leave the orientation toward being more ? It leaves it where men and women have placed it throughout the history of their struggles. It leaves it in human nature, historically conditioned. That is exactly why being more is an orientation, not a given fact, nor fate. It is an orientation or, if distorted, dehumanization. That is why living out this orientation implies fighting for it, otherwise it cannot be realized. It is in this sense that freedom is not a gift we receive, but instead a right that we acquire; at times we preserve it, at times we improve it, and at times we lose it. While ontological, the humanization forwarded by the orientation is not inexorable, but problematic. As much as it may be realized it may also be frustrated. It depends on what we make of our present.

The future is not a province some distance from the present which just waits for us to arrive some day and perform the operation of adding this ready-made tomorrow to today, which both become old and obsolete. The future is born of the present, from possibilities in contradiction, from the battle waged by forces that dialectically oppose each other. For this reason, as I always insist, the future is not a given fact, but a fact in progress. The future is problematic and not inexorable. Only in a controlled dialectic can the future be thought of as something already known. From a truly dialectic perspective, the dream that moves us is a possibility for which I must fight so it can be realized. And if I fight with many others for its realization, it is because there are forces that—in opposition to our reason for fighting—struggle to maintain unspeakable privileges that result in a reign of alarming injustices: millions of famished individuals, millions of children kept from school, millions expelled soon after entering, and innumerable people dying from the lack of minimum health and medical assistance. This arbitrary disrespect for the barest minimum of rights for the majority of the population is practiced by the minority in power. I fear that shamelessness, which has been causing hopelessness in the majorities, may be coming to the boundaries of its possible limit.

It is in the concrete, dynamic, and contradictory present that the battle is waged from which the future emerges. Only the past, while lived time and available for our analysis and comprehension, cannot be transformed. It can be accepted, understood, refused, but never changed. It is not possible for us to intervene in it, but by understanding its contradictory movements, it is possible to perform better in the present. The present and the future are times under construction, transitioning into the past.

One of the biggest misconceptions of reactionary practice and thought is to judge that immobilizing the present can transform the future into a repetition of the present. It just so happens that when today's tomorrow becomes a new today, in light of a new, problematic, and uncertain tomorrow, the new today is never a repetition of the previous today.

I am convinced that in the today under construction, one of the experiences to be emphasized the most in improving democracy, considering our strong authoritarian tradition, is creating a taste for freedom. This is a taste that does not grow or strengthen in the absence of responsibility. There is responsibility in the exercise of freedom that takes on the limits that make it more authentic.

Posing situations to learners—so that they can express themselves about the respect or disrespect for rights and duties, the denial of freedom, and the lack of ethics regarding public property—is an indispensable practice in progressive education.

Involving the young in following the developments uncovered by the Congressional Investigative Committee on the Budget, both through the print media and through television, is a practice of undeniable value. Even better would be if young students, summoned by their organizations, take to the streets and, supporting the effort of the committee, criticize the disloyal and demand their punishment.

We cannot, regardless of our age, color, gender, or sexual orientation, allow our developing democracy to drown once again in a sea of mud.

It is possible to teach democracy. First, however, one must give testimony to it and, in doing so, fight for it to be lived and put into practice on a global level. What I mean is that the teaching of democracy cannot be done just through discourse about democracy, often contradicted by authoritarian behavior. The teaching of democracy requires discourse not about abstract democracy, but about it as practiced and experienced. It requires a critical discourse, well founded, and which concretely analyzes its disjunctures and incoherences, as well as a theoretical discourse that emerges from a critical understanding of practice and is ethically based. We cannot reconcile the democratic radicalism for which we fight with a gray, tasteless, and cold understanding of educational practice, an understanding that takes place in classrooms isolated from the world, with educators who merely deposit content into the supposedly empty heads of submissive learners.

Considering the lack of democratic experience in which we grew up, we must be careful in teaching democracy never to have an opinionated manner or to say, "Do you know who you are talking to?" or "Because I said so, there's nothing more to discuss."

Our democracy, in the developing stages, has to avoid both authoritarianism and permissiveness, to which our democratic inexperience always exposes us. We need not the insecure teacher who cannot assert authority, nor the arrogant teacher who abuses authority, but the teacher who never denies either authority or learners' freedom.

Authoritarianism and permissiveness are not paths leading to democracy or its improvement.

Teaching democracy is possible, but it is not a job for those who become disenchanted overnight just because the clouds turn heavy and threatening.

Teaching democracy is possible, but it is not a job for those who, too patient, wait for so long that they miss the train of history, or for those who, too impatient, end up spoiling their own dreams.

Teaching democracy is possible, but it is not a job for those who perceive and act mechanistically, the willful owners of history.

Engaging in democratic experiments, outside of which there is no teaching of democracy, is the permanent job of coherent progressives, who, understanding and living history as a possibility, never tire of fighting for democracy.

This is what is demanded of us progressives in contemporary Brazilian society, a movement that embraces, contradictorily, antidemocratic traditions and popular traditions while overcoming the cycle of military governments that started with the coup d'état of April 1, 1964.

This is the demand of present Brazilian society: that we not waste time, that we not leave for tomorrow what we can do today when it comes to the democratic, ethical character of our practice. The more dramatically we live the contradiction between our antidemocratic heritage and our recently acquired taste for freedom, the more competently and responsibly we stimulate the taste for freedom.

The fight for democracy in Brazil is measured by a number of political and pedagogical rights—the right to justice, without which there is no peace; to life, which implies the right to be born; to eat; to sleep; to have good health; to have clothing; to pay respect to the dead; to study; to work; to be a child; to believe or not to believe; to live one's sexuality any way one deems appropriate; to criticize: to disagree with the official discourse; to read; to play regardless of age; to be ethically informed about what happens on a local, regional, national, and world level; to move, both to come and go; and to not be discriminated against, whether on the basis of gender, class, race, or any other reason, such as being too fat or too thin.

There is a fundamental duty that relates to all of these rights: the duty of being committed to making them viable. Once these rights are recognized beyond a doubt, we must fight incessantly for them, regardless of our role or occupation in society. Critically implemented educational practice makes an indispensable contribution to this political struggle. Educational practice is not the only key to the social transformation required to gain human rights, but no transformation will take place without it.

The greater clarity that education gives the popular classes to "read the world" may bring political intervention that advances the democratic learning process.

What progressive educators need to do is bring life itself into their classrooms. They need to critically read day-to-day life and analyze, with learners, the shocking facts and disjunctures of our democracy. They need to expose learners to examples of discrimination taken from daily experience (race, class, and gender discrimination), and examples of disrespect for public things, examples of violence, examples of arbitrariness. These examples should be analyzed to reveal their aggressive contradiction of what I have been calling men and women's orientation toward being more, which has been constituted as our nature throughout history. Also, they contradict the authenticity of democratic life. In fact, a democracy where discrimination and disrespect occurs without punishment still has a great deal to learn and to do in order to purify itself.

Not that I believe it possible for there to be, some day, a democracy so perfect that such disrespect will not exist.

The possible dream is that of a democracy where disrespect occurs, but its perpetrators, whoever they may be, are severely punished according to the law. The value of democracy lies not in the sanctification of men and women, but in the ethical rigor with which deviations are dealt with, deviations that we are all capable of as historical and incomplete beings. No democracy can expect that its practice will have sanctifying power.

A good democracy warns, clarifies, teaches, and educates. It also defends itself from the actions of those who, by offending their human nature, deny and demean democracy.

While it is necessary that we critique ourselves, we must also recognize that the explosion of scandals—such as the former president's direct participation in corruption, along with ministers, senators, representatives, business people, and judges—has been publicly denounced. This represents undeniable democratic advance. Another advance for which we must fight will be the rigorous punishment of the disloyal. It is also important to emphasize that not one representative, not one senator, not one president made it to the house, the senate, or the presidency without someone's vote. The conclusion is that we need to vote better and that we should add more democracy and never substitute it with authoritarian governments. Democracy is not learned or improved with a coup d'état. It is pure naiveté to accuse only the Brazilian democracy of ethical deviations and arbitrary acts, as if the authoritarian governments were historically immune to corruption. On the contrary, it is exactly because our democracy has improved, or made itself more like a democracy, that we are uncovering such shocking sandals.

Due to a poor understanding of the reasons behind the facts, the naive perceive virtue as a flaw. Without the democracy we experience today, despite all its fits and starts, we would know nothing about ethical problems.

A coup d'état today would set us back just as much, maybe more, than the one in 1964, and it would leave as many scars.

Authoritarian regimes are in and of themselves a contradiction, a profound negation of the nature of human beings, who, poor and incomplete, need freedom to be, just as birds need a horizon to fly.

May the possibility of a new coup—the dream of incorrigible reactionaries, those lovers of death and enemies of life—rest in peace far away from us.

Fifteenth Letter

~

Since the beginning, even at my most indecisive, I visualized the process of liberation as more than the individual struggles of men and women. I also, however, refused to believe that it was a purely social phenomenon or a pure manifestation of class in which the individual was diluted.

THE TASTE FOR FREEDOM, which I have had since my earliest childhood, made me dream of justice, equality, and overcoming the obstacles to realizing the human orientation toward being more, and made me engage, to this day and in my own way, in the fight for the liberation of men and women. A taste for freedom generated itself into a love for life and a fear of losing it.

This central and fundamental theme I have addressed, at times explicitly, at times not, in all the texts I have written. It has also been a central theme in the majority of conferences I have participated in, both inside and outside of Brazil.

In my books *Education as the Practice of Freedom, Pedagogy of the Oppressed, Education and Change, Cultural Action for Freedom, Pedagogy of Hope,* and *Teachers as Cultural Workers,* I may have been more explicit in addressing the theme in question. In some more than in others, I may have made clear the ontological matrix of struggle, which is that human nature has historically and socially become oriented toward being more. Unfortunately, we are oriented toward but not inexorably destined to being more. Thus it is as possible for this orientation to be realized as it is for it to be frustrated.

Since the beginning, even at my most indecisive, I visualized the process of liberation as more than the individual struggles of men and women. I also, however, refused to believe that it was a purely social phenomenon or a pure manifestation of class in which the individual was diluted.

On the contrary, complex and plural, the liberation process involves many dimensions, as many as mark the human being: class, gender, race, and culture.

Just as I could never accept that the fight for liberation could be restricted to the struggle of individuals, I could never accept that it could be reduced to the fight of women against men, of blacks against whites. The fight is one of all human beings toward being more. It is a fight to overcome obstacles to the humanization of all. It is a fight for the creation of structural conditions that make a more democratic society possible. The fight is not, as I said in the previous letter, for a democratic society so perfect it suppresses sexism, racism, and class exploitation once and for all. The fight is for the creation of a society capable of defending itself by punishing with justice and rigor the perpetrators of abuse; it is for a civil society capable of speaking, protesting, and fighting for justice. The final struggle is not to satisfy men and women, but to recognize them as finite, incomplete, and historically bound people who are capable of denying goodness and becoming evil, but also of knowing goodness and becoming loving and fair.

In the struggle for liberation we cannot forget or minimize specific aspects that characterize male-female, black-white, working class–elite relations. But for me, recognizing such specificities is not enough to allow any one group to contradict the focus of the whole process and demean the importance of others. I cannot discount the struggle of women or the struggle against white oppression, but I also cannot afford to discount the role of class, even in a society as complex as the North American one, in understanding racism and sexism. I cannot for the sake of my tactics in my own struggle.

Sometimes I am criticized for not having given enough attention to those individuals who experience the role of the oppressed and subsequently that of the oppressor. First of all, I should say that I have referred to this type of ambiguity, even insistently in some texts, when I discuss the virtues of progressive educators. Among such virtues I emphasize coherence, which demands humility and eschews behavior that contradicts our verbalized belief. We must not adopt a progressive discourse and then engage in a reactionary practice. Such a case, for example is a professor who fights against gender discrimination but adopts an oppressive pedagogical practice. Within his or her academic practice as an advisor of graduate students, helping them develop their theses, he or she behaves in such an authoritarian manner that students have little room to be intellectually adventurous. This hypothetical professor, one easily found in actual schools, is both oppressed and oppressor; that is, incoherent. His or her struggle against sexism loses its strength and becomes inconsequential babble. In order for the struggle to gain authenticity, he or she must overcome incoherence, getting past lip-service, and shorten the distance between what is said and what is done.

As long as the professor in our example reflects critically upon practice, he or she will realize the failure to balance authority as the professor against students' freedom, which has resulted in oppressing them and contradicting antisexist discourse and practice. The professor is left with one of two options: to cynically accept authoritarianism and falsely continue the antisexist struggle, or to revise his or her relationship with the students in order to continue honestly the antisexist struggle. Another case of incoherence is a man who labels himself a progressive, speaks vehemently in favor of liberation for the working class, but at home is his wife's owner.

That is why I defend unveiling the contradictory and the practice of never giving examination a rest. After all, cynicism is not the weapon that will rebuild the world.

Let us insist, however, that incoherence is a possibility and not a fact of our existence. The very viability of incoherence challenges me not to become entangled in it. Humility helps me by warning me that I too can fall into incoherence. At the same time, accepting that there are as many possibilities for incoherence as there are for relationships between dominator and dominated within individuals is not enough to block the liberation process. I remember that in *Pedagogy of the Oppressed* I quoted Franz Fanon and Albert Memmi.[1]

Deep down, the oppressed internalizes the oppressor, who then begins to live within him or her. This is the ambiguity of the oppressed, who grows the oppressor within him or herself.

Engaging in what Fanon called "horizontal violence"—in which some oppressed hurt and mistreat other oppressed as if they were oppressors—the oppressed kill the oppressor within the oppressed.

Another side must be thought out in progressive education; that is, what pertains to the teacher-student relationship.

In the studies that followed *Pedagogy of the Oppressed*, I sought for more clarity as I attempted to analyze teacher-student relations. I have insisted on making it clear that teachers and students are different, but if the teacher has opted for democracy, he or she cannot allow this difference to become antagonistic. This means that he or she must not allow his or her authority to become authoritarian. Once again, we are faced with the incoherence I spoke about: the teacher who adopts a democratic discourse while engaging in an authoritarian practice.

I explained this in *Pedagogy of the Oppressed.*

> The educator places himself or herself before the learners as their necessary antagonizer. He or she recognizes the absoluteness of their ignorance as the reason for his or her existence. The unaware learners, very much in the manner of slaves in Hegelian dialectics, recognize their ignorance as the educator's reason for existing, but unlike the slaves in Hegelian dialectics, they don't get to discover themselves as the educator's educators.
>
> In reality, as we will discuss later, the reason for liberating education lies in its reconciling impetus. Thus, liberating education implies overcoming the opposition between educator and learner in a way that makes both educators and learners.
>
> In a banking model of education ... it is not possible to observe such an overcoming.

If a teacher truly believes in democracy, he or she has no option, upon realizing his or her incoherence, than to shorten the distance between what he or she says and does. No progressive, man or woman, regardless of profession, can escape the possibility of contradicting himself or herself, a possibility that can only be overcome by exercising coherence. From the point of view of our political-pedagogical perspective—whether feminist, radical, critical, liberating, or constructivist—if we are progressive we will have to seek to overcome the contradiction that incoherence represents.

How can a racist teacher speak about democracy, unless it is a very special democracy, one that sees blackness as diminishing it?

How can a sexist teacher speak about democracy, unless it is a democracy indifferent to the presence of women?

How can an elitist teacher speak about democracy, unless it is a democracy for the aristocracy that dwindles in the presence of the popular classes?

No doubt racist, sexist, and elitist teachers who speak about democracy and call themselves progressive must become truly committed to freedom, must undergo their own Easter: They must die to their old selves as sexists, racists, and elitists and be reborn as true progressives, enlisted in the struggle for the reinvention of the world. What is not possible is to continue in the ambiguity that their incoherence brings on—progressive discourse, reactionary practice. Since it is what one does that judges what one says, they will be seen and understood as antidemocratic and reactionary. Their fight for democracy is neither ethically valid nor politically effective.

It is not the necessary authority of teachers that makes them obstacles to liberation. The teacher's authority, as I emphasized in the previous letter, is indispensable to the development of the learner's freedom. What may frustrate the process is the abuse of authority by the teacher, which makes him or her authoritarian, or the emptying of authority, which leads to permissiveness.

The teacher's accumulated knowledge, which obviously reinforces his or her authority, is not in itself a reason to set the poles of educational practice against each other.

The arrogant teacher, full of and certain of the absolute ignorance of students, becomes a figure irreconcilable with democracy and freedom.

Thus, the teacher's authority and real knowledge are not what works against freedom, but his or her authoritarianism, arrogance, and mistaken view of what constitutes knowledge.

I find it important to emphasize this point because sometimes we are lead to believe that the contradiction between teachers and students is irreconcilable. In fact, it is not. The original contradiction between teachers and students can be irreconcilable or reconcilable.

If my political-ideological belief is democratic, liberating, and I am coherent, the contradiction I experience with students' freedom is reconcilable.

That is why I said in *Pedagogy of the Oppressed*:

> In reality, as we will discuss later, the reason for liberating education lies in its reconciling impetus. That, however, does not mean that the educator stops being an educator and stops teaching or that the learner stops being a learner and stops learning. What the educator needs to do, if he or she is truly and coherently democratic is to "take good care" of his or her authority by exercising it. And the best way a teacher can take care of his or her authority is to respect the freedom of the students.

Since *Education and Present-Day Brazil*, my graduate thesis, completed in 1959,[2] I have recognized that the actions of men and women take place within the time-space continuum in which ideas are generated. I have also recognized the impossibility of ignoring the historical, cultural, ethical, racial, and class conditioning to which we are subjected. Neither realization allows me to forget the ontological reason for my decision to fight in favor of the liberation of the oppressed.

A taste for freedom, a love for life that makes us afraid of losing it and places us in a permanent search, an incessant pursuit of being more as a possibility, never as a destiny or fate, constitutes human nature. One of the things that pleases me the most about being a person is knowing that the history that shapes me and which I shape is about possibilities, not determinism. That is why, in facing the possibility of being or not being, I see my struggle gain meaning. To the extent that the future is problematic and not inexorable, the human praxis—action and reflection—requires decisions, severance, and choice. It requires ethics.

The concrete conditioning of gender, race, and class, which I cannot minimize, cannot overturn ontological reason. That is why, in spite of identifying myself as a Northeast Brazilian man who was born to a certain social class, family, and generation and received certain influences in childhood, adolescence, and adulthood, my commitment in fighting for liberation is to be loyal to our taste for freedom, our love for life, and our sense of justice.

Our struggle as women, men, blacks, workers, Brazilians, North

Americans, French, or Bolivians, is influenced by our gender, race, class, culture, and history, conditionings that mark us. Our struggle, nevertheless, departs from these conditionings and converges in the direction of being more, in the direction of universal objectives. Or else, for me at least, the fight would make no sense.

One of the reasons, as I see it, for the failure of "realist socialism" was its lack of a taste for freedom, its authoritarianism, its mental bureaucratization, which reduced life to immobility. It was a mechanistic understanding of history which denied history as a possibility and nullified freedom, choice, decision, and belief, and ended up terminating life itself.

Sixteenth Letter

~

It is not possible to create without serious intellectual discipline; likewise it is not possible to create within a system of fixed, rigid, or imposed rules.

AT THIS POINT, I WOULD LIKE TO MAKE SOME COMMENTS about a problem constantly discussed in the hallways of our universities.

I am referring to the problem of advising those writing graduate theses and doctoral dissertations.

I start from an understanding that the advising task is necessary to the candidate writing an academic piece, and that the help offered to the candidate must enable him or her to help himself or herself.

The advisor's role, then, cannot be one of programming the candidate's intellectual life or establishing rules about what the latter may or may not write about. The true advisor's role, besides listening to the candidate's questions and adding to them, is, in an open and friendly manner, to both comfort and stimulate the candidate. To comfort with good answers, appropriate suggestions, and useful bibliographies. This should, however, return the candidate to questioning. Quietude cannot be a permanent state. Only within a relationship that is agitated can quietude make sense. Life is a constant search that cannot, even when writing theses and dissertations, be immobilized. The relationship between advisor and advisee is more than a strictly intellectual one and must be warm, respectful, and capable of creating a climate of mutual trust rather than curbing the advisee's production.

The advisor's role is to discuss—as many times as may be necessary within the limits of the advisor's time—the development of the advisee's research and ideas; the depth of the advisee's analysis; the simplicity or beauty of the advisee's language; the difficulties the advisee faces with the topic, the bibliography, or the very act of reading and studying; and the loyalty with which the advisee writes about topics or people. Obviously, such discussions should not be used to impose the advisor's method for studying, analyzing, reading, or quoting, but should support the advisee's methods or make the advisor's position clear when the two disagree.

The advisor's role is to value the advisee's effort or to criticize the advisee's lack of effort. Being silent in the face of serious productive effort is as harmful as being silent in the face of contempt for the task. Deep down, the progressive advisor cannot perform either authoritatively or permissively. He or she cannot be quiet in the light of advisee merit or lack thereof.

The advisor's role is to notify the advisee about information on the advisee's topic, to call attention to rarer documents, and to stimulate and mediate meetings between the advisee and other intellectuals in the same field. It is to help the advisee to help himself or herself. After all, what really matters to academia, the advisee, and society is that the advisee receive the best scientific education possible.

The advisor's role, from a democratic perspective, is not one of appropriating the advisee, choosing a dissertation topic or title, imposing a style, assigning the number of pages to be written, determining the piece's political-ideological orientation, or limiting the length of quotes.

Both advisor and advisee have the right to choose not to work with each other. There is no time limit on either one putting an end to their relationship either. The minute that there is a lack of compatibility for any reason between an advisor and on advisee, academia must accept the two establishing new relationships.

What an advisor cannot do for any reason, having shown intellectual solidarity with the advisee during the advising process, is surprise the advisee with comments contrary to the thesis on the day of the exam. An advisor who behaves in such manner can only feel free to do so if he or she is never evaluated. The worst aspect of such behavior is what it tells students about ethics; it makes academia look bad and demeans us.

When convinced that an advisee has made an error an advisor must, in a committed and passionate fashion, call the advisee's attention to the problem and orient him or her to understanding and overcoming it.

In some cases, the matter isn't one of error, strictly speaking, but of diverging interpretations. A master's or doctoral candidate is supposed to demonstrate not whether he or she thinks like the advisor, but rather whether he or she dares to think independently, regardless of the mistakes he or she may make. To err is not a sin, rather it is part of the discovery process.

A dissertation that demonstrates an author's curiosity, risk-taking, and adventurous spirit may be of more value than a well-behaved one that reveals fear. It is not possible to create without serious intellectual discipline; likewise it is not possible to create within a system of fixed, rigid, or imposed rules.

A good advisor, thus, is one who is humble, is alert to the contribution he or she must offer the advisee, and recognizes, without insecurity, the important subsidy the advisee brings to the advisor's field of study.

Academia cannot and must not become an inhibiting context that limits the ability to think, argue, inquire, doubt, or go beyond existing models. That is why those loyal to their critical objectives must not become trapped in one way of thinking, running the risk of sectarian narrowness.

I also believe it is important for the advisor, at the beginning of his or her work helping someone develop a dissertation, to discuss with the advisee what it means to write such a text. What it means to write a text necessarily implies what it means to read one. It is almost impossible to overcome some of the difficulties that writing presents without the critical exercise of reading. I read what others write, and I write for others to read. To the extent that I exercise my critical curiosity through the reading of a text, I gradually master the process of its intelligence. If I look for that intelligence ready made, lying there in the text, left by the author, I am not preparing myself to write. The prospect of participating in creating the meaning of a text enables me to rewrite it.

The best course for those who want to write is to read a lot and well, especially reading that corresponds in topic and is elegant. Writing daily is also good, such as notes about the TV news, letters (even if they aren't sent to anyone), or comments on books or magazines.

The important thing is to write with a care for the clarity of the text, saying what needs to be said, and using tasteful language.

I have insisted in previous articles that there is no conflict between writing with rigor and writing beautifully. I have emphasized that searching for beauty in producing a text is not just the duty of artists, but of all of us who write.

For that reason, supplement the reading of fundamental texts for a thesis with those of good writers, novelists, poets, biographers.

One can only gain from acquiring a familiarity with the tuneful sentence, clear exposition, and a light style. Obviously, the tunefulness of a sentence or lightness of a style are only of value when associated with important content. Thus I speak of tuneful sentences and a light style and I oppose babble. Empty words do not meet the requirements of serious academia or the rigor of good publishers. That is why a text that does not make a good thesis does not make a good book either. What seems strange to me is to say that a text makes a good book but not a good thesis. In this case, someone is wrong, either the publisher or academia.

Once, when I coordinated a summer program at a foreign university, which included two hours a day of conferencing with students, I had a long conversation with one of the students about her thesis project. It was a well-written text that clearly described the steps of the project. At a certain point, I disagreed with her argument about the neutrality of education. With a sad look on her face, she told me that she was not satisfied with the treatment she had given education in the text either, but that it was what her advisor believed.

I am totally convinced that in this case the proper conduct for the advisor would have been to disagree with the advisee, describe her position, and justify it. If, however, the advisee still insisted on the nonneutrality of education, it would have been the advisor's place to withdraw from the advising task or, as a sign of tolerance, continue advising while reserving the right to oppose the position during the exam. Instead, the advisor imposed her position on the advisee, who bowed to this authoritarianism.

At the Pontifical Catholic University of São Paulo, I participated with Professor Ana Maria Saul, currently the university's vice-president, in an excellent experiment in the area of advising thesis and dissertation writers.

We met every fortnight with graduate students to discuss the students' reports on developing a thesis or dissertation.

These were three-hour meetings with one short coffee break. During the first stage, students spoke about their arrival in the program, their initial interview, their doubts, and the difficulty or ease with which they asked the questions that would lead them to define their topics, still vague and nebulous. In other words, they talked about their writing journey, the moments in the broader project of producing an academic document.

Next, we initiated a debate about each student's report, making inquiries and suggestions.

Each of the participants saw himself or herself in the experience of the others, in the difficulties each faced in putting on paper comments that were still being formed as thought, and in expressing ideas in written language. The oral exercise of presenting and debating their academic practice—describing how they thought about their topics, read the fundamental bibliography, or worked with their advisors—ended up contributing to the effort of writing the thesis or dissertation.

In fact, speaking about one's project is part of the process of writing a thesis. The oral moment must precede the writing moment, which we also need to talk about as much as possible. Talking about what one intends to write and what one has already written about helps one to better write what one has not written and rewrite what has not been finished.

Sometimes this or that student's advisor attended the seminar and contributed his or her critique or commentary to the discussion.

We never did conduct objective evaluations of the seminars, but judging from their richness, the increasingly critical participation of the students, and the personal comments of some, there is no doubt that they were effective and holding them was the right decision.

The diversity and variety of topics addressed in the meetings contributed to expanding the spectrum of challenges and student curiosity. All participants had an opportunity for enrichment. Often a student would engage in discussing topics other than his or her own and venture an analysis that revealed aspects of the topic not yet considered by the presenter.

In the final analysis, these group meetings provided new perspectives on certain problems and revised points of view. New views and revised views lead students to perceive previous perceptions and knowledge. Realizing how one previously perceived and knew reconfirms what was previously accepted or firms up what is a new way of seeing, an indispensable exercise for those who conduct graduate studies.

It is still necessary that the advisee take on his or her role responsibly. Writing can be a pleasant activity, but it is always a demanding one. Writing becomes pleasant when we, with humility and persistence, overcome this or that difficulty in putting on paper our thoughts on a subject.

The joy we experience as we write is the reward we receive for our determination and commitment to the task of recording our understanding of the subject.

Still, it is not possible to write about what one does not know. I must, therefore, know what I will write about and determine the scope of my search. I should be clear about my question and more or less clear about my answer to it. Without working through these demands with my advisor, without developing a basic bibliography that addresses my topic, it is impossible to write a thesis.

Without rigor, without seriousness, without intellectual discipline, the advising process is frustrated and fails to meet expectations.

Writing about a topic presupposes previous and parallel readings, as well as the reading of one's own writing. And none of that can be done without effort, dedication, and responsibility. It is absurd for an advisee, especially someone on a scholarship, to pretend to study instead of really studying, to give the impression of working when in fact not taking the task seriously.

The ethical demands of the advising task are not restricted to the advisor. They necessarily apply to the advisees as well.

We must recognize and emphasize, however, the importance of the advisor's role in the advising process, including the stimulus the advisee receives from the advisor and the impact of an advisor's lack of courteousness toward an advisee's work. After all, the advisee is just as human as the advisor. As such, he or she feels, suffers, dreams, knows, and can know more. Human, not inhuman.

Seventeenth Letter

~

Only the mechanists, who unknowingly lose the ability to think dialectically, can accept a compartmentalization of men and women as simplistic as the one they describe.

NOW I WOULD LIKE TO DO A DIFFERENT EXERCISE. I would like to critically approach a few of the many questions posed to me in the seminars I have coordinated inside and outside of Brazil, and posed in letters. These questions, in general, gravitate toward certain basic themes, certain fundamental concerns about domination, be it of class, race, or gender.

It cannot be said of any question that it is the first. Every question reveals a dissatisfaction with previous answers to previous questions. To inquire is to take on the curiosity of those who search. There is no knowledge outside of inquiry or outside of surprise. Those who ask, however, must become or already be committed to the process of an answer, as much as they expect those they ask the question of to be. In other words, the question cannot be satisfied with waiting. Of course, whoever asks a question expects an answer, but those who inquire critically are willing to deal with the answer obtained and also to attempt their own answer. Furthermore, some questions already contain the inquirer's answer; the inquirer only seeks to ratify or rectify it. Those who ask this kind of question seek to submit their answer to the judgment of others.

I have here, on my desk, four questions that have just arrived from North America. They repeat, almost exactly, many other questions I have received from there.

1. How can the high levels of school failure among students of color in so-called progressive societies be explained?
2. Can the oppressed truly work as real subjects in progressive programs with the oppressor?
3. How can it be explained that gender, class, and race discrimination endure in so-called progressive societies?
4. Can a liberating educational practice eradicate the power of gender, class, and race discrimination in a progressive society?

I believe the starting point to answering all these questions, regardless of which one you begin with, is to discuss domination and liberation as contradictory, nonmechanical processes. There can be no domination that does not produce in the dominant and in the dominated, positions and attitudes, values and ways of reading the world that are contrary to each other. Nobody, no person, no class, no group under domination until yesterday and demonstrating ambivalent and dual behavior, goes on to be different today. A new man and a new woman will never be the result of mechanical action, but only of a deep and complex historical and social process. A new man is born little by little, gradually; he is not born full-grown. Only the mechanists, who unknowingly lose the ability to think dialectically, can accept a compartmentalization of men and women as simplistic as the one they describe. We harbor within us, at times vigorously, democratic inexperience, which has marked us since colonial times and is in contradiction with new expressions of and impulses toward democracy. Colonial marks endure to this day.

It is, in fact, necessary to insist on the process that is history's nature. Historical, progressive practice is not an exception. No democratic dream, even that of socialism, can feed the ideal of sanctification for men and women. That of being more, yes, for it is their historical orientation. This orientation, however, which is just an orientation and not a fate or destiny, may gradually consolidate through the liberating struggle or it may gradually deteriorate and intensify existing dehumanization.

One of the problems all revolutions have faced and which the mechanist mind could never understand is the permanence of old superstructures within the new ones, contradicting the infrastructure being created by the revolution. Yesterday's ways of being, valuing, thinking, and certain beliefs and knowledges penetrate the revolutionary today. New ways of valuing and thinking do not become instituted from one day to the next, like magic. It is not like moving a table from one spot in the house to another, in which physical strength is all that is required. Changing cultural habits is a different story. For example, it would be hard to convince most Brazilians that tofu *feijoada* tastes good.[1]

The old elitist and authoritarian education, which even before the revolution was incoherently lived by revolutionary educators, extends into the revolution, making it more difficult to institute the new education. On the other hand, some aspects of the new practice of education that contradict society's old superstructure became gradually instituted through process, through struggle. Involvement in this conflict stirs up our consciences.

Sometimes contradictions ensue between the new revolutionary time and the revolutionaries' idealistic thinking. For them, the new infrastructure was instituted overnight and the new superstructure likewise, mechanically.

Let us then, having described these considerations, take up the first question: How can the high levels of school failure among students of color in so-called progressive societies be explained? The explanation is that even though such societies think of themselves as progressive, perhaps even adopt a system of antidiscriminatory laws, they are not applied equitably, they have not yet died to their racist selves or experienced their rebirth as democratic selves.

As long as racist ideology is only fought on paper and the discriminated feel disempowered in seeking legal protection, students of color will continue at a disadvantage in the struggle for better standards of education.

The high level of incoherence that such societies exhibit within their populations tends to contribute to this mismatch. On the one hand, there is the passionate democratic discourse of those who mysteriously recognize their role as teachers of world democracy and guardians of human rights and, on the other, there are evil racist practices that aggressively contradict democratic ideals. The struggle against racism, sexism, and class discrimination is an undeniable demand in a democratic society and indispensable for its development.

Regardless of the educational setting where progressive educators may work—elementary, secondary, tertiary, professional, popular, informal—they have no choice but to ensure coherence between their democratic discourse and their equally democratic practice.

It is not possible to talk about democracy and, at the same time, accept the contempt heaped on the educational space and the education itself of poor, working class, and black children, as if they were mere objects, ontologically or innately inferior. Extended contact with such mistreatment tends to encourage a solidarity with it, a feeling that makes those who are small smaller, and makes then chose that contact as an ideological-political option.

In such societies, it would be surprising if students of color did not show high levels of failure.[2]

With a certain anger, we must insist on two obvious points: first, the failure of students of color represents the success of a dominant racist power; second, the failure of black students is not their responsibility, but that of the policies discriminating against them.

The second question: Can the oppressed truly work as real subjects in progressive programs with the oppressor?

Regardless of whether a practice is implemented using exploitative, violent tactics by the dominant class or whether it is contradictorily accepted by those who misrepresent themselves as progressive, an oppressive practice is incompatible with the progressive dream and a progressive practice.

The white, male oppressor who discriminates, which is a form of oppression, against women and blacks while defining himself as progressive can more easily overcome his contradiction than can the oppressor who does so while affirming and defending his class and power. The oppressor who defends his class and power may even call himself democratic, but his democratic ideal has excessively narrow horizons that cannot include closeness to the person of color. The democracy defended by this type of oppressor feels threatened if the popular classes fill the streets and public squares in defense of their rights and interests. Democratic substance requires more ethical radicalism. A democracy must not look the other way regarding any kind of discrimination. From this point of view, in order for the progressive to work side by side with the authoritarian, the antidemocratic person, the progressive must become reactionary and the project abandon its progressive nature or the authoritarian must convert to the progressive struggle.

Another alternative, which would not fit the spirit of the question, is situations in which an individual is democratic only as a matter of survival while working within a progressive environment and has to learn how to deal with his or her discomfort.

The third question is centered on something that I have already addressed in dealing with the previous questions: How can it be explained that gender, class, and race discrimination endure in so-called progressive societies? A society's official discourse about itself and its social practice are two very different things. A society's social practice defines its profile, not its official discourse. The official discourse, however, does have some historical value and must be used by progressives to benefit their struggle. It must be used to demonstrate the lack of coherence between their discourse and social practice and to demand a shortening of the distance between the two.

I have no doubt, however, that one of the reasons why discriminatory practices endure in a society that to some extent defines itself as progressive, and may even show signs of it, is the difficulty faced by minorities seeing themselves as majorities.

It would be easier for the so-called minority groups to accept their differences and unite in fighting discrimination than to pursue their separate objectives and become debilitated by fighting for each minority group alone.

The gradual overcoming of all forms of discrimination is part of the dream of liberation, of the permanent search for happiness, of life itself. Critical and revealing education plays an undeniable role in this process, and it will be all the more effective as the power of discriminatory processes decreases. We cannot expect a liberating educational practice from a reactionary educator. Likewise, real democratic action will have little effect if taken in a heavily racist context.

It is indispensable for the fight against domination that political practice engage mature men and women who critically recognize the need for unity in diversity, in itself a pedagogical practice.

The struggle for a less unjust democracy, one more ethically based, is also a work of art that awaits us.

Liberating education may help in the process of overcoming discriminatory power when political agents are prepared to intervene and transform the political and economic structures of the state.

Eighteenth Letter

~

> The master-slave relationship, regardless of how colorful
> its disguise, dehumanizes the slave and the master. From
> an ethical point of view, and as the radical importance of
> ethics only grows, both the dominator and the dominated
> are dehumanized.

AT THIS POINT, AS I COME TO THE END OF THIS SET OF LETTERS,
I would like to propose some topics that have been posed to me as fin-de-
siècle problems. Some of these have emerged recently; others have been
long present in history and are only now gaining visibility, new colors.

I know it is not easy to list all that is problematic at the end of a century
touched and challenged by world wars; local wars with worldwide impact;
radical social, political, economic, ideological, and ethical transformations;
scientific and technological revolutions; the overturning of some beliefs and
myths; the rebirth of others, like the Nazi myths of nation and race; and the
return to doubts that challenge excessive certainty about modernity. It is not
easy to list what is problematic for those living in the last decade of the old
century and for those who will live in the beginning of the next one.

Some points of undeniable complexity, involving politics to episte-
mology, may be inventoried.

North-South Relations
While the center of power, the North has become accustomed to framing
the South. The North "gives a north" to the South.

One of the tasks that I hope the South will impose on itself is to try
to overcome its dependence by acting as the subject of its own search, to
be a "being for itself" and not "for the other," as it has been.

What I hope for is more than a shift in positions, if that is even possible, but for the South to stop seeing in the other its "north" and start giving them a "south." I have no doubt that a shift would not be the way to go. Instead we must aim for an interdependence in which the one cannot be if the other is not. While giving the South "a north," the North would be given "a south," and vice-versa.

Impossible dream? No! Utopia. A possibility.

In reality, the imbalance between North and South—from which results the domination of the latter and the violence of the former, the exaggerated power of the North and the exaggerated weakness of the South—ends up affecting the North's interests and jeopardizing the advancement of global democracy.

The master-slave relationship, regardless of how colorful its disguise, dehumanizes the slave and the master. From an ethical point of view, and as the radical importance of ethics only grows, both the dominator and the dominated are dehumanized. There is, then, no happy choice between dominating and being dominated. The undeniable material advantages for those who dominate become gradually empty in the face of resistance by those who, offended, fight for the return of freedom. Between being a dominator or dominated there is the path of utopia, of the possible and concrete dream of freedom. That path is one of tireless struggle, one that is to be lived well, strategically planned, with the savvy and skill of a serpent and not just the docility of a lamb. For this reason, it is important to emphasize that we must not choose immolation or surrender, but instead affirmation of the critical fight that searches for authenticity.

This is not an easy struggle. It is a struggle for stubborn people, those who are persistent, hopeful, and patient. It is for skillful people, the curious, those who are always willing to learn, willing to extract knowledge from their antagonizers. It is for the politically competent, those who do not isolate themselves, but on the contrary work to increase the number of fellow fighters. It is for those who know that politics without compromise is impossible and for those who know that compromise does not necessarily mean conniving.

The problem of bringing about the unity of the dominated in order to face a common dominator in favor of a higher objective, that of resolving differences at some point in the process, is nearly impossible. Using tactics as old as they are effective, the dominator divides the dominated and continues to reign.

Unity among the different must be self-imposed if they intend to be effective in their just struggle.

It is interesting to observe that in 1968 nobody had foreseen what was to take place in May in Paris, New York, and around the world, to a greater or lesser extent, in different societies. No one could predict that an entire generation would demand freedom and personal affirmation or that they would shake the foundations of traditional, authoritarian power.

A few fellows in exile in Santiago had just arrived from Paris in April 1968, having met with both Latin American and French political scientists of the highest order, and no one, not for a moment, had suspected the rebellion about to explode.

Again, a similar phenomenon took place recently, in a more profound manner, which changed and continues to change the face of the world: the collapse of "realist socialism" and not, as I understand it, of the socialist dream or utopia.

If anyone had, ten years before, predicted what was to happen in Eastern Europe he or she would have been deemed a lunatic and no one would have paid any attention. The collapse of the Berlin Wall? You must be crazy! In reality, however, it would not have been the ravings of a lunatic, but the thoughts of someone with a taste for freedom.

The Issue of Hunger

Worldwide hunger—to whose statistics we contribute 33 million out of a population of 149 million Brazilians—is a horrible reality that constitutes a kind of pornography.[1]

It is impossible to live in peace in light of the statistics about the problem of hunger around the world. Hunger gradually expands into tragic realities, each of which constitutes an enormous challenge.

It is undeniably shameful that in Brazil we end the century with such high numbers of brothers and sisters who die for lack of food to eat.

The challenge that sociologist Herbert de Souza, Betinho,[2] has been posing to the country through his antihunger campaign has generated questions about whether the campaign leads to conscientization or not.

Even though I have written countless times about the concept of conscientization, I will run the risk of repeating myself. It is crucial to distinguish, even if briefly, between conscientization and consciousness.

Consciousness is when my conscious body adopts a spontaneous position toward the world, which is the concreteness of singular objects. Consciousness is the presentation to my conscience of the objects I perceive in the world in which I find myself and with which I interact. These objects are presented to my conscience and are not within it.

On the desk where I work, write, and read, and which has accompanied me like a brother since my arrival in Geneva in 1970, I now have books, papers, a stereo, a telephone, and some pens. I am conscious of them. All these objects are presented to my conscience but are not within it. Consciousness is a starting point. It is by becoming conscious of an object that I can account for it. Yielding to my curiosity, the object is known by me. My curiosity, however, before the world, which is "not-me," perceives the object without reaching an understanding of its reason for being. This curiosity, if it undergoes a transformation process, becomes what I call epistemological curiosity and may perceive not only an object but also the relationships among objects, allowing me to realize their reasons for being.

In consciousness, fragmented knowledge halts at sensing the object or phenomenon. In conscientization, by perceiving the relationships among objects and their reasons for being, the cognizant subject derives an understanding of the objects, the facts, and the world. The cognizant subject knows critically, without that meaning that he or she makes no mistakes or errors. This is what I have been calling the reading of the world, which precedes the reading of the word. Reading context and reading text: the one implies the other.

In consciousness as well as in conscientization, we read the world and then can read the word. In the case of consciousness alone, our reading is naive, whereas consciousness combined with conscientization gradually makes us more critical.

This explains why illiterate communities, having suffered injustice, attribute the hunger that destroys them to destiny, fate, or God. Only in the struggle for survival do they begin to overcome the naive and magical perception of phenomenon. Conscientization changes one's perception of the facts, based on a critical understanding of them.

A person who has reached conscientization is capable of clearly perceiving hunger as more than just not eating, as the manifestation of a political, economic, and social reality of deep injustice. If that person believes in God and prays, his or her prayer will certainly focus on asking for the strength to fight against the deprivation of dignity to which he or she is subjected. The person who has reached conscientization and is also a believer in God sees God as a presence in history, but not one that makes history in lieu of men and women's actions. In fact, it is up to us to make history and to be made and remade by it. It is by making history in a different way that we will put an end to hunger.

The person who has reached conscientization is able to connect facts and problems and to understand the connections between hunger and food production, food production and agrarian reform, agrarian reform and reactions against it, hunger and economic policy, hunger and violence and hunger as violence, hunger and the conscious vote for progressive politicians and parties, hunger and voting against reactionary politicians and parties, whose discourse may be deceptively progressive.

A person who has reached conscientization has a different understanding of history and of his or her role in it. He or she will refuse to become stagnant, but will move and mobilize to change the world. He or she knows that it is possible to change the world, but impossible without the mobilization of the dominated. He or she knows very well that victory over misery and hunger is a political struggle for the deep transformation of society's structures. It is clear that overcoming hunger will require the creation of jobs both in the countryside and in urban areas, which in turn requires agrarian reform.

One of the conditions of understanding a fact, phenomenon, or problem within its network of relations is for us to perceive it, to emphasize it. First, we must comprehend it as an entity on its own and then understand its relationships to other facts or data.

I believe that is exactly what Betinho's hunger campaign has been doing. It has been making hunger into something that is perceived as its own entity although it has always been concrete. It is making hunger a shocking, uncomfortable, and undignified presence among us. I have no doubt that Betinho never intended to organize a solely charitable campaign, for I know he can distinguish between charity and assistance. Assistance is necessary. In fact, it can trigger, as it has, the process of conscientization; it underlines the need and fuels the curiosity of the "assisted," gradually making it possible for them to accept themselves as subjects of history, through their involvement in the political struggle.

I recently read a statement by Betinho that relates to this discussion. "I have never known," he said, "of any hungry person who responded to someone who brought food by saying, 'Thank you, but I cannot accept your gesture; it's just charity.'" The discourse of the hungry is the act of eating the food. It is through lessening the need that hurts them that they speak. It is from the starting point of this concrete thing (food) that they respond to this other, equally concrete thing (hunger). Once the hungry understand hunger better and comprehend the reasons for it, they can become involved in the necessary struggle against the injustice of it. Furthermore, by engaging countless people who eat, dress, listen to music, and live well, the campaign will move many to change the ways in which they see and think about Brazil. The campaign will bring them to conscientization and convert them.

I myself have heard from many people who used to believe that agrarian reform, critical education, and liberation theology suggested subversion and authoritarianism and were just ideological manipulation. They now say that it is urgent that the scandal of hunger be ended and that we fight for Brazil's reinvention.

The moment will come when the power of young Brazilian business people, who are beginning to learn of the losses they incur due to the uneven distribution of income in the country, will add to the pressure for agrarian reform as one of the central moves in their game. It is not possible to overcome hunger without agrarian reform, job creation, and fair income distribution. Critical capitalists and progressives agree on this.[3]

Recently, a Brazilian businessman who is a good friend of mine told me about a conversation he had had with a U.S. counterpart, whom he had asked for a perspective on Brazilian reality. After some positive comments about the Brazilian economy, the North American told him, "You have some obstacles you must overcome in order to move forward—the terrible distribution of income and the incredible and unsustainable reluctance to conduct serious agrarian reform. Changes in those areas would result in the development of your internal market, which offers undeniable potential."

In fact, with thirty-three million people starving and many more below the poverty line who have close to no buying power, we are faced with more needs than freedoms.

The antihunger campaign has been emphasizing this limit, which represents a fundamental step toward conscientization.

In closing, I should note that the antihunger campaign is not an isolated movement, hidden in some "corner" of history. The campaign is taking place at an important historic time, a unique one in our political history.

It is a time marked by the impeachment of a president, with all its implications; the Congressional Investigative Committee on the Budget; an alert press; a restless and demanding civil society; and a youth back demonstrating on the streets. We are living in a climate of confrontation between critical optimism about the country's life and pessimism and disillusionment.

I do believe, however, that the predominant position is that of optimism, just as I believe the 1994 elections[4] will bring results more in the direction of optimism than of pessimism.

The Issue of Violence

The issue is not just one of direct physical violence but also of disguised or hidden violence: hunger, the economic interests of the superpowers, religion, politics, racism, sexism, and social classes.

The struggle for peace—which does not mean a struggle for the eradication or denial of conflict but for their fair and critical confrontation and a search for solutions—is an imperative demand of our times. Peace, however, does not precede justice. For that reason, the best way to fight for peace is to make justice.

Nobody dominates anybody, robs anybody, discriminates against anybody, or mistreats anybody without being legally punished: not individuals, not peoples, not cultures, not even civilizations. Our utopia, our sane insanity, is the creation of a world where power is based on ethics. Without it, the world crumbles and cannot survive.

In such a world, the main task for political power is to guarantee freedom, rights and obligations, and justice, not to support the arbitrary actions of a few against the suffering majority. Just as we cannot accept what I call "neoliberal fatalism," which implies the deproblematized and inexorable future, we cannot accept domination as a given. Nobody can categorically tell me that a world made of utopias will never be built. This is, after all, the substantively democratic dream to which we aspire, if we are coherently progressive. Just dreaming of this, however, will not make it concrete. We need to fight unceasingly to build it.

It would be horrible if we were sensible to pain, hunger, injustice, and violence without perceiving the reasons for all this negativity. It would be horrible if we could feel the oppression but could not imagine a different world. It would be horrible if we could dream about a different world as a project but not commit ourselves to the fight for its construction. We have made ourselves men and women by experimenting in the dynamic of these understandings. Freedom cannot be gained as a present. One becomes richer in the fight for it, in the permanent search for it, even if there can be no life without the presence, however, minimal, of it. In spite of that, we cannot acquire freedom for free. The enemies of life threaten it all the time. We must fight to maintain it, recover it, and expand it. In any case, I do not believe that the fundamental core of life, freedom and the fear of losing it, will ever be suppressed. Threatened, yes: a threat to life understood in the broadest sense as not just human life. Life implies freedom as movement and constant search; it also implies caring for freedom and fearing the loss of it. Freedom and the fear of losing it become melded in the deepest core indispensable to life, that of communication. In this respect, a regrettable contradiction is adopting a progressive, revolutionary discourse and a life-negating practice. Such practice is polluting the air, water, fields, and forests. It destroys trees and threatens animals and birds.

At a certain point in *Das Kapital*, while comparing human labor to other animals' labor, Marx says that no bee can be compared to even the most "modest" of human workers. Even before producing an object a human being is capable of idealizing it. Even before working, the human worker has the work blueprinted in his or her head.

This inventive ability, which implies communication, is present at all levels of life experience. Human beings express their creative and communicative abilities with marks exclusively their own. Communication exists, but human communication is processed through existence, another human invention.

The same way that a worker has a blueprint of what is to be produced in his or her workshop, men and women who are workers or architects, doctors or engineers, physicists or teachers also have in their heads a blueprint of the world in which they would like to live. This is the utopia or dream that propels us to fight.

The dream for a better world is born from its opposite. For that reason, we run the risk of so idealizing the better world that we become detached from our concrete one. We also run the risk of becoming much too "adhered" to the concrete world and submerging ourselves in fatalistic immobility.

Both of these positions are not illuminating. The critical position holds that by gaining a certain epistemological distance from the concrete world, I can know it better and make the dream of a better world a reality. Thus, accepting the dream of a better world means accepting the process of building it. This is a process of struggle strongly rooted in ethics. It is a process of struggle against all violence, including violence aimed at trees, rivers, fish, mountains, cities, and the physical manifestations of cultural and historic memory. It is a process of combating violence against the weak, the defenseless, the attacked minority, and the discriminated against, regardless of the reason. It is a process of struggle against the lack of punishment that currently encourages crime, abuse, and disrespect for the weaker and for life. In the tragic despair that is the reality of certain segments of our population, life is no longer a value, or is an unimportant one. Life is seen as something with which one plays for a time, and for which only random fate can account. One can only live while one can provoke life.

It is a struggle against the disrespect for public things, the lies, and the lack of scruples. These problems will bring moments of disenchantment, but it should never take away our hope. Regardless of what society we live in, or belong to, we must fight with hope.

The Rebirth of the Nazi-Fascist Threat

The rebirth of the Nazi-fascist threat—not only in Europe but around the world, as if the world had lost its memory—is a serious problem.

Violent and necrophilic, the Nazi-fascist ideology hates life and the joy of living and adores death. Thus, this movement does not tolerate doubt, movement, or the taste for inquiry. Any curiosity that might lead an individual to doubt the myth of Fascist certainty is violently drowned and silenced. The only truth is the word of the leader, whose validity is sealed by the turmoil of the domesticated masses.

This fascist threat may grow to the extent that, overwhelmed, the Left vacillates between denying itself by believing in neoliberal discourse (about the death of ideologies—and it is only possible to destroy ideologies ideologically—of history, of social classes, of utopias, of the dream, and of socialism) and reactivating Stalinism, a huge denial of the experience of "realist socialism." One of the greatest flaws of this socialism was its authoritarian framework, while the most positive aspect of capitalism lies in its democratic frame, even though evil is the very nature of capitalism. To make capitalism more human is an impossible dream to which angelic spirits or incorrigible deceivers are devoted.

The way to go for the Left is not to deny itself, closing doors and operations in guilt or despair, which can only strengthen antagonizing forces. It is not to succumb to the tragedy of Stalinist authoritarianism.

Undeniably, the role of the Left today is to believe that it does exist and to abandon authoritarianism and dogmatism. It is to overcome historical, philosophical, and epistemological errors; for example, that of setting socialism and democracy against each other.

The Issue of the Role of Subjectivity in History

As a philosophical, historical, epistemological, political, and pedagogical problem, which relates both to modern physics and to educational practice, the role of subjectivity has been questioned before the theory of knowledge and democracy at the end of this century. Such a theme has always been present in human concerns, and today it has been revived, overcoming a certain mechanism of Marxist origin—but not Marx's exclusive responsibility. Such a mechanism reduced subjectivity to a pure reflex of objectivity, avoiding the repetition of a certain naiveté that made the importance of subjectivity absolute and resulted in lending subjectivity or consciousness the role of maker of the world. One of the fatal consequences of the mechanistic understanding of subjectivity was an equally mechanistic understanding of history, a deterministic understanding, in which the future was seen as inexorable and unproblematized. It is in history as possibility that subjectivity takes on the role of a subject and not just that of an object of the transformations of the world. The future then stops being inexorable and becomes that which it is historically problematic.

Notes

~

Here I am, once again writing to Paulo Freire's readers for strong, profound, and simple Paulo, who asked me to complement his work by writing the notes to this book, *Letters to Cristina*.

I thought the experience of being a note-taker would make me more concise. I was totally wrong. Stimulated by the letters, the reality in which they are immersed, and the knowledge that in writing about this reality, I am doing a little of what Paulo does a lot—analyzing, reflecting, denouncing, criticizing, and writing; in other words, reading the world and writing the word equivalent to the world he speaks of—I wrote a lot.

Paulo in his letters and I in my notes critically read the facts, situations, and people of our society, intentionally trying to be aware of the possibility and necessity for the transformation of the perverse, corrupt, and unjust Brazilian world into a new Brazil in which men, women, and children have equal space and time.

Given such important topics, I was not content with nor could I restrain myself from elaborating short and "objective" notes, while trying not to bore Paulo's readers.

I continued building (although without being able to say it to the author of the book) a space for the notes, which could not help being themselves. They also had their own soul, a certain and needed autonomy.

I could not remain only the note-taker who neutrally explains and disappears so that the notes do not carry the sentiments and motives of the one who writes them. I did not want that.

I refused, but I also made sure that I did not invade Paulo's text. I passed on detailed information (and my own reflections!) to his readers when he preferred, for various reasons, not to provide that information in the text.

I enjoyed discussing Northeast Brazilian culture, although I still owe the reader a few explanations, such as of *bumba-meu-boi* and the *maracatu*, which for lack of time and distance from the Northeast I could not research. I had to speak and write about the problems of Brazilian culture, which changed so much over the 1930s, 1940s, and 1950s, but which contradictorily remains the same.

It is interesting to report that when Paulo sensed that some of his readers misunderstood his system of theoretical, political-pedagogical thinking, he abandoned that system, which others associated with pretentiousness or formality.

He denied it by writing poetry, and he denied it by writing these "letters." Both of these denials are visible ones. These forms of Paulo's expression do not prevent or untwist the systematization of his theoretical yet practical way of thinking.

In reminiscing about his childhood—which Paulo exposes in the most intimate way, describing its most difficult moments—he did not idealize or romanticize those days. He described them because those were the years that fed the critical thought of his adulthood.

In writing letters instead of essays—which in their most traditional form are characterized by a sequence of logically unconnected ideas that begin, develop, and end in each letter, forming the totality of the text—Paulo did not follow tradition. In fact, he wrote essays, but the essays were in the format of letters. Without denying the value of traditional essays, he chose the less common form of letters, believing that texts composed this way are the most communicative. Each one speaks for itself.

Paulo's painful childhood should be told and retold, not as a complaint, lament, or to torture the reader, but because it was not an isolated experience in the Brazilian context. It was an historically rooted way of living. His childhood translates the Brazilian moment.

Through letters it was easier and more profound for Paulo to analyze Brazil's many problems metaphorically, using Lourdes's piano, his father's neckties, "Mr." Armada's ruthlessness, the cloth pads on the heads of the piano movers, the *calungas* of the trucks, the soldiers of the handkerchief gang, the houses of the working men, the ghosts, his mother's hope of becoming the secretary of the Jaboatão High School, the premature death of his father, Olegário Mariano's house, the scream of the painted faces, bean-soup, and many other instances. Using these images to talk about the experiences and frustrated dreams of the people, Paulo talks about the most distinct facets of Brazilian reality: the lack of hope; the presence of oppression, authoritarianism, exploitation, and domination; the dreams of what is possible; the striking social differences; the deficiencies of education and the schools; the poverty, hunger, unemployment, and underemployment; and, finally, the deprivation of the many and the opulence of the few.

The close relationship of these letters to Paulo's life did not reduce them to subjective texts, but rather charged them heavily with subjectivity; they translate real moments of the objectivity of Brazilian history, a history that he participated in as a subject.

One more thing I should make explicitly clear to readers, especially foreigners: the presence of the profound and grave problems denounced in this book does not imply that they are sanctioned by the real citizens. Although many do not know how to change our society, they know that they should, want, and need to change our society. This book is dedicated to them.

Not just the organized institutions of civil society have been giving clear signals that it is necessary and possible to change Brazil. There is a wider political will. The population of Rio de Janeiro, the most violent city in our country, recently demonstrated conscience and the political will to change. The city stopped for five minutes.

Almost everyone dressed in white, and men, women, and children stopped doing what they were doing: eating; studying; teaching; driving a car, bus, or train; selling and buying; singing or playing ball at the beach; screaming on the floor of the stock exchange; or walking and praying at mass. Hand in hand, around the Church of Our Lady Candelaria, on the train, on the bus, at home, at the office, at the store, at the plaza, at the school, everywhere, wherever they were in this beautiful city, they stopped for five minutes of silence—disturbed only by the church bells—a time for reflection and brotherhood, solidarity and justice, hope and peace, in longing for a less violent, more just society in control of itself.

Although I respect other cities and peoples of other countries, I cannot see this event happening anywhere but in Brazil. In a country of impunity, corruption, and oppression is found, contradictorily, a country of relaxed joy, hard work, and creative power.

It is a daring, abundant, and vigorous creation of sounds and letters, colors and pictures, stories and novels, living carnival and dancing soccer, science and philosophy, universities and planned cities, and so on.

The organized institutions of civil Brazilian society, through acts of courageous resistance, have been mobilizing communitarian urban and rural movements by addressing issues from education to politics. In particular, students have organized for better education and ethical politics; the Catholic Church for children, prisoners, workers, and those without land; educators and parents for free, quality public schools for all; and the street children for themselves. Campaigns have been launched to distribute food and employ the poor; to end violence against women, Indians, homosexuals, blacks, and prostitutes; to reject the sexual exploitation of young girls; to prevent AIDS and assist those with AIDS; and to stop torture, censorship, and drugs. The varied agendas are ensuring sex education; supporting education at all levels and grades; ending illiteracy; preserving forests, rivers, oceans, fauna, and flora; improving public health, housing, transportation, prisons, and political systems; and, finally, enforcing the rights of all people, regardless of gender, class, race, religion, or age.

Thousands and millions of Brazilians daily think, discuss, and decide. They are instrumental in pressuring those in political power and the dominant classes by looking for feasible alternatives to better their families' conditions with the positive consequences of the Brazilian social body.

Brazil is contradictory. Tactlessness and the abuses of the few have hit many cruelly, but the unknown efforts of so many, which have not yet totally materialized, have furthered progress even while setbacks have discouraged us. The flame of hope, based in the struggle and persistence of the great majority of oppressed people, remains lit, and undoubtedly changes the country day by day.

We are not just an irresponsible country with a high birthrate and high infant mortality rate, a major concentration of wealth, and a popular culture that only worries about samba, carnival, and soccer, as many in the North accuse.

We are a people full of vitality who value and spend much of our time in the samba, carnival, and soccer, but who also built, through hard work, the ninth largest economy in the world.

With joy and conviction, I present these notes—although they are accusations that show the ugliest face of Brazil, I have faith in the Brazilian people. They are capable of establishing a true democracy.

—*Ana Maria Araújo Freire*

Notes to the Foreword

1. The president in question, Fernando Collor de Mello, who won a second term in the 1989 elections with thirty-five million votes, was impeached on March 15, 1990, by the Brazilian nation, two-and-a-half years after he took office.

   The initial enthusiasm of voters changed rapidly into disappointment and resentment, regardless of their class.

   The authoritarian, drastic, and inconsiderate measures of the president and his ministerial cabinet left Brazilians stunned.

   For eighteen months, any savings accounts exceeding one thousand dollars were frozen. The day he took office Collor deposited their value into his own savings and bank accounts. The population viewed this as an unconstitutional confiscation. The measure certainly had dramatic repercussions in the daily lives of citizens, businesses, factories, and artists.

   The president then created another currency. He dismissed thousands of federal employees, who received only part of the salaries due them, and prohibited them from working. To benefit his supporters, he sold the residences built for ministers at the birth of Brasília. He also prosecuted the *marajas* (named such after the governor of the very poor state, Alagoas). During his campaign for presidency, many employees of the government benefited through his efforts, as from the public monies—these demagogic measures, he proclaimed, were to make public monies and public morale healthy.

   He initiated a process of privatizing state businesses without scruple, favoring large Brazilian and foreign corporations who treated them like junk, as we say, and caused damage to the nation.

   His initial economic policies—the Plan for Economic Stabilization—was intentionally recessive and inflationary, although Collor and his ministerial cabinet denied this.

   Besides projecting the image of austerity that he wanted to impose, he used a powerful television system to show himself in a positive light. The president, who was governing the nation within the parameters of liberal modernism, appeared on our television screens every Friday, broadcasting from the Palace of the Planalto—headquarters of the government in the federal capital—with groups of inexperienced guests, his followers who came from various corners of the country, to reinforce his appearance as a popular statesman. In reality, he was only emptying the public's savings.

Collor completed the image by supposedly piloting the supersonic planes of the Brazilian Air Force or the submarines of the Brazilian Navy; by racing automobiles and bicycles; and by navigating powerful jet skis through crowded public beaches.

He thought he was promoting the image of a young, strong, athletic, intelligent, sports-oriented, bold, modern, courageous, decisive, enterprising, liberal, flexible, and popular president. He spoke to the people by addressing the "homeless" as "my people."

He choose to live in a family residence and not in the presidential palace, a project of Oncar Niemeyer's, when Brasília was built. On "Dinda's house," as he called his mother's residence, he spent public money without the taxpayer's knowledge, evidently in compliance with his uncontrolled and grandiose wishes. He renovated the building; built a platform for a helicopter landing, which he used daily as his means of transport; and landscaped an enormous area with expensive Brazilian rocks, a waterfall, and Japanese fish.

A year into his term, disappointment with his economic program and with him escalated. There was a general rise in suspicions about his lack of dignity in public office.

Stories of corruption took over the front pages of newspapers and magazines and filled television screens and radio programs. The opposition parties mobilized themselves more and more; news reporters dedicated themselves to disclosing the unlawful and unethical deeds of the president on a daily basis. This went on while he continued to prepare his propaganda for the written, spoken, and televised press.

Produced in marketing agencies and on television, his projected image of a bright young man capable of modernizing the nation was falling apart. Millions spent on advertising neither improved nor sustained his image.

A crisis activated in the midst of family members, divides them. Pedro Collor de Mello, feeling the economic and moral damage done by his own family members, denounced the network of extortion headed by the former treasurer of his brother's presidential campaign—Paulo Cesar (P. C.) Cavalcanti Farias—a network that continued to benefit himself, the president, and their small group of supporters.

To the "remaining funds of the electoral campaign"—which actually were enormous donations from large- and medium-scale national and multinational corporations that feared the victory of the Labor Party and illegal donations from the Brazilian electoral board—were added new fortunes in monies from corrupt trustees of the government's capital.

The accusation from Pedro Collor was confusing to the public since it came from a reliable source; from someone who knew the private and public life of the accused ones. Pedro Collor did not spare any accusations in stating his suspicions about P. C. Farias's conniving with his brother, the president. The fall of President

Collor seemed imminent after his brother's comments to one of the main news magazines in May 1992.

The president took advantage of his right to speak on television and, enraged, "apologized" to the Brazilian people for the inconvenience caused by "the groundless accusations of my insane brother Pedro."

Pedro Collor's accusations directed at his brother and his treasurer were aimed at eliminating both, especially his brother, who was sinking, day by day, due to the contradictions and inconsistencies of his defense.

The Congressional Investigative Committee on the Budget (CPI)—which examined the activity and origin of P. C. Farias's corporations as it was established by congress to do—shocked Brazilian society.

The self-interested and false statements of the shock troops connected to the president did not help, since they claimed repeatedly that the president had no opportunity to defend himself. His cause was not helped either by the commissioner's revelations regarding the money extorted from Brazilian and multinational corporations.

Witnesses faced real fear in confirming the network of corruption, from the simplest government maids to the secretary of the unscrupulous undertaker who had set up a farce to acquit the president.

On September 29, 1992, the House of Representatives initiated the process of impeaching President Collor.

On October 2 of the same year he was summoned to court. His lawyers prepared his defense, using judicial strategies because his innocence was nonexistent, but the process was irreversible. Judicial nitpicking did not help, the nation demanded the resignation of the president. Everyone knew that he was not able, politically or ethically, to govern the country.

On December 29, 1992, by joint deliberation of the legislature and a judge of the Federal Supreme Court, the population's hopes and dreams were met when punishment fell on Collor. At the assembly, in a strategic measure, the lawyer nominated by the judiciary power (due to the withdrawal of the two lawyers initially chosen by the accused) read Fernando Collor de Mello's resignation letter a few minutes before a compulsory resignation was imposed on him.

All of us Brazilians knew, however, that he had not resigned. We knew that we had prevented him—with a democratic judiciary, legal procedures, and organized pressure from millions of men, women, and children who walked and rallied on the streets and in the city squares (see note of the fourteenth letter) from continuing to govern the Brazilian nation irresponsibly by dilapidating and vilifying it.

2. The Collor era left the suspicion that corruption had infiltrated various segments of our political society.

On October 1993, the economist José Carlos Alves dos Santos—former director for many years of the unions' budget, who had hid millions of dollars, some of it counterfeit, in his house and who probably killed his wife—denounced a corruption scheme in distributing and using public monies. This was certainly a tactic to distract from his own crimes, which in a few days were revealed to the nation.

Immediately after, the senator of São Paulo, Eduardo Suplicy of the Labor Party, asked Congress to use its power to set up a Congressional Investigative Committee (CPI), which did not have the power to punish, but did have ample power to investigate those denounced by the economist, including deputies, senators, ministers, and even the state governors in office.

Ninety-four days of arduous work resulted in a report of 558 pages, which was read by its compiler, Deputy of Pernambuco Roberto Magalhaes, a member of the Party of the Liberal Front (PFL), from 9:30 A.M. to 5:45 P.M. on January 21, 1994.

The economist moved with ease through numbers, prices, values, expenses, and revenues that suggested that large corporations influenced contractors (such as large engineering firms or hydroelectric factories) to inflate their invoices beyond the actual cost and connived with corrupt politicians to publicly embezzle in order to benefit their private bank accounts and supporters, and that those managing philanthropic entities were stealing from them.

Alves dos Santos was lying when he accused the deputies, who are much respected for their ethics by the Brazilian population. He was lying when he stated that he did not participate in and was not behind the barbaric death of his wife.

The nation, frightened almost to death, watched the live television broadcasts of the investigation into the accused's actions, which they could not explain, or read the newspapers. They listened to the absurd and inconsistent answers. Then, working and creative people manifested the political will that the accused be punished for their crimes and the nation not be punished for the embezzlement of public monies.

The CPI, impeccably presided over by Senator Jarbas Passarinho of the Social Democratic Party (PSD), in approximately three months of hard work, investigated documents, tickets, and the banking activities of the forty-three people accused by the economist. Eighteen were fired (or if elected, were recommended for termination); fourteen continued to have their bank accounts examined by the House of Representatives, the federal police, and the public ministry; and eleven were found innocent.

The investigations now proceed in diverse areas, directed by the official organizations, while the population awaits final decisions that will put an end to immunity from prosecution, which is the very nature of the crimes committed by the political or economic elite of Brazil. We want, as citizens, to put an end to corruption.

By "eating" its own members, Congress manifests the intention to clear its office staff of corruption and show that its own interests do not surpass the interests of the nation and that it is possible and necessary—even with pressure from interest groups to prevent it from taking place—to wipe from Brazilian public life all disgraceful men and women.

There is, unfortunately, a segment of civil society that believes that "all of this" is a product of a democratic government that allows the operation of legislative houses. For that reason, Freire emphatically states that they are needed to improve our democracy.

On the contrary, it is the lack of freedom that fostered corruption and the imposed silence of our dictatorial history that implicitly favored and sweetened such behavior, not the open and transparent operation of Congress, the state legislative assemblies, and the town councils.

Our people already know what they want, what they need, why they are exploited, and what their dreams for their children and the nation are, but they need to recognize who will represent their legitimate interests and elect their true representatives to Congress. In this manner, they will not be disappointed and their votes will not be insulted.

Notes to the Introduction

1. At this exhortation of Freire's, I cannot help talking about an indictment by some Brazilians who also screamed the same phrase, "Never again!"

A study of "707 completed lawsuits and dozens of incomplete official documents" done in secrecy resulted in the book *Brazil: Never Again,* which was published under the protection of the World Council of Churches, headquartered in Geneva, Switzerland, and the archdiocese of São Paulo. It was authored by Dom Paula Evaristo Arns and published by the publishing company Vozes of Petropolis. All quotes are taken from the fourth edition, published in 1985.

Taking as a principle that "torture is the cruelest and most barbaric crime against a human being" (p. 17) and relating the torture of Brazilian political prisoners to the historical formation of Brazil through colonialism and slavery, a group of Brazilians worked from August 1979 to March 1985 to describe the acts of repression by the military government from April 1, 1964 to March 15, 1985.

The main objective of this pioneering group was the same as that of Freire and all those who had been tortured: that "never again should the violence, ignominy, injustice, and persecutions of the recent past in Brazil be repeated" (p. 26).

The populist government of João Goulart fought for more humane conditions and for the integration of the poor into the citizenry. The predominant civil and military sections—impregnated and compromised by the ideology of national security, which originated in the United States with its ideological complements of the cold war between the Western and Christian block and the Eastern and pagan block—saw this as a destructive act to be vigorously punished (see notes of the first and fifth letter).

The M. Pitany coup d'état of April 1, 1964 had as its proclaimed objective the battle against inflation, corruption, and subversion. In the name of that battle, torture was established as a legitimate way to extract information from political prisoners, those subversive to social order, and those who consciously fought against the situation lived by the masses in Brazil—that of social, political, economic, and cultural injustice.

Many did not want to know and could not know (for instance, the thousands in exile)—certainly very few followed Father Tito, who, physically and psychologically destroyed by torture, committed suicide in 1974 in Paris—what it was like running away, living clandestinely in the most precarious of circumstances, being in prison, being tortured, surviving by looking at the shadows of persecutors, dying in the prisons or in the barracks under torture, or even being "run over" on the streets, "drowned" on the beaches, or shot when they tried to "run away" from the sieges by political, military detectives.

Many families received explanations such as these from ministers of justice and military officials while looking for their "missing" relatives. Just as many times, they were told not to look for them, to be silent, or to find them as "refugees" in the guerrillas of neighboring countries.

The many recently discovered mass graves have restored the bodies of loved husbands and wives, sons and daughters, brothers and sisters, fathers and mothers that were killed in so many different and degrading ways. Others researching in the "archives of horror" found pictures of their relatives, who were killed by torture and buried anonymously.

Brazil: Never Again cataloged 695 torture lawsuits that the authors had access to—therefore, far from the total of all torture cases. In all, "7,367 names were brought to the prisoner's dock as the subject of political lawsuits filed in the military justice court." Some of those accused in these lawsuits had more than one charge against them; 284 sailors and marines were denounced. Approximately 88 percent of those accused of torture were male while only 12 percent were female. Of that total, 38.9 percent were twenty-five years old or younger—2,868 cases— of which 91 were minors, less than eighteen years of age. Among the 4,476 accused, whose level of schooling was stated in the charges, 2,945 had a college degree and only 91 were illiterate (during this period Brazil had about twenty million illiterate people). The National Army was directly responsible for 1,045 arrests and more than 884 arrests were carried out by the Office of Information for the Center for the Operation of Internal Defense (DOI-CODIS), which was spread throughout the country. DOI-CODIS was lead by officers of the National Army and organized in 1970 with the financial cooperation of national and foreign corporations. In 3,754 cases (51 percent), the charges do not mention the organization that executed the arrest (pp. 85–86).

The book reports that 1,997 of those arrested and tortured were executed before the investigations opened. Of them, 3,572 were born in the interior and 1,833 in the capitals of the states, while 4,077 resided in the capitals and only 1,894 resided in the interior. The highest number were those living in Rio de Janeiro (1,872) when they were processed and 1,517 living in São Paulo. Thus, they were mostly urban and members of the middle class (pp. 86).

According to the same report, those most often tortured were from the military and related organizations, 4,935 cases; those who participated in violent or armed action, 1,464 cases; those who participated in the ousted government in 1964 or had even a simple political association with it, 484 cases; those who revealed ideas through the press, in the classroom, or in speeches, 145 cases; and those who were artists, 18 cases (see pp. 85–87).

Regarding the communication with the judge by those executed: "No communication, 6,256 cases (84 percent)"; "communication within the legal deadline, 295 cases (4 percent)": and "communication outside the legal deadline, 816 cases (12 percent)" (p. 87).

About 10,034 others were only investigated; 6,385 were indicted but never appeared on the list of the indicted, and the "3,649 remaining appeared as witnesses or informants, not being able to exclude themselves from the hit list, since countless episodes were recorded in which they had also been detained during the investigation, and even tortured" (p. 88).

The social sectors most affected by the military government's repression were those countering the navy, army, and airforce, and the military brigade of Rio Grande do Sul. Thirty-eight lawsuits were brought against those who had made "a systematic effort to eliminate from the military all those identified with the ousted government and its nationalistic project"; thirty-six lawsuits against those in the unions; fifty-six lawsuits against students; twenty-two lawsuits against politicians in congressional office, in executive positions, or running for reelection; fifteen lawsuits against professionals of the press; and fifteen lawsuits against those countering the Catholic Church (pp. 117–19).

Brazil: Never Again argues that eleven Brazilians were executed because of the "testimony of people who witnessed, in Brazilian prisons, the death of other political prisoners under torture" (p. 247) and that arbitrary detention or imprisonment favored the disappearance of victims, who added up to a total of 125 missing persons (pp. 291–93).

We know today, thirty years after the military coup d'état, that General Emilio Garrastazu Medici arrested about 50,000 people, both Brazilians and foreigners, thereby immolating the greater part of our idealists.

We also know that the majority of the cases of torture, which resulted in the death and disappearance of political prisoners, took place during the presidential period of General Medici (October 30, 1969 to March 10, 1974). During this time, it is important to remember, the majority of Brazilians were enjoying songs that incessantly repeated "I love you, my Brazil"; were dedicated to the Brazilian soccer team, which received the Jules Rimet Cup and the World Cup in Mexico; and were proudly announcing to the world our "economic miracle" by shouting "Go forward Brazil!"

Consequently, overpowered by the "great Brazilian destiny," which was finally happening, many slept peacefully and did not know about or believe that—at the bottom of the organizations of repression, on the streets, on the roads, in the Amazon forest, under the leadership of officers of the armed forces formed to defend the nation against an external enemy—many were dying or being mutilated for committing the crime of dreaming and fighting for a Brazil we all could be proud of for its real democracy.

"Brazil 1964: Never Again!" we all should shout, not only in the name of those who were tortured and killed and their relatives and friends, but also in the name of those who lost their historical conscience through alienation.

2. After the military coup d'état of 1964, the institutional acts normalized dictator-ship in civil and political society, legalizing persecution of everything that was or could become, from the point of view of the new owners of power, subversive.

The Institutional Act, No. 5 (AI-5), of December 13, 1968, was signed by the second military president after the coup d'état of April 1, 1964, General Artur do Costa e Silva (who ruled from March 15, 1967 to August 31, 1969). It was certainly the hardest and most arbitrary of the acts in the republic's history and imposed the most destructive consequences on the population.

In the name of securing "the authentic democratic order, based on freedom, respect for the dignity of human beings, the fight against subversion and ideolo-gies contrary to the traditions of our people, [and] the fight against corruption," the president, emboldened by the National Security Council, granted himself the right to proclaim the following, enabled by the retreat of Congress, the legislative assemblies, and the town councils: in regard to intervening in the states and municipal politics, he gave himself the right to nominate governors and mayors; to "postpone the political rights of any citizens for a term of ten years and cancel federal, state, and municipal elective mandates" when the citi-zens might threaten security (enacted by "guarding them and prohibiting them from attending certain places or leaving a certain domicile"); to suspend their political rights, extended to restrictions or prohibitions "on the exercise of any other public or private rights"); to "dismiss, remove, or make available" publicly elected officials or employees of public corporations or of mixed partnerships; to "dismiss or transfer to the military reserve or members of the military police" during a state of siege; to confiscate goods after investigation "of those who have grown rich illicitly"; and to suspend "the guarantee of habeas corpus, in the case of political crimes against the national security, the economic and social order, or the popular economy."

Indeed, this "right" to exercise the freedom of choice, centralization, and author-itarianism, did not stay in the literal meaning of the law. The Complementary Act, No. 38 of December 13, closed the doors of Congress.

From that time on were years of persecution and terror, even after the reopen-ing of Congress, while the agents of the "counterrevolutionaries" fulfilled, item by item, the cruel and perverted code that had been proclaimed ostensibly to estab-lish the "authentic democratic order, based on freedom, respect for the dignity of human beings," and so on.

It inaugurated "postmodern" torture, which leaves neither marks nor proof. It separated families. It initiated the greatest exodus ever of scientists and intellectu-als from this country. It censored the lyrics of popular songs and the pronounce-ments of the press. It dismissed and deprived. It built mass graves.

It allowed the rise of corruption and a lack of ethics without precedent in the history of our country due to the lack of a transparent political society and a civil society prevented from knowing and/or participating in what was happening in the sphere of power.

On December 31, 1978, near the end of General Ernesto Geisel's term (March

15, 1974 to March 15, 1979) Brazil commemorated the end of the AI-5 and began, as a result of the battles of its people, to have a new voice.

3. The studies done by the group that published *Brazil: Never Again* declare that two-thirds of the legal proceedings they studied referred to organizations forbidden by Brazilian legislation before the military coup d'état of 1964.

Almost fifty clandestine movements were the target of repression, many of them of Marxist orientation and born from the Communist Party of Brazil (PCB), founded in March of 1922. They had an aim in common: the search for a socialist society in which workers conquered power, only differing in the tactics they used to achieve that power, including whether they sanctioned the use of violence or not.

Some of the clandestine movements wanted to mobilize the rural sectors, while the majority intended to reach and affect the major urban centers of the country. Their ranks were swelled by young students and intellectuals, especially university professors; members of the military, from soldiers and marines to majors and captains; members of the unions; workers; and peasants.

Internal conflict within these movements' subdivisions and new alliances showed clearly the small likelihood of them being forces capable of taking power or overcoming the repression of the military regime.

Two things weighed on the movements: their small number in relation to the violent, armed population embodied in the armed forces and police and the lack of a steady civil society.

The March of the Family with God and for Freedom was a parade organized by the women of São Paulo, thousands of whom took to the streets to ask for the end of the "communist government" of President João Goulart (September 7, 1961 to April 1, 1964). By the beginning of March of 1964, the middle class had already adhered to the wishes and interests of the dominant class.

The clandestine movements were distinguished by their ingenuity, which was nearly suicidal. Their militants intended to conquer the armed forces and the organized police almost solely with idealism and dreams, using them to over-whelm institutional acts, soldiers, officers, and civil personnel trained to capture and torture "subversives"; and expecting to receive generous shares of the nation's budget and foreign capital to do so.

The main revolutionary clandestine movements, largely demobilized by repression and almost always resulting in their leaders' violent death, included the following:

1. The National Liberation Action (ALN) was led by the former deputy Carlos Marighella whose motto was "Action creates the vanguard." He intended through his National Liberation Army to defeat the military regime. The ALN, which operated from 1968 to 1973, in cooperation with the Revolutionary Movement of October 8(MR-8) kidnapped the U.S. ambassador to Brazil in 1969 as a tactic to demand the liberation of fifteen political prisoners. Marighella was killed in an armed ambush led by the

much feared torturer, the Police Deputy Sérgio Paranhos Fleury, on an elegant residential street of São Paulo in November of 1969. His successor, João Camara Ferreira, was kidnapped and tortured to death in October 1970 by the same deputy, Fleury, in a place used for such purposes in the state of São Paulo.

2. The Popular Revolutionary Vanguard (VPR) was formed in 1969 when a captain of the army, Carlos Lamarca, headquartered in the army barracks of Quitauna in Osasco, São Paulo, decided to take a large quantity of arms and to lead other military officers in an armed movement against the established regime in 1969. Between 1968 and 1971, the group carried out important revolutionary battles. In 1970, the VPR faced the armed forces and the military police, which had surrounded their guerrilla training area in the poorest region of the state of São Paulo, the Vale da Robeira. That same year, the movement kidnapped three diplomats from Japan, Germany, and Switzerland serving in Brazil. The VPR was destroyed in 1973 when Cabo Anselmo, a police agent, infiltrated the movement and took his "fellows" into a massacre while supposedly intending to reorganize the VPR in Recife. Indeed, the VPR was effectively shattered when its major leader, Carlos Lamarca, was killed in the wilderness of Bahia in September 1971 and was already corroded by hunger, fatigue, solitude, and the lack of support of rural populations, frightened by the ideological preaching of the right and intimidated by the arms of power, who had abandoned them to their own destiny.

3. The Revolutionary Movement of October 8 (MR-8), which immortalized Che Guevara by using the date of his death in 1967, had its origin in 1966 in the university. By 1969 it began to be persecuted after having helped the ALN to kidnap the U.S. ambassador to Brazil. In 1971, it incorporated the militants of VPR, including Carlos Lamarca, who died as a member of the MR-8. In 1978, almost all of the militants of the MR-8 who were being persecuted in Brazil escaped to Chile, dismantling the organization.

4. The Popular Action (AP) was initially a political movement inspired by the ideology of French thinkers. Since the colonial days of Brazil, French thinkers have influenced us, including Jacques Maritain, Mounier, Theillard de Chardin, and Padre Lebret. The AP was formed in 1962 by many students of the Catholic Youth University (JVC) and one of the sectors of the Brazilian Catholic Action, also originating in France. The AP controlled the management board of the National Union of Students (UNE), and many of its members worked as volunteers in one of the most important movements at the beginning of the 1960s in Brazil, the Base Movement of Education (MEB), organized by the bishops of the Catholic Church through the National Conference of Bishops of Brazil (CNBB). Between 1965 and 1967, the AP adopted more and more Marxist positions until it defined itself as a typical Maoist organization, assuming a political course similar to the Communist Party of Brazil (PC of the B) (a faction that in 1962 withdrew from the PCB, initiating its activities as the PC of the B and today having the acronym PPS).

It had orthodox and Stalinist tendencies, although it rarely took part in guerrilla actions. The identification between AP and PC of the B was complete around 1972–1973. After that, two of the major leaders of the AP—Paulo Wright and Honestino Guimaraes—were arrested and killed by DOI-CODI, which contributed to the disappearance of the movement in 1974.

5. The Communist Party of Brazil (PC of B) organized a guerrilla movement in the Amazon region in southern Para State which lasted from 1966 to 1975. Its militants, who survived in a harsh region, had to face 20,000 soldiers of the National Army. In those battles, around sixty-one members of the Guerrilla Forces of the Araguaia died due to the armed forces cruelly repressing the local population in order to locate the guerrillas.

I shall only mention some other organizations named in *Brazil: Never Again,* as the reader can find details about them there on pages 89 to 113: MOLIPO, TL, TLNE, PCBR, CORRENTE, FALN, PCR, MRT, MRM, OP-COR, PRT, POLOP, COLINA, OLAS, VAR-PALMARES, POC, PORT, FBI, OSI, MIM, MAR, FAP, CSR, and MEL.

4. Institutional Act, No. 2 (AI-2), dated October 27, 1965 and signed by the first president of the military government, Marshal Humberto de Alencar Castelo Branco (April 15, 1964 to March 15, 1967), concisely says in article 18: "All actual political parties are extinct and their respective records canceled" and "regarding the organization of new parties, the exigencies of Law No. 4,740, dated July 15, 1965, and its modifications still hold."

The Complementary Act, No. 4, dated November 20, 1965, based on AI-2 and the cited Law No. 4,740, stipulated the rules for creating two new political parties. The members of parliament had to make their choice and begin to annex themselves to either the National Renovating Alliance (ARENA) or the Brazilian Democratic Movement (MDB), which were officially antagonistic.

Through the Program of Action in the Political Planning of the MDB, elaborated in the 1970s, the "opposition" party explicitly opened the space for actions that forced a break with the norms and that repudiated dictatorship. It ended up actually supporting the opposition.

I. Implanting normal democratic conditions and consequently condemning: a) all types of dictatorship; b) the establishment of regimes beyond the law; c) the continuity of fighting ... ; VI. The Brazilian Democratic Movement [MDB] will pursue: a) the revocation of AI-5; ... c) the revocation of the decree No. 477, which represses students and teachers: d) the revision of laws against the press to free them from Draconian norms and the abolishment of the death penalty, life sentences, and exile; e) broad and total amnesty for all civil and military people hurt by the acts of lawlessness and freedom of choice practiced from April 1, 1964 on; VII. Freedom of related organizations." (*Documentation and Political News* 9 [October–December 1978], pp. 73–81).

At the end of 1979, during the previous military government of General João Batista Figueiredo (March 15, 1979 to March 15, 1985), Brazilian society cried out for "broad, total, and unrestricted amnesty." The ARENA and the MDP were abolished.

Therefore, the MDP was transformed into the Party of the Brazilian Democratic Movement (PMDB)—which officially started, although only for a few years, to carry the flag for the real and true democratization of Brazil.

Brazilians owe much to Deputy Ulysses Guimaraes, a militant of the MDB-PMDB, who was the greatest leader of the party and who bravely fought for the political and social democratizing of Brazil. Ulysses was one of the most lucid, critical, and serious statesman in all our history. Through humor, patience, and knowledge, this politician from São Paulo knew, as very few do, the right moments to speak and to be silent, to love and to hate. He saved lives from the war of repression and, with the protection of civil and political societies, commanded the reinstatement of Brazilian democratic institutions. He was attentive since the coup d'état of 1964 to the obstruction of President Collor. Brazil misses him.

5. In regard to torture, one of the great Brazilian psychoanalysts, Helio Peregrino, wrote the following. I transcribe the text, in part, so that the reader can better understand Freire's narrative about a friend of his who was tortured by the memory of what she had suffered in Brazil and also so that readers can understand more clearly the way torturers deprive us of humanity.

> Torture, unbearable corporeal punishment, introduces a wedge that splits the body and the mind. More than that: it sows discord and war between the body and the mind. Through torture, the body becomes our enemy and persecutes us. It is this basic model on which rests the action of any torturer.... In torture, the body militates against us, demanding that we speak. From the intimate thickness of our own flesh a voice is raised which denies and intends to split from us, a voice that we abhor, since it is the negation of our freedom. Alienation reaches its crucial point here. Torture imposes upon us the total alienation of our own bodies, which become foreign to us and our enemy.... The project of torture entangles itself in a total negation of the person, who is embodied. The center of the human being is freedom. This, in turn, is an invention that the subject makes, through the word that represents him or her. In torture, speech, which the torturer searches to extract from the tortured, is the absolute and radical negation of his or her condition as a free subject. Torture aims to turn freedom inside out. According to this measure, such speech, through intimidation and violence, is the degraded word of a subject who, at the hands of the torturer, transforms himself or herself into an object. (Helio Peregrino, "Political Torture," *Folha de São Paulo* [June 5, 1992], p. 3; quoted in *Brazil: Never Again*, pp. 281–82.)

The techniques most utilized in torture by the military regime of Brazil are listed in *Brazil: Never Again* in an appendix titled, "The Methods and Instruments of Torture." They were the *arara* stick, electric shock, cayenne pepper, tension doublers, drowning, the dragon chair (one in Rio de Janeiro and another in São Paulo), the freezer, insects and animals, and chemical products.

The torture that Freire's friend was submitted to (and with whom Paulo Freire dialogues through the act of silent solidarity) was the arara stick, a common practice from ancient times until today in the prisons and police stations of Brazil. It was described by two other victims of repression:

> The arara stick consists of an iron bar across which is laid a person's tied wrists and folded knees. It is placed between two tables, keeping the body of the tortured hanging above the floor about twenty or thirty centimeters. This method is almost never used on its own, its usual complements are electric shock, flat paddles, and drowning.... (Augusto Cesar Salles Galvao, twenty-one-year-old student from Belo Horizonte; a letter in his own handwriting from 1970).
>
> The arara stick was a metal structure that could be disassembled, consisting of two triangles of galvanized pipe in which one angle was shaped like a half moon. It was placed under a person's knees and between the hands, which were tied together and to the knees.... (José Milton Ferreira de Almeida, thirty-one-year-old engineer from Rio de Janeiro; act of inquiry in 1976). (Quoted in *Brazil: Never Again*, p. 34.)ET

At that time—in the military regime—torture acquired sophisticated techniques to make victims suffer and to degrade them physically and psychologically. Using "scientific methods" never before known in the organizations of national repression and with the connivance of some doctors, such torture left no signs or marks on those who had their bodies humiliated. Priests, pregnant women, and children were not spared. The torturers did not discriminate against any class, race, age, gender, or religion.

The fact is that we brought in industrial technologies; capitalist consumption; economic and financial methods; and organizational and educational structures to ally us to "Christian and Western" postmodern torture so that we could exorcise the imaginary witches of our McCarthy era from the bodies of our youngsters by training on beggars to efficiently destroy "dialectical Marxism."

> The teaching of this method of violently extracting confessions and information was not simply theoretical. It was practical, with people really being tortured as guinea pigs in this gruesome apprenticeship. One of the first to introduce such pragmatism to Brazil was the U.S. police officer Dan Mitrione, subsequently transferred to Montevideu, where he was finally kidnapped and killed. When he was an instructor in Belo Horizonte, in the first few years of the military regime, he used beggars from the streets to instruct the local police. Treated cruelly in the classroom, the poor men said that students learned the various ways of creating, in the prisoner, the split between the body and the soul, by hitting him or her in vulnerable areas. (A. J. Langreti, *A face oculta do terror*, [Rio de Janeiro: Civilizacao Brazileira, 1979]; quoted in *Brazil: Never Again*, p. 32).

Mitrione's "school" established a bitter knowledge in Brazilians—civil, police, and military, many of whom subsequently got special "degrees" in torture from various countries of the North—that was used in an efficient way and relegated thousands of Brazilian families to eternal mourning for their young idealists, who only dreamed of a more serious and more just country that would no longer submit to external orders and interests.

Notes to the First Letter

1. These huts, called *mocambo,* are typical of the coastal region of Northeast Brazil. They belong to the poorest populations and are built in the large cities in the area of the mangroves or hills.

   The huts are built with material taken from the surrounding areas, are simple, and (if, it were not for the problems they posed in terms of hygiene, which possibly could be amended by competent health officials) are an ecological alternative suitable to a tropical climate, poor region, and Third World country.

   In order to build mocambo, one needs coconut tree leaves, twigs, boards, timber for the roof, and clay. Coconut tree leaves are placed in the sun to dry, and are then called coconut tree hay, a greatly durable construction material.

   On the ground, which is "pressed" (see note of the twelfth letter), the walls are raised, which consist of a canvas of dried coconut tree leaves tied to vertical poles fixed in the ground and covered with moist and smooth clay. After they dry, the walls built in this manner, with clay, are reasonably resistant to the elements.

   Sometimes the huts have indoor partitions, a few windows, and two doors, which consist of two boards, the top one kept open for fresh air, as if it were a window, and the bottom one kept closed to prevent the animals from coming into the house. The mocambo always has a rectangular shape, with the windows set in the long walls of the house and the two doors set in the short walls at the front and back of the house. In the mocambo are a clay stove for cooking and, rarely, a bathroom.

   The mocambos are also roofed with coconut tree leaves, which before drying are folded along the length of the leaf by cutting the central stalk. Atop the dry walls go the roof timbers, and over them the folded leaves, one next to the other, almost overlapping, secured to each other and the timbers, so that the rooms of the mocambo are protected from the burning sun in the summer and the torrential rains in the winter.

   Traditionally, the children of the mocambos who lived in the mangroves searched for crabs to nourish their families and sold them, helping the family to survive.

2. In Northeast Brazil, we pick the fruit when it is the right size but not yet ready for consumption. This is done so that the animals, especially the birds, do not eat them before we do. Therefore, fruit picked "for good" is customarily covered up with dry banana tree leaves or old newspapers so that they can ripen. Ripeness, in the majority of the Northeast Brazil bananas, is shown by the golden color of their peels.

3. To fly a kite, locally called *pipa*, *arraia*, *cafifa*, *pandorga*, *quadrado*, *tapioca*, or *balde*, has been over time, one of the most popular and widespread pastimes of Brazilian children.

Easily built by the child, who for that reason feels creatively challenged, he or she chooses the most satisfying size, color, and shape of his or her kite, preferably as different from his or her classmates as possible. The kite only requires, beyond imagination and love, a bit of tissue paper, some small rods, a little glue, and a few meters of fine, strong thread.

Kites have been a boy's toy typically, since flying them to great altitudes requires the expanse of the open sky and the ample space that only streets and plazas can offer, which in the *machismo* society was forbidden to girls until very recently.

In the city of Campinas, the kite has been used as an instructional tool to teach the elements of physical sciences and mathematics to children.

A small group of science professors at the State University of Campinas (UNICAMP) introduced the study of measurement, counting, and geometry through the process of constructing and flying kites with the children from the city's slum, São Marcos. The joy and pleasure everyone experienced in this act of teaching-learning did not make it any less systematic, scientific, or appropriate for the children.

Subsequently, this same group—Professors Eduardo Sebastiani, Ubiratan D'Ambrosio, and Carlos and Zoraide Arguello—joined Adriano Noguerira, a philosopher concerned with educating the popular classes, and about twenty students from the colleges of mathematics, physics, and engineering, to create the *Museu Dinamico de Ciencias*, the Dynamic Science Museum.

The museum, which is still operated today in the Parque Portugal, in the district Taquaral of Campinas, invited children to participate in the experience in a social rather than academic spirit.

Between 1985 and 1990, every August when the winds blow strongest almost all over Brazil, the museum sponsored the *Festa do Papagaio*, the Kite Festival.

On those occasions, the group taught the children how to build kites as a way for them to learn and apply basic knowledge of physics and mathematics in an easy, suitable, and efficient method. The unity of theory and practice was joyfully lived and understood.

In speaking to me of that experience, one of the professors relived the joy of the times in which boys and girls—girls were initiated then—filled the skies with colored tissue paper and thread, learning about height and distance, perpendiculars and hypotenuses, atmospheric tension and pressure, space and time, catenary curves and lines, the infinite and the finite, winds and air currents. In a spectacle of joined hands, heads, and souls, people of different degrees of knowledge, distinct classes, genders, and religions had only one goal—the act of learning without competition.

The outdoor class avoided focusing on who made the most beautiful kite or the longest or the most colorful tail or who flew it the highest. The aerodynamics class, in the open sky of August, had an open love for the acts of creating, observing, comprehending, and applying scientific knowledge without having it imposed on them by the teacher, who usually forces the formulas on the students and requires equations and rules to be memorized and written on the blackboards of closed and sad classrooms.

Freire, who has valued the world as a fountain of knowledge, a source of common sense, as the beginning of scientific, systematized knowledge (in fact the group began from Freire's premises) could not have the kite as his first science class, except for the pleasure of flying it.

Notes to the Second Letter

1. At the end of the past century and the beginning of this one, when the newly liberated slaves were settling themselves in the biggest and most important Brazilian cities, they evidently occupied the areas despised by the middle class and local elites. The narrow paths between the mountains and hills have been their leftovers ever since.

   The narrow paths were no more than what many continue to be: gutters in which filthy, polluted, green water passed through. In them, even clean rain water turned to sludge due to trash, including that from the sewers. The imprudent children spent their leisure time swimming these waters before they reached the ocean and rivers. On its fetid banks, in areas prone to floods, the very poor built and continue to build their houses.

   The residences in the hills do not present more comfort than those located on the banks of the narrow paths. The inhabitants have to descend and climb the slopes on foot, and if their houses are spared floods, the strong winds and torrential rains of the tropical zone can easily destroy them.

   The mocambos endure the damage of inclemency better than the residences built with urban debris. The houses of the hills and narrow paths are without running water, electricity, sewage, or garbage collection.

   In this manner, when Freire speaks of the "world of the kids who were from very poor neighborhoods on the outskirts of town" he is speaking about the excluded children, the children of the mocambos and of the hills. They are excluded from eating, attending school, being clothed properly, sleeping well, taking baths in clean water, and waiting for better days.

2. About the meaning of gimmick or *manha*, consult my note 29 of Freire's *Pedagogy of Hope*.

3. Chicken thief was the name used in Northeast Brazil, before the violence of burglars had reached its cities, for those who committed small thefts to survive, having no job due to a sluggish economy.

   The term indicated a thief who stole, almost accidentally, things he found in the backyards of the well-to-do—clothes, fruit, or even chickens.

   "Little people" is the Brazilian term that arrogant middle-class and upper-class people call, even today, people deprived of material goods. Besides being discriminatory, the term is intended to hurt the individual, and rob him or her of the dignity of belonging.

It is as if being poor or miserable was disgraceful and worked against possessing moral or ethical qualities because of a nonprivileged social status. Therefore, "little people," men or women, were considered inferior individuals to whom we ought not give any respect or esteem. This term is highly pejorative, therefore, Freire uses it in quotes.

Notes to the Fourth Letter

1. We used to shout *calungas de caminhão* in Pernambuco in the past to the men—because it was one of the hardest jobs of the time it "naturally" fell on blacks—who loaded and unloaded the trucks.

   Since this transportation service depended on human labor, the trucks carried the necessary five or six men who stood upright in the truck, holding on for a modicum of safety during the trip. In the driver's seat or hidden by the wooden sides of the truck, these men appeared to the elite, as "little puppets" or "short people," a reading of disdain by a discriminatory and authoritarian society. The term *calungas de caminhão* is probably related to the divinities of an African religion called *calungas* because the men were generally black. The African men, who came to Brazil as slaves from the sixteenth to the nineteenth centuries, were called Angolans, Cabindans, Benguelans, Congolese, or Mozambicans according to their African origin.

2. Northeast Brazil has the tradition of celebrating its dearest and most respected saints on June 24, Saint John's Eve, and June 29, Saint Peter's Eve. More than any other holidays of Catholic origin, such as Christmas and Easter, these June feasts touch all social classes.

   The fireworks include *traques* (small packages of tissue paper with a minute amount of gunpowder that explodes on contact with the ground); sparklers that spray drops of colored fire from the children's hands; the *rojoes* (gunpowder pistols that explode with an enormous bang like thunder at high altitudes); and *busca-pe* (a "fire" that follows the person who runs from it, only to explode at his or her feet). Flare rockets, great bonfires, and strings full of little flags in colored tissue paper make the religious feast a pagan one, full of noise and joy prolonged until day breaks.

   The little boys dance the quadrille with the little girls in rustic dress. The quadrille is an imitation of the dances of European royalty, animated by the orders of the *puxador* and popular music, especially the *baiao, xaxado, xote, rancheira,* and *mazuzka.* In between are celebrated the "weddings" of "pregnant" young girls and "reluctant" grooms, officiated over by the police and parents preoccupied with the "sin."

   Both simulations—the quadrilles and the weddings—eternalize social values and give special life to the June feasts in an authentic Northeast Brazil atmosphere.

   It is the season when young girls ask Saint John or Saint Anthony to find them real grooms (actually on June 12, but traditionally celebrated closer to the end of June, when the feasts are). It is the season when they see, in the shadowy dark, their destiny in aluminum water, preferably the face of a loved one whom they will soon marry, or when they walk on the burning, ash-covered coals left by the fires at daybreak. If their feet do not burn, this is a sign that they will not die before the next June.

Food is an essential part of these feasts. Sweet potatoes or corn cobs roasted on open fires are added to *pamonhas* and corn soup, called *canjica*.

Pamonha is cooked inside a corn husk. First, green corn is grated and the resulting cream passed through a sieve; then sugar and coconut milk are added. After being tightly wrapped in the corn husk, the cream cooks for hours in enormous pots of water. Served very hot, to the point that butter melts over it, it invites us to taste.

The canjica that Freire speaks of is prepared similarly to the pamonha, being cooked for hours on end in copper pans until it reaches the consistency of a smooth pudding and a golden color. At that point, the canjica is placed on plates, sprinkled with cinnamon, which causes a bouquet of aromas when mixed with the unique, delicate flavor of *manjica*, and served cold.

Consequently, June in Northeast Brazil is the month when superstitions and Catholic faith mix with the dreams of the nobility and money, with music, noise, dance, and "weddings"; a month of popular foods, colorful clothes, and fire, which all explain the passion for Brazil that rises from a people who have experienced so much suffering, especially in the wilderness. Praying and waiting for the gift of rain makes the dried vegetation flourish into an exuberant green, as strong as its people and their feasts.

3. Using "hands" to describe an amount of green corn, Freire remembers a measurement already outdated in Brazil which indicated the number of corn cobs. In Pernambuco, a hand was equal to fifty corn cobs, in Alagoas to twenty-five corn cobs, in São Paulo to sixty corn cobs, and in Rio Grande do Sul to sixty-four corn cobs.

Notes to the Fifth Letter
1. Since General Dantas Barreto, minister of war to President Hermes da Fonseca (November 15, 1910 to November 15, 1914), was introduced as a candidate for governor of Pernambuco by Pinheiro Machado, who openly ruled as the supreme chief of the nation, Barreto was considered elected.

In fact, he was elected with the intervention of the federal government in Pernambuco using the local army—today the seventh military regiment—for electoral fraud. This and other vices were registered in the books settling vote counts. The person whom the forces in power had decided should take power (see note of the fourteenth letter), Dantas Barreto instilled terror after taking office,. His mission was to replace the oligarchy of Rosa e Silva and to frighten the news reporters and the most daring colonels, thereby establishing a stronger military government.

In order to do that, Dantas Barreto created the "handkerchief gang," *Turma do Lenco*, that Freire speaks of. It was so called because the members hid their faces with a handkerchief during their "actions." A few officers and soldiers of the Military Police of Pernambuco were involved, commanded by Colonel Francisco Melo, who had a compromised past and at least one act of cowardly massacre. He had commanded the shooting of sailors who had already received a pardon for their role in the Revolta da Chibata. Under the leadership of a bold sailor, João Candido, they had refused the application of the cane as a punishment on board ship.

The handkerchief gang showed their excellency in service by beating the important and respected news reporter Mario Melo and expelling the news reporter Assis Chateaubriand (who had founded the *Associated Daily*, still kept as an important chain of newspapers), among other actions of institutionalized terror.

The famous news reporter whose murder Freire laments later in this letter is Trajano Chacon. At the age of thirty four, at the peak of his professional career, he was the greatest victim of the perversity of the handkerchief gang when on August 11, 1913, in the open street of Imperatriz at the center of Recife, he was beaten cruelly to death after a commemoration of the creation of juridical degrees in Brazil.

Those present at the scene, who were scared and frightened, but also revolted and enraged, kept silent during the barbaric crime because they could not do anything and because they understood that the punishment that the general governor and his gang were performing in the dark, since all electricity had been conveniently shut off, was meant not only for those who were there, but for all the people of Pernambuco, including the governor's political adversaries and especially the critical news reporters.

Trajano Chacon's despicable death was to revenge two editorials supposedly written by him that criticized the cowardly actions of the governor, published in the newspaper *O Pernambucano*, the property of Henrique Milet, a law professor in Recife, a friend of Trajano and his whole family.

Milet, revolted by the death of his friend and collaborator, concluded his eulogy at the crowded funeral with a sentence that seemed prophetic and explained what history has done and does so often to those who are executioners of the people.

"Trajano Chacon is being buried dead, General Dantas Barreto is being buried alive!"

In fact, Dantas was not able, as was usual at the time, to elect his successor. In spite of the political terror spewed by the government of Dantas Barreto, the people faced the terror and those who committed it, and elected the leader of the opposition—Manuel Borba—to succeed him.

Trajano's nephew, Vamireh Chacon (without whom I would not have been able to write this note since history books proved unfruitful), now a professor of political science at the University of Brasília, promptly told me (with the passion of someone who has been one of the great students of the history of ideas in Brazil and not just an affectionate nephew) that this savageness toward his uncle was the straw that broke the back of the political career of Dantas Barreto, who died in obscurity in Rio de Janeiro.

The history of oppressors' impunity in Brazil has here a clear and sad example. The murderers were taken to court, but declared not guilty because the governor kept dismissing the prosecutors in charge of the wrongful death cases of Chacon, Francisco Barreto Campelo, João de Deus, and Mena Barreto de Barros Falcao (no relation). The handkerchief gang at the doors of the press had not intimidated the prosecutors, who carried out their obligation of denouncing and not disguising the murderers. Two prosecutors were replaced and Dantas found another who, by defending the police officers, acquitted them all with the connivance of a jury picked by hand and composed of public officials, in spite of the accused having confessed in detail how they had killed Trajano.

Rui Barbosa—a remarkable jurist and one of the well-to-do public men who was lucid, courageous, and critical—placed himself, as he always had done, in support of justice by pronouncing in the federal senate an obituary for the murdered news reporter from Pernambuco that exhibited his revulsion at the government of Pernambuco and its crimes and aligned himself with the family of a dead friend.

Trajano Chacon, who knew how to honor his citizenship by fighting for his country—he had held arms while yet very young, beside Placido de Castro, to annex today's state of Acre to Brazil—is honored today for his work in critical and conscious journalism as the patron of the Press Association of Pernambuco.

2. The movement that Freire speaks of is known in Brazil as the Revolution of 1930.

For years after the proclamation of the republic in 1889, Brazil had been governed by the agrarian aristocracy of the coffee plantation.

The two states of the federation—Minas Gerais and São Paulo—that were the biggest producers of national wealth had chosen and "elected" the president of the republic as if public power were private, only there to protect and serve them.

Discontentment was emerging through the 1910s and 1920s against this politics of an export-oriented, agrarian monoculture that exposed a great part of the population to misery (the popular classes), to survival (the middle classes), or to business (the clientele of the state, which overloaded public offices with officials, whether they were needed or not). Many fought for the few jobs created in the three productive industries initiated by the private sector or improvised small and precarious jobs in the parallel economy, which has grown until it is now the only possibility for income among the popular classes.

An armed movement erupted in October 1930 to stop these types of activities under the leadership of Getúlio Vargas. He was a former minister of the treasury for the president in office, Washington Luíz and the former president of the province of Rio Grande do Sul (until 1930 the actual governors of the states were called presidents), who had lost the election of March 1930, which was carried out under the legal rules and practiced vices of established power.

The assassination of João Pessoa in July 1930—who was then president of the province of Paraiba and who had formed with Vargas a defeated ticket as vice president—was the spark that started the conflagration of the armed movement, even though the assassination was not related to the crises of electoral fraud or the poor economy, which affected all. The assassination gave a political advantage to the "revolutionary forces," who knew how to encourage the climate of defeat and proclaimed themselves indignant at the "political assassination" of João Pessoa.

On November 3, 1930, the "revolutionary government," having ousted President Washington Luíz a few days before he was to assume office on the victorious ticket of the governmentalists, headed by another person from São Paulo, chose its leader Getúlio Vargas for the highest office of the nation, as announced by the Junta Pacificadora.

After various difficulties and conflicts, a representative assembly was elected by direct vote in 1933. The new constitution was proclaimed in 1934, which stated that the president should be elected by Congress for a four-year term. This was an act against Vargas's maneuvers to guarantee himself continued power. While the country was preparing for elections, three years later, Vargas engineered a coup d'état on November 10, 1937. He governed Brazil in a declared dictatorship until he was ousted on October 29, 1945.

We owe his fall to the contradictions evident between his way of governing and the country's wish for freedom, created by the climate of the Second World War and widespread not only in Europe and the United States but also in Brazil.

With the undeniable authoritarian talent of a military leader and in the very Brazilian tradition of a high ability to govern, Vargas was certainly the person who most revolutionized the political and economic history of the country.

Therefore, the people again elected him in 1951 for a term that should have lasted five years. It was abruptly interrupted by his suicide on August 24, 1954, an answer to the enemies accusing him and his family of corruption.

The year 1930 was one of awakening progress. It was the watershed between an archaic and regressive Brazil and a modern Brazil, complete with the creation of a bureaucratic state; the rise of a more homogenous and numerous middle class; a concern for social problems (it was Vargas who created the Ministry of Labor and the Ministry of Public Education and Health in 1930); a respect for the working class demonstrated in the act of decreeing labor laws, although, of course, this was partly due simply to the typical values of a populist government; and the creation of the political, economic, and legal infrastructure necessary to industrialization.

Brazilian historians disagree on how to interpret the Revolution of 1930. Was it promoted by the bourgeoisie, who wanted to obtain power until then retained by the latifundio owners, or was it a movement of the civil and military middle class, who wanted to establish social and political justice in Brazil?

I can't help pointing out Vargas's political willingness to lead the construction of a better, more serious, and more just country, dynamic in all its aspects.

A short, fat man, Vargas was a cigar smoker with a profound and communicative look who liked to receive, read, and keep in his pockets the notes people sent on the rare occasions when he appeared publicly. He was cheerful and polite and had the great power of persuasion. Serene or jovial when it was convenient, he lived a reserved and methodical life, was agnostic but not above taking advantage of the Catholic clergy, was charismatic and possessed of an easy smile. A military leader, a peacemaker, and a statesman all at the same time; a man of clemency, but implacable with his worst enemies; a lucid and agile politician who was serious about his duties and wise about national problems—Vargas was our best example of a Brazilian populist.

In this manner, by assisting and valuing the proletariat, he let their demands be consecrated, granted them protectionist laws, and coerced them. At the same time, he burned extra stock to protect the coffee growers and he aided the bourgeoisie by creating industrial measures, which did develop the country but also helped this new dominant political faction grow enormously rich.

Vargas, especially in the first fifteen uninterrupted years of his administration, activated the Brazilian nation at all levels and angles, but unfortunately did not activate political consciousness.

He had a utopian project for which he fought fearlessly, without distancing himself from nationalism or populism.

He dictated and imposed, but he also changed and built—with his democratic idealism and patriotic sensibility—the country's possibilities, which the Brazilian people had not yet been able to realize, through his despotic way of governing for so many years, thus encouraging our new, fragile, and democratically inexperienced republic.

3. Wladimir Herzog was a respected news reporter who, at the age of only thirty eight, was summoned to testify against the repression of the military regime.

He reported on the morning of October 25, 1975, and by the afternoon of that same day had died in the branch offices of the DOI-CODI—the security organization created in 1970 during General Medici's administration of the armed forces (October 30, 1969 to March 15, 1974)—after having been barbarously tortured.

The commander of the Second Army in São Paulo, who was responsible for the death, sent a statement to the press announcing the suicide of Herzog.

The body of the news reporter was also insulted: it served as a prop in the farce they photographed to "prove" he had hung himself. The chair placed in front of his inert body was displayed as "evidence" that he had climbed it to throw himself off. It proved the opposite, however, as it showed his feet touching the floor, his waist level with the chair, his knees bent, and his legs parallel to the floor.

His family and Brazilian society started an investigation on October 25, 1978. Judge Marco José de Morais declared a verdict: the state was responsible for the arrest, torture, and death of Wladimir Herzog.

Likewise, Rubens Beirodt Paiva was arrested at his residence in Rio de Janeiro on January 20, 1971, after a telephone call in which a man asked for his address under the guise of delivering a letter from Chile.

Right after that, six persons in civilian dress, all carrying arms and no identification, invaded his house and took the federal deputy to the branch offices of the army police, where the DOI-CODI was.

This division of the army denied, in spite of proof, that Rubens had been detained there. He had been seen by other political prisoners and his family had signed a receipt for the delivery of Rubens's car, which the deputy had driven himself to police headquarters.

Since he was young, Rubens Paiva had been connected to nationalist causes, such as the fight to create Petrobras, whose motto was "The Petroleum Is Ours." When he was still a deputy, he had been one of the members of the Congressional Investigative Committee of the Brazilian Institute of Democratic Action, which straightened out the scandal of generals behind the military coup receiving large sums of dollars from the government of the United States in 1963 (*Brazil: Never Again*, pp. 269–70).

The investigation, so compromising for the corrupters (U.S. rulers who believed and divulged to the whole world themselves as the makers and masters of democracy) and for the corrupted (the generals who led the revolution in the name of battling corruption, among other motives) caused them to punish Paiva for having been one of their denouncers. The Institutional Act, No. 1, dated April 9, 1964, canceled his congressional team.

After being arrested and accused of the "crime" of maintaining correspondence with Brazilian political deportees who lived in Chile, Paiva was subjected to the "findings": torture his body could not endure.

"Disappeared," his death was only recognized ten years after his kidnapping and death. His remains were never handed over to his family and those who admired him as one of the greatest public men of Brazil.

Miriam Verbena was raised alongside Freire's children as if she were a cousin. She was born in Belem do Para into a family dear to Esther Monteiro, one of Freire's aunts, who had extended herself to Freire almost as a mother during the days in Jaboatão. Miriam came to live in Recife at the age of seven, sheltered by the generosity of Esther. She was raised alongside Esther's child, Dona e João, as one more sister. At that time, only a stone wall and always open gate separated Paulo's house from his Aunt Esther's. It was a large family that dreamed of a new Brazil.

In the 1970s, Miriam, one of the innumerable young people of her generation to do so, enrolled herself in a clandestine revolutionary movement that fought to establish a less evil, more just, and humane society, as Freire used to say. Therefore, she was assassinated by the forces of repression, along with a colleague while they were traveling by car on a road in Pernambuco.

As in all the other cases, the powers that be did not take responsibility for the deed. The official statement claimed the case as the kind of simple car accident so common on our roads.

Today, April 1, 1994, as I write this note, Brazil remembers the military coup d'état with sorrow. Many shout, "1964: Never again!"

Never again: the death and torture of Herzogs, Rubens, and Miriams. "Never again!" we all have to shout.

NOTES

4. The quote is from Pe. Antônio Vieira, *Obras Completas, Sermões*, vol. 3, books 7–9 (Portugal: Lello e Irmão, Editores Porto, 1959), pp. 342–43. It is important to read the analysis of his work in E. L. Berlink, *Ftores Adversos na Formação Brasileira*, 2nd ed. (São Paulo: Impressora IPSIS, 1959), pp. 86–87.

5. Ibid.

6. The quote is from Joaquim Nabuco, *First Centennial Publication Celebrating the Old Representatives of Pernambuco,* (Rio de Janeiro: House of Representatives, 1759), p. 64.

7. The quote is from Paulo Cavalcanti, *O caso en conto como o caso foi—Da columa Prestes à queda de Arraes, Memórias* (Rio de Janeiro: Editora Limitada, 1979), pp. 284–85.

8. The Collored PCs, or *PCs colloridos,* are all those who kept themselves faithful to P. C. Farias and Fernando Collor de Mello. De-Collored PCs are those who became disbelievers in the same. Both are those who have been growing rich by dishonestly wasting public monies, embezzling public monies for their pockets or billing public works with inflated invoices and other distortions, cheating the society with illegal or shadow business, exploiting the working class by paying little attention to their poverty; and provoking the latter through outrageous consumer prices— all corrupt and unspeakable practices of Farias and Collor, who saw them as natural and valid.

   Freire obviously refers, in this part of his work, to the disrespect shown the population through various forms of political, ethical, and social behavior—which we have learned from our political and economic elites, who, through the P. C. and Collor ways, damaged the whole Brazilian population and were protected by almost total immunity from prosecution—which has been active in Brazil since its invasion by Portugal in 1500 (see notes of the first and twelfth letter).

9. Brazilian historiography has registered the character of the Brazilian people as docile. That ideological interpretation has not been confirmed, however, by the last years of our history.

   The great contradictions—generated by the miserable conditions of many of the oppressed on the one hand, and the arrogant, authoritarian, and discriminatory tradition of the oppressors on the other (which, let it be said, has come to generate terrible differences between the classes)—have been transforming our society as episodes of deplorable and shameful violence against some leave the people in a climate of unbearable insecurity.

   At this moment, I speak more of the events against which the oppressed cannot defend. I speak of the systematic extermination of the less socially valued in Brazil by institutionalized power, by those police officers who carry out destructive activities during their off-duty hours or by those alternative groups that call themselves righteous.

   The Brazilian state and institutionalized governments have been favoring the practice of vigilantism on the part of bad police officers and other groups who consider themselves as having the legal power to "make justice with their own hands" and form an armed power parallel to that of the state.

Therefore, in the large Brazilian metropolises we have what scholars call "double control," policing by the authority of police officials and policing from the social milieu.

The police commanders at headquarters preach every day, as legitimate representatives of the repressive apparatus of the state, about how police officers should treat "outlaws" with rigor, in this concealed way preaching violence toward the popular classes.

The population in general—ill advised about the real motives of delinquency, tired of being victimized, and desirous of proving that workers are not "that kind of people"—instigate along with small merchants a demand for those trained by the police force, on police missions, or in "righteous" groups, and who have access and experience in deadly weapons to use them to "clean" the city of undesirables, "extinguishing them" forever.

I do not advocate, far from it, the indiscriminate protection of criminals or a forgetfulness regarding the responsibility of those who have committed antisocial actions. The crimes committed in Brazil today by "outcasts" from the political, economic, and social process have left almost the whole population in a panic and terribly scared, because many of the acts have been barbarous and hideous. They deserve, indubitably, punishment for their acts, even if we know that they are the product of our society, which has been terribly unjust. It is also true, however, that Brazilian society cannot continue to expose its members to all types of massacres. The immunity from prosecution has to end. Criminals should be judged and punished as human beings by a judiciary power composed legally for that purpose and not as objects by any groups who believe themselves to be "righteous."

The police, the only state institution that can use force legally in the name of internal security, must stop the abuse of power by laying the foundation and self-imposing sanctions on the indiscriminate use of physical force, beatings, the infringement on rights, false arrests, humiliation through torture, and murder. Such sanctions should be leveled on both their "legal" activities and on those who, without political conscience or humanitarian sentiment, prefer to chastise the victims of the political, economic, and ethical problems of the nation instead of fighting the oppressor who truly tortures almost all of us of the Brazilian nation.

The systematic extermination of minors is a sinister practice that has been widespread in various corners of Brazil for the last few years. For instance, vigilante groups carried out, with a high degree of secrecy on June 23, 1993, the killing of eight street children who were sleeping completely wrapped in blankets on the streets of Our Lady of Candelaria Church, one of the symbols of Brazil. Police officers, dressed in civilian clothes, fired a machine gun without even checking who they were killing, simply because the children smelled, were starving and homeless, had been abandoned by their families, and, therefore, unfortunately, had to steal in order to survive.

Brazil's true citizens cried, were ashamed, and mourned these deaths.

In an authoritarian and unpunished way at the end of 1993, the military police of Rio de Janeiro invaded a slum called Vigario Geral. Under the silence of night, some men dressed in civilian clothes and covered with hoods retaliated against drug dealers who lived in the hills and had not paid an illegal bribe as promised by killing innocent people. Some of them were women and some were men, some were drinking beer and peacefully talking in a bar and others were sleeping the few hours they had left after a day of hard work.

At the bar, seven people were shot. The police then invaded a house and shot eight people of the same working family, people whose evangelical faith was the cornerstone of their lives, leaving only a child alive.

After washing away the blood, that tenacious community transformed the house into a cultural and resistance center.

Walking the streets, the police officers claimed six more victims, even some who cried out loudly for their lives and shouted desperately that they were working people and not vagabonds. Everybody saw and heard. They could not do anything but get desperate. Twenty-one innocent people paid the ultimate price for living in the hills of misery, injustice, and the bribe that was not received.

Their families and society continued shouting for justice and peace, which still has not arrived. The hills of Rio de Janeiro continue to be daily persecuted by the police, the "righteous," the drug dealers who make their headquarters there, and misery.

One year ago, another such episode, equally frightening, took place in the city of São Paulo. To make the situation worse, the violence fell on convicted men under the guardianship and responsibility of the state in the most progressive state in the country, the state of São Paulo.

The prisoners of pavilion 9 of the detention house at the Carandiru Prison were the target of unrestrained tyranny by those who believed themselves to be the makers of justice and order. The massacre took place on October 2, 1992, but it only became public the next afternoon so that the elections for the mayor of the capital could take place according to the interests of the owners of power.

After a dispute among the prisoners of that pavilion (one of them, a "drug smuggler," had received his money but had not delivered the drug—drug traffic being a common practice in the military prisons, sponsored by the corrupt police officers), the "zealous" public incarceration officials screamed that there was a rebellion.

Without being qualified to do so, the guards on the prison walls telephoned the metropolitan police headquarters. Immediately, the commander arrived, accompanied by famous troop experts in violence: Tobias Aguiar Visible Patrol (ROTA), Special Operations Control (COE), and Special Action Tactics Group (GATE). The assistant secretary for the prison and the judges of the criminal courts also arrived and all met in the director's office of the prison. During a telephone call, the secretary of public safety sent a message to the director of the detention house to "transfer authority" to Colonel Ubiratan, commander of the metropolitan police headquarters.

In this manner, by giving the order, the secretary gave up his civil and political power in the public safety arena and delivered it, improperly in this case, to the military police, who massacred the prison population.

The colonel, imbued with ample powers, did not want any civilians in his "war operation," leaving for "his" field of action once he heard the voice of the judges—who, at that moment were already in the prison—to pursue a military action in a civilian area, something unheard of in the prison history of Brazil.

Barricades set up by the prisoners did not prevent the troops from entering pavilion 9 and executing the occupants of cell after cell in a few minutes.

Rusty cell doors that did not open saved some for a few minutes; men who were in the rush of killing could not wait to open them with more effort than simply kicking them with their feet. Three hundred police officers armed to the teeth acted against approximately a thousand unarmed men.

Those who survived, hurt and terrified, were placed in the central courtyard of the pavilion and sat totally naked, with their heads down. Obedient to all orders, they evidently felt conquered. Those who moved were bitten by dogs trained to kill. Others, after being questioned about the crime they had committed before being arrested, were taken from the courtyard and disappeared. Ironically, the person who had caused the quarrel was saved because he was in the infirmary for treatment.

It is a common practice in prisons all over the world to keep prisoners naked after rebellions and riots, sometimes for many days. Although common, it is humiliating, degrading, and reproachable in this as in many other cases because the prisoners already feel conquered.

This has been one of the arguments of the São Paulo criminal lawyers who have prosecuted the torture and death of the 111 men killed that day. Their families demand compensation from the state, declaring that their relatives were not trying to run away, did not retaliate, and that the massacre was barbarous, intended to eliminate some "elements" detained in the prison. The principle is obvious: naked prisoners do not object or run away, they only obey and submit themselves as a strategy to try to survive. To murder unprotected prisoners is a crime against human rights.

Upon first hearing the news of the "rebellion," at the end of the afternoon on Friday, October 2, two members of the Human Rights Commission of the Order of Lawyers of Brazil (OAB)—which has been one of the most attentive and concerned institutions in the last few years regarding the political, juridical, and ethical issues of Brazilian society—made their way to Carandiru but were not allowed in. They heard from the director that the prison was under military police command, which was not authorizing anybody to enter. The two members were Flavio Straus and Margarida Helena de Paula.

On Saturday, October 3, the first act exposing the "secret of the state" was when two other members of the OAB went to the prison, entered, and gathered information about the dimension of the tragedy. They returned and then informed civil society. They were João Benedito de Azevedo Marques and Ricardo Carrara.

The OAB, through its Human Rights Commission and other vigilant organizations that had been witnessing the political and social injustices the oppressed segments of Brazil had been suffering, summoned the national and international press, so that another disgrace would not remain in the silent conscience of the oppressors.

On Monday, October 5, the criminal lawyer Jairo Fonseca—a jurist with a clear and explicit political preference for the oppressed, a member of the most active OAB of São Paulo and the person who provided me with the details for this note—was able to enter and converse with the survivors of pavilion 9. He was accompanied by the press. Survivors confirmed that they were in their cells and were not trying to run away as their aggressors alleged. They added that some fellows seen in the courtyard had disappeared from the prison. They told other terrible details of that afternoon of horror.

The majority of the prisoners of pavilion 9 were first-time offenders awaiting trial, a few were serving their prison sentence, and others had already served and were still there on account of the slow and unjust judiciary machinery of Brazil.

Various national entities mobilized, followed by America's Watch, which immediately sent a representative to the scene of the massacre, and Amnesty International, which demanded settling the facts so that those responsible could be punished. Unfortunately, Brazilian authorities concluded, after months of investigation and questioning, that proof was lacking in order to incriminate top police officials. The police officers were indicted for having acted on "superior's orders." All were protected by the institutionalized immunity from prosecution of the oppressors, because, as of today, they have not ended their inquiries into the matter.

The Legal Medical Institute in São Paulo, in its verdicts, has pointed out that the cause of death in the 111 prisoners was perforation of their bodies by knives, bayonets, bullets, and dog bites.

ROTA was entitled to its infamy, having been responsible for the third story of pavilion 9, where eighty of the total 111 people murdered cruelly were found.

The prisoners had with them, at the time of the massacre, many steel weapons: iron bars and daggers that they made themselves inside the prison by sharpening metal blades to protect themselves from other prisoners and prison agents. Officially, they had thirteen guns, one of them inexplicably belonging to the National Army, but all were rusty and showing signs of disuse, which was reported by the experts of the Criminal Institute of São Paulo.

The presence of these weapons was highly suspect. One highly compromising fact for the invaders of Carandiru was that all of the prison officials' weapons were locked up on the night of the "rebellion," when the pavilion was without electricity and covered with wreckage and water, due to running faucets and burst water pipes, which contributed to eleven bodies being found the next day. So one can have an idea of the extent of the police officers' fraud when one knows that only five fire arms had been recovered from the detainees' hands over the last twelve years. Obviously, police "efficiency" planted the weapons after the slaughter, proving themselves the good repressors that they are.

It is important to point out that no police officer was hurt by the detainees nor anyone else killed during this episode. Since electricity to the prison had been cut at the end of that rainy afternoon, darkness made some police officers crash into rough walls and obstacles on the way and, for that reason, some police officers and their chief had skin abrasions.

It is important to emphasize that the nature and degree of wounds on the bodies of the police officers and on the bodies of the detainees were qualitatively and quantitatively different. Some wounds were from the oppressors, who were capable of everything, others were from the oppressed, who were capable of little.

Lines of relatives formed in front of the detention house of Carandiru, in the center of the most important city in the country, when the massacre was revealed. They are a signal of the impotency and indignation of those who did not know the destiny—alive or dead?—of their husbands, fathers, sons, or brothers, and who waited during long days and nights. They learned about the resignations of the director of the prison and the secretary of public safety with tears of despair and pain, hopelessness and revolt, and looked upon the naked bodies of their relatives, exposed side by side in open coffins, who were displayed to the world without dignity.

Notes to the Sixth Letter

1. The shed-like company stores, practically nonexistent today, were the grocery stores of yesterday. Built next to the owner's house, this store was where the peasant who plowed the owner's land got the necessary supplies for survival.

In the store, the peasant, or "live-in farm helper," and his or her family would buy "on credit"—that is, without paying cash at the moment—and carry the goods to their humble, often uncomfortable house. They bought only basic foods—such as beans, manioc flour, sugar (which the peasant produced at the mill), salted and dried meat, coffee, vegetable oil, bread, and dried coconut. These they added to what the family could produce on its own: small pumpkins, sweet potatoes, manioc, and pigs and chickens. The store also provided them with kerosene for their oil lamps, candles, matches, soap, ropes, brooms, sandals, clothes, sheets, and canvas "beds." They needed very little more than that in order "to lead a life," that is, to have the minimum to survive and work from dusk to dawn, which cracked the skin and aged the body.

The store had a political function as great as that of supplying goods which was never explained and which many of its users never understood during the centuries of its existence. That is, at the end of the month, peasant consumption at the store was often larger than the family's monthly salary. While the peasant tried to save in order to pay these bills, which were accumulating month after month, year after year, the peasant continued to struggle on the plantation, cleaning and cutting cane, grinding and purifying sugar at the mill, being submissive and thankful to the owner, who "generously" advanced food and "services." This kept the peasant just where the owner wanted. Such were the characteristics of slavery, which remained in many perverted ways after "liberation."

Good transportation (which meant that the peasant could move from place to place with a certain easiness), the increasing consciousness of the rural worker (see notes of the twelfth letter), and the nomadic work, from mill to mill, plantation to plantation, ended the company store. Named after the way that people eat today—taking the food to the fields and eating it cold with the saucepan as the plate—"cold-floating" is condemned by the same owners who prevented the peasants from leaving before and who dismissed them after labor legislation helped the rural worker in 1963. All this determined the bankruptcy of the company store owned by the mill or plantation owners.

2. Aluízio Pessoa de Araújo is discussed in note 4 of Freire's book, *Pedagogy of Hope*.

3. Osvaldo Cruz High School is discussed in note 2 of Freire's book, *Pedagogy of Hope*.

4. The question of water pollution in Brazil is very serious, either of ocean or river water. All kinds of garbage is thrown, including sewage and industrial waste, into these waters. The factories and sugar mills that Freire speaks of, denouncing their madness, are just two contributors to the waste dumped in the waters, long-ago polluted, of a countless number of our rivers.

The production of alcohol from sugarcane—a common practice in Northeast and Southeast Brazil to create, among other things, fuel for automobiles so that we can industrialize on a large scale—has been one of the biggest polluters of many of the rivers of our country.

After grinding sugarcane, a juice is obtained. By cooking and purifying it, it turns into a syrup. Afterward, microorganisms are added to ferment the syrup and the result is alcohol after the surplus is cleared away, such as water.

This process, simplified here, well illustrates the carelessness of contractors and rulers in the name of progress, who let the beautiful old rivers of limpid water transform themselves into motionless rivers that sadly exhibit algae and dead fish. This stillness is caused by *calda*, a rich organic material that needs oxygen and so "steals" it from the river water. It kills the true inhabitants of the river, microscopic and macroscopic animals and vegetables, through lack of oxygen, which was natural, original, and totally theirs.

5. We know that in many parts of the world, knowledge is enriched by learning ghost stories, hearing about the shadows of dead people who haunt houses and palaces, preferably on dark nights or by the light of the full moon.

But I believe that in Northeast Brazil there is a special love, driven by fear itself, almost paralyzing terror, for talking about and raising to life the dead, who are homeless and restless, as if discovering stories could make history.

During my childhood, I became acquainted with one thousand and one of these stories by listening to Maria, my "black mother," and her father from Rosinha who was called Candido—faithful and dear servants for decades on end—and from Corina, a dear friend, who lived next door to my family. I also lived the stories, experiencing them when I lived in an enormous house that my father was able to buy because it had been abandoned by the landlords due to the haunted "souls in pain" who made the rounds and hide themselves in the countless rooms.

My father bought it at a public auction for a low price, which was due not so much to the work and expenses that its size demanded, but because in those years of the 1940s in Recife there rambled through the house the soul of a German housekeeper who had been killed by soldiers during the Revolution of 1930 (see note to the fifth letter). Besides this despicable act, they had targeted a large mirror that, consequently, the faithful say, attracts haunted souls. I, as a young girl, would look at myself in the mirror, afraid of seeing her face instead of mine and coming upon the souls of other dead people in that house, children whose illness had taken them to the "other world."

Recently, in a visit to the governor of Pernambuco—in which we discussed French architecture and the site chosen by Mauricio de Nassau for the palace of the government—Paulo, Secretary of Education Paulo Rosas, the governor, and I strayed to discussing ghost stories, which are so loved by the people of Pernambuco.

The governor narrated, then, with humor and a respectful laugh, the different stories that the employees of and visitors to the palace have told, both believers and nonbelievers, for decades, about the haunted souls of the governor's palace.

One of them is about Agamenon Magalhaes, who was a mediator with the state for many years and who frequently appeared after ten o'clock at night wandering through the bedrooms and living rooms where he had lived. Sometimes he was seen in full, sometimes without his head, sometimes running after people or flying through the wide, long hallways, other times overlaying his Chinese features on the faces of the oil paintings of other governors, all in line in the portrait gallery, as if he were suggesting the end of the power of his successors. Agamenon, a real statesman from Pernambuco, almost always appeared while moaning or screaming and always asked for masses and prayers. He always demonstrated his concern for people, to whom he dedicated so much of his attention while governor.

I believe that these frightening images of Agamenon were propagated by his political enemies, who wished to destroy his public image, and by the creative ability of our people.

People have believed that Agamenon's "tormented soul" has returned to the world to pay for his sins as an authoritarian ruler by suffering the fear he causes in the living and to prevent himself from being forgotten as a ruler concerned with the social and economic problems of the popular classes.

These mythical stories verbalize the popular unconscious and embody both sides, almost antagonistic, which we carry inside ourselves: good and evil. Ghost stories, which still so terrify children and adults, make us understand, as they did with Freire, the unity of good and evil, the real and the imaginary, a unity that life itself demands in the historical process.

Notes to the Seventh Letter

1. The quote is from Van-Hoeven Veloso Ferreina, *Jaboatão de Meus Avós*, (Recife: Biblioteca Pernambucana de História Municipal, 1982), p. 184.

2. The quote is from Manuel Bandeira, *Poesias* (Rio de Janeiro: Livraria José Olímpio Editora, 1955), p. 192.

Notes to the Eighth Letter

1. The "chamber pot of heaven," as Freire says, is a popular term that indicates the high rainfall in certain areas and demonstrates the irritation of urban residents with the rains, which are seen as an inconvenience. It shows a lack of respect that men and women of the countryside, in need of rain, would never display.

   The expression "chamber pot of the sky" is the same as the "chamber pot of the world," already explained in note 23 of Freire's book, *Pedagogy of Hope*.

Notes to the Tenth Letter

1. From that time onward and as a result of the social circle of curious intellectuals who met around the packing cases of imported books that brought ideas from "other worlds," Freire began to put together his own library.

   His book, which lists the literary works he acquired, begins in 1942 and proceeds—patiently listing author, title, cost or "gift," and number of volumes—year after year, until 1955. There I find catalogued literary works by national and international authors published in the south of Brazil or by publishing houses in Spain, Argentina, Mexico, France, England, the United States, and even Portugal. The books were always published in Rio de Janeiro or São Paulo and "imported" by the bookstores of Recife.

   From this handwritten record of 572 books, we notice that he began reading books in Spanish in 1943; in French in 1944; and in English in 1947; that is, if we assume that after the books' purchase, he read them.

   I would mention some of the foreign authors that constantly appeared in his book of acquisitions: Aguayo, Claparede, Dewey, Lasky, Ingenieros, Maritain, Balmes, Taine, Sforza, Snedden, Duquit, Kant, Ortega y Gasset, Trancovich, Mourrais, Max Beer, Durkheim, Chersteton, Aldous Huxley, Burchardt, Raymond Aron, Croce, Vaissiere, Gerald Walsh, Macnab, Labriola, Plato, Schopenhauer, Haechel, Berdiaeff, Campanella, Andre Cresson, Gustavo Le Boun, Horne, Aristotele, Messer, Elizando, Charlotte Burkler, Bastide, Adler, Toynbee, Weigert, Enrique Pita, Brunner, Vico, Spengler, Shakespeare, Nordeaux, Reinach, Rousseau, Bally, Backhauser, Vosseler, Maeterlinck, Saussure, Douzat, Bernanos, Montavani, Leite de Vasconcelos, Tomás de Aquino, Sarmiento, Renan, Gurvitch, Nietzsche, Lucien Lefevre, Dante, Lascki, Jean de Lery, Piaget, Fritz Tiahn, Fouillé, Scheller, Saint Augustine, Mallart, Bergsan, Werner Jaeger, Ballesters,

Guillermo Dilthey, Richard Wickert, Lorenzo Lujuriaga, Paul Monroe, Espasandier, H. Marrou, Riboulet, Rene Hubert, Richard Lewis, Wilcken, Virgil Gheorghin, Martin Grabunann, De Hovre, Lewis Mumford, Peter Petersan, Bühler, Gregovius, Winn, Dottrans, José Forgione, Luella Cole, Adolf Meyer, Charles Norris Cochrane, Butts, P. Barth, Hobbes, Klineberg, Juan Gomes, Arnold Rose, L. C. Dunn, Michael Leiris, Homer, Louis Halphen, Charles Bemout, Roger Doucet, Erwin Rohde, Kilpatrick, Zaniewski, Pierson, Erich Kahler, Lowie, Spencer, Roger Ginot, W. A. Lay, Ernesto Neumann, Frank Freeman, Hermann Nahl, Spranger, Margaret Mead, Huizinga, Castiglioni, Kaufmann, Radice, Vanquelin, Eça de Queiróz, Gentile, Olsen, Fernandes Ruiz, Ponce, Bode, Perkins, Skinner, Kronemberg, Charmat, Zulliger, Richepin, Ebagné, Nicholas Hans, Maugier, O'Shea, Gonzague de Reynold, Roger Cousinet, Nelly Wolffneur, James Conant, Charlotte Wolff, Nicholas Hans, Ernest Schneider, Kieffer, Findlay, Julius Koch, Karl Roth, Herbert Read, Andre Beley, Geronimo de Moragas, Stekel, Schumpeter, Krieck, Baudonnin, Elmer Von Karman, Comenius, Bodin, De Havre, Dostoyevsky, Frederick Eby, Ernest Green, J. B. Bury, M. A. Block, Slavson, Emile Callot, Labrousse, Wilhem Dilthey, James Campbell, Betrand Russell, Sidney Hook, Berenice Baxter, Rose Marie Mosse-Bastides, Pierce, John Wynne, Volpicelli, John Scott, Pitirim Sorokin, and Harry Brandy.

Among the national authors constantly on Freire's list, I would mention: Tristão de Atayde, Gilberto Freyre, Joaquim Ribeiro, Artur Ramos, M. Querino, Leonel Franca, Pedro Calmon, Otávio de Freitas Júnior, Anísio Teixeira, Hermes Lima, Otto Maria Carpeaux, Oswald de Andrade, José Veríssimo, Oliveira Viana, António Candido, Florestan Fernandes, Alfrânio Peixoto, Adonias Filho, Murilo Mendes, Plínio Salgado, Valdemar Valente, Carneiro Ribeiro, Euclides da Cunha, Pinto Ferreira, Silvio Romero, Amaro Quintas, Joaquim Nabuco, Sérgio Buarque de Holanda, Silvio Rabelo, Viriato Correa, Fernando de Azevedo, Pascoal Leme, Carneiro Leão, Graciliano Ramos, Olívio Montenegro, Machado de Assis, Carlos Drummond de Andrade, Manuel Bandeira, Vinicius de Moraes, Mauro Mota, and Ruy Barbosa.

Freire read more foreign authors on his topics of interest—anthropology, linguistics, philosophy, literature, grammar, history, and education—than Brazilian authors. This does not indicate a deliberate choice by Freire of foreign books, whatever their validity, but rather, the small national production of books in Brazil during the 1940s and 1950s.

It is important to understand and emphasize this.

Previously to the formation of his genuinely Brazilian thinking about the national reality, Freire was occupied and preoccupied with more than a hundred European, North American, and Latin American authors. He chose masters of thinking, clear speaking, and good writing who were concerned with the beauty of language and the correctness of speech and the "reading of the world." Few then existed who were theoretical masters of education in general and Brazilian education in particular.

He lived, therefore, the contradictions between the ideas of so many bright, foreign thinkers ("experiencing" their educational experiences) and those of national thinkers as well as of his childhood experiences, creating his unique way of thinking of Brazil and Brazilians. From all those influences, he gave back to the world his "readings" and critically elaborated experiences.

Unfortunately, Freire did not proceed with his book record, which would have enabled us to accompany his readings, comprehension, and expression in regard to them; his reinvention of read texts; and his intellectual production.

Freire's book record until 1955, meanwhile, is not sufficient to entirely explain his renovation of pedagogical Brazilian thinking—whether in the Second Congress on Adult Education in 1958 or in the elaboration of his dissertation in 1959 (see note 46 in *Pedagogy of Hope* and note to the fourteenth letter in this book)—much less his writing from *Pedagogy of the Oppressed* on.

His book record failed to mention Karl Marx, Merleau-Ponty, Alvaro Vieira Pinto, Antonio Gramsci, Albert Memmi, Franz Fanon, Barbu, among others who influenced him so much from the 1960s on.

Notes to the Eleventh Letter

1. School grade retention (that is, holding students back a grade) is a serious problem in Brazil, indicating one more time that Brazilian society is elitist, authoritarian, and discriminatory, banning the most socially deprived from its privileged spaces; in this case, the schools.

   The educational census of 1988—compiled by the Ministry of Education, the secretary of general administration, the Department of Regional Planning, and the Department of Planning Information—points out in the *Statistical Summary— Regular Elementary Education* that the total number of students registered in primary schools from ages seven to fourteen in 1988 who repeated a grade was 4,933,863 students (p. 73). The total number of students in elementary school was 26,754,501 (p. 37).

   The census does not indicate how many times the student had been held back. Yet, we know this distortion to be common in schools, especially in the first year of elementary education. Unlike in the United States, where the student receives automatic promotion, he or she begins to repeat grades during the second year when the attempt at recuperating is almost always frustrating. Such a suffocating experience right at the beginning of school learning is terribly unjust and cruel because children stay away from school to never again return, almost always without having learned to read and write.

   Another point of failure happens in the fifth year of elementary education, which shows clearly that elitism persists after the first barriers to school learning are removed. We comprehend this better if we compare the two Brazilian educational structures, the one previous to 1971 and the one after, when primary and secondary curricula were united into one curriculum for eight grades as proclaimed by law. The high rate of students who are held back in the fifth year demonstrates that elitism was separating those who could make it from those who could not make it into the second phase of elementary education. The fifth year is equivalent to the first year of secondary education and represents the selective role in regard to school retention.

School retention, which falls upon the popular classes once or successive times, leads inexorably to school drop-out or to what experts call, and Freire repudiates, "school evasion."

In the same document, we learn that 3,212,734 students were "distant" from or "abandoned" by elementary education in 1987 (p. 79).

Another fact speaks of the popular classes' disregard for public schools. Of the "distant and abandoned" students, 61.8 percent attended elementary schools maintained by the state administration; 32.2 percent attended schools maintained by the city administration; and 0.4 percent attended schools maintained by the federal administration (very few schools in the country are federal, most are trade and general education schools). Only 5.5 percent of "distant and abandoned" students were from well-to-do families, who could attend private schools with better learning environments and teaching than all the elementary public schools put together (p. 82).

Unfortunately, this is the most recent official data. We know that the situation has not improved in the last five years.

2. In regard to the paddle and the use of the paddle, the reader can consult note 12 of Freire's book, *Pedagogy of Hope.*

Notes to the Twelfth Letter
1. The Movement for Popular Culture (MCP) was the first of a series of political educational movements that emerged in the 1960s in Brazil. MCP tried to redeem popular culture by having intellectuals lead the people to revolutionary practice for transforming the country.

MCP was officially created in Recife on May 13, 1960. Its statutes were published in the government bulletin of Pernambuco dated August 23 and September 12, 1961. MCP was registered on September 19 of the same year in the notary's office of Bel. Emilio T. R. dos Santos of Recife.

According to its statutes, the purpose of MCP was educational and cultural. Its goals were:

> 1. to promote and stimulate, with the help of the private and public powers, the education of children and adults; 2. to pay attention to the fundamental objective of education, which is to develop all of the aspects of the human being through integral education on a communitarian basis, including, according to the constitution, optional religious education; 3. to promote the peoples' cultural level by preparing them for life and work; 4. to collaborate for the betterment of the material level of the peoples through specialized education; 5. to form departments designed to interpret, systematize, and transmit the multiple aspects of popular culture (*Diary of the MCP*, vol. 49 [Recife: Foundation of the Culture of Recife, 1986], pp. 56–57).

2. The maracatu is a group dance to a percussion band; the bumba-meu-boi is a popular, fast-moving dance; and the fandango is a lively Spanish dance.

3. Fernando Collor de Mello, who wants to return to the Brazilian political scene, frightened and intimidated the nation with his specious legislation, which allowed disgraceful aberrations and was obviously intended by the dominant class to preserve itself and to further its advantages and privileges (see notes of the first and fifth letter).

   The former president intended to remain in the city of São Paulo, not his state of Alagoas, so that he could run for federal deputy in the elections on October 3, 1994, as a representative of the people of São Paulo, who magnanimously gave him the votes to be elected president in 1989. The process of punishment, which almost all Brazilians have been waiting for since his impeachment, has still not been completed. Meanwhile, as I write this note in February of 1994, we are already sure that only in the next millennium will he be able to run for public office. By decision of the executive, which ratified Congress' measure at the time of his impeachment, he has lost his political rights for eight years.

   P. C. Cavalcanti Farias is also no longer a fugitive. After being indicted by the justice of Brazil, he ran away from Lagoas to Pernambuco and from there to Paraguay, Argentina, and Europe.

   Located by the Brazilian press in London, he escaped to Thailand even after the diligence of the Brazilian government joined British justice in seeking his extradition.

   Arrested in Bangkok on November 29, 1993 by twenty police officers from Thailand, P. C. returned to Brazil after 156 days of evasion and is being detained by the military police in Brasília, where he awaits trial and sentencing by the Federal Supreme Court.

   P. C. has thirty-nine indictments for illegal acts, including fraud, counterfeiting, gang formation, ideological disloyalty, use of false documents, embezzlement, corruption, prestige exploitation, and corruption of witnesses.

   Therefore, Fernando Collor de Mello and P. C. Cavalcanti Farias are symbols of corruption, cynicism, and lack of civic ethics, all of which the majority of the Brazilian population repudiates. More than that, they want to see the beginning of the end of immunity from prosecution for the elite, which finally seems to be emerging in Brazilian society.

4. To journey to this place was an act of courage. Paulo, Father Sérgio, and I left on a Saturday morning in 1991 in an extremely old car to travel from Pelotas to Bage. The night before we had traveled from Porto Alegre to Pelotas. Where the asphalt ended, the educators were waiting for us in a run-down house. They wanted to join us so we could caravan to the place called "Conquest of the Frontier" in Rio Grande do Sul. Conquest, it's true, but of the landless. Frontier, it's true, but of Brazil with Uruguay.

   It was a cold, damp, and depressing winter day. A better car and a real pilot, indeed a simple driver, would have been hard pressed to accomplish the mission, during which it was necessary to traverse, at great danger, the almost sixty kilometers of muddy road that separated "civilization" from the place. Very few other cars were on the road—drivers of chartered buses refused to go on this adventure—and their colors were obscured by the dark and slippery mud of that region.

We knew, then, that the efforts of the residents combined with the local public power had been ineffective in building a road with gravel and rocks. Each prolonged period of rain brought to those who planted a harvest of lost food.

The "concession" of donating lands to those without land did not include the benefit of a plantation self-administered by those families, many of whom were illiterate and worked the land peacefully. From the oppressor's point of view, it was better if the experience was not successful. In spite of the mud, lack of asphalt roads, and illiteracy, the tenacity of that people was "being successful" in aiming to overcome all negative factors.

5. We use the term "pressed ground" to describe floors without wood, tiles, cement, or brick. Pressed ground floors are very common in the houses of the poor in Northeast Brazil, either in mocambos or other lodgings (see notes of the first and second letter), consisting of ground prepared so as not to raise dust when one walks on it through basic techniques of compacting the ground.

6. Francisco Julião left Brazil and lived in Cuernavaca "Northeast Brazilian style," as Freire says, after the military coup d'état of 1964, when he was persecuted for his political fight for the Northeast Brazilian farmers.

The exploitation of workers in that region has been, since colonial times, one of the most terrible and cruel. Slavery until the nineteenth century, lack of work, low salaries, financial exploitation, (see note of the sixth letter), assassination of leaders, and terrorizing of those who simply requested salaries not received for days or months, has been the daily lot of people in Northeast Brazil.

The first expressions of revolt against the miserable life that they still lead happened in 1955 when the workers of the Galileia Mill in Pernambuco founded the Agricultural and Cattle Breeder Society of the Workers of Pernambuco. Their rural league aimed at fighting for the possession of land and for agrarian reform.

The singer-guitarists who played at local fairs and markets of Northeast Brazil interior managed to spread the league among the farmers. Historically, one of the functions of those "literate men" has been to perpetuate old knowledge and transmit new ideas to those who do not know how to read.

Through their own verses, often spontaneously improvised, or those of other poets (often appearing in the "cheap literature," consisting of almost handwritten leaflets sold in places attended by the popular classes, which address politics and sexual scandals, when they are exposed, and wood carvings are seen, hung from ropes tied from one tree or post to another), the singers spread the ideas of the league, by translating old and profound dreams.

As a result, the illiterate population organized itself around an association in order to push for better days for them and their families.

Julião—lawyer, state deputy, federal deputy, and socialist—stimulated the formation of other leagues. They proliferated under his leadership. It is estimated that in 1963, 218 leagues had sprung up throughout the country, from only 64 in Pernambuco.

By 1961, the rural movement had acquired a national character. That same year, the leagues organized the First Congress of Farmers and Agricultural Workers, whose list of demands included agrarian reform, the right to freely organize and the extension of the rights of urban workers to the rural workers.

Besides Julião, the others who directed the organization of leagues were priests of the Catholic Church, from the north and Northeast Brazil, and communists of various stripes, for example, the Union of the Farmers and Agricultural Workers of Brazil (ULTAB) which acted in the center and south of the country.

The political consciousness and organization of the movements led the latifundia owners, especially the powerful factory owners, to express horror at losing a bit of their privileges.

The situation became more and more unbearable for the privileged groups when the voice of the countryside was heard and translated into a determination to legalize their working rights by the federal government in 1963. The Governor of Pernambuco, Miguel Arraes, was elected in 1962 by a coalition that included socialists and communists, who openly supported the farmers' battles.

The elite from Northeast Brazil, connected to the sugar industry and forming a powerful aristocracy, united itself against all those who conspired against their established power, mainly the populist government of João Goulart and the governors united in meeting the needs of the popular classes.

Because the rural leagues were divided, they were destroyed easily by the military regime. Their major leader—Francisco Julião—took refuge in Mexico.

By 1979, country people were still active. The movement of the Landless was strong even though many of their leaders, unjustly and cruelly, were silenced for ever.

7. According to the testimony of Paulo Rosas himself, then coordinator of investigations for the MCP, only a short article came to be published, entitled "Two Memories of the Carnival in Pernambuco." Other investigations were conducted and material collected toward an unfinished article, "A Century of Carnival, 1861–1961." Its objective "was to study not only the carnival itself, but also to use the carnival to analyze changes in behavior and social values over the period." The *Book of Luck* had the same objective, to study the carnival, as did still "The Level of Critical Thinking Among the People."

In brief, but important testimony, the psychologist and respected Brazilian educator, Paulo Rosas, always generous in his assistance, told me that "A documentary about periodical publications for children and young adults (which I put together for MCP) was sent formally by MCP and the University of Recife to the president of the republic [Jânio Quadros] as an accusation and request for action."

In regard to the first work, "Two Memories," a small group of the MCP investigators, led by Maria Isabel Araújo (Lins), it is possible to say a little something.

After a short introduction, the first part was about the formation of the carnival of Pernambuco (1860 to 1890). It analyzes the Carnival of the Street, including horses, music, masks, maracatu, fandango, bumba-meu-boi, and *pastoril* (outdoor folk plays); and the Carnival of the Club, including music, dances, and decoration.

The second part was about the days of freedom (1910 to 1920). It analyzes the Carnival of the Street, including the parade, association marches, decorations, music, and motorcades; as well as the Carnival of the Club.

8. According to *SUDENE: Ten Years*, a document published by the Ministry of the Interior in 1969, the Superintendence of the Development of the Northeast (SUDENE) was created by Law No. 3,692 on December 15, 1959, with the objective of developing Northeast Brazil. The creation of SUDENE, a product of a new mentality, implied the introduction of new administrative methods and modifications to the operation of the government of the region and views of the law. The following were its goals:

1. to study and propose directives for the development of Northeast Brazil;
2. to supervise, coordinate, and control the development and implementation of projects at the expense of the federal organizations in the region specifically related to its development;
3. to implement, either directly or through subcontract, the projects related to the development of Northeast Brazil, attributed to them by law;
4. to coordinate the programs of technical assistance, and their national or international input, to Northeast Brazil.

As a work instrument to implement SUDENE, directives, a director's plan, was to be established by law that would delineate regional sectors, enterprises, and works to be developed. The SUDENE would still, with the cooperation of the organizations active in Northeast Brazil, create an emergency plan to battle results of droughts and assist the populations affected.

In a strategic move to the establish development, the area of Northeast Brazil was redefined to include the states of Maranhão, Piauí, Ceara, Rio Grande do Norte, Paraiba, Pernambuco, Alagoas, Sergipe, Bahia, the Territory of Fernando de Noronha, and part of Minas Gerais. They make up what is called the "Drought Polygon."

The law, foreseeing the resistance SUDENE would encounter as an agency with renewed purpose and an eminently technical character, tried to structure SUDENE in a way to protect its authority as a planning organization through political regional representation by establishing SUDENE as a member of the deliberative council, that is, the governments of the nine states in the redefined area of Northeast Brazil. Cohesion of federal performance, consequently, would be assured by the participation in the deliberative council, of the director of the National Department of Works Against Drought (DNOCS), the superintendent of the Commission of the Valley of the San Francisco (CVSF), a representative of the armed forces, representatives from the financial agencies of the government (including the Bank of Northeast, Bank of Brazil, and the National Bank of the Economic Development), and a representative of each civil ministry (p. 29).

SUDENE—created during the government of progressive President Juscelino Kubischek through the competent efforts of the economist Celso Furtado, his first superintendent—started from the real needs of the region and was designed with the intent of diminishing the internal contradictions generated by the different stages of economic development and conditions of the populations of the northeast, center, south, and southeast of the country.

> Northeast Brazil stood out, ten years ago, for its underdevelopment, an area of the Brazilian territory untouched by the delinked development of central and south Brazil. The great disparity in the levels of economic growth attained by the two regions of the country, along with a serious problem in the continuity of Brazilian development, resulted in the rise of threats to national unity, threats that originated in divergent positions regarding the solutions to be adopted to correct disparity.
>
> The creation of the Superintendence of the Development of the Northeast (SUDENE) in 1959 constituted an answer to the Brazilian nation about the challenges of development in Northeast Brazil. SUDENE, through the explicit objectives of a plan of regional development, was to direct and guide development efforts with a view toward solving the problems of a region in which one third of Brazilians live (*SUDENE: Ten Years*, p. 11).

9. The Superior Institute of Brazilian Studies (ISEB) was, as the name explains, a center for the study of our political, economic, social, and cultural problems, a concern centralized in progressive nationalism.

It was born of a group of intellectuals debating Brazil's problems, not as a simple academic exercise, but with the intent of formulating a project for national development. They were concerned about the underdevelopment of the country and the increasing misery of its people. The Second World War had exacerbated the Brazilian contradictions. Its climate of freedom and hope for better conditions, created toward the end of Vargas's dictatorship (1930–1945), favored intellectual debates and dreams of equality and peace.

From the intellectuals, who met in the National Park of Itatiaia in 1952, the ISEB was officially formed on July 14, 1955, by decree of President Cafe Filho. He had replaced Vargas after his suicide in 1954, completing the presidential term for which they had been elected by popular vote in 1950.

The members of the ISEB created a philosophy or ideology of development that they hoped would influence the actions of governments, intellectuals, students, unions, and the military, and would, therefore, transform Brazil into a developed and just country without concentrated wealth and with agrarian reform, among other necessary measures.

The main themes of discussion (they maintained training courses) were whether to industrialize or not, whether to maintain an "essentially agricultural country" or not, whether the state should participate in development projects or just draw up the plan, whether the state should intervene in the private sector or free market, whether to accept foreign capital or not, whether to associate with national capital and nationalism (or *entreguismo*, to yield to international imperialism), and whether national economic models were capable of development. Autonomy or dependency, qualitative or quantitative changes of the production process, education of the masses, and the value of national culture and the levels of consciousness or alienation of the Brazilian people were also topics.

Freire's dissertation (see note of the fifteenth letter) shows the undeniable influence of Alvaro Vieira Pinto, one of the members of the ISEB, in forwarding the categories of "genuine consciousness" and "critical consciousness."

Juscelino Kubischek and João Goulart, presidents of the republic during the golden period of the ISEB, had a close relationship with the institute, applying the theories developed there to real government action and availing themselves of existing ideologies to make political stands of great importance.

The ISEB was one more Brazilian institution that closed its doors after the military coup d'état in 1964.

10. One of the former teachers present at this meeting remembered the story of a man who, having obtained the teacher's address in the city of Natal and asking the other students for financial help, had at great risk traveled from Angicos to the capital of the state.

Having located her and "beaten" her door—a term used in Northeast Brazil to describe how people clap their hands at the door of a house—he wanted to have a conversation with her. He had a simple question: what was the reason for her "mysterious disappearance," and that of all the other teachers of Angicos? Why had they stopped the tasty treat of reading that they had been teaching?

She was terrified and spoke to him at the gate of her house, without even inviting him onto the shade of the porch, as is common in Northeast Brazil to do. She nervously said, "Return, return to your house! Return to Angicos! I don't know why we stopped teaching you! I don't know! I don't know! I don't know!"

The man left and she thought, "I hope that one day he will understand what happened, the reason why I could not invite him to come in to my house, the reason why I could not inform him about why we had interrupted our work." She looked in all directions to make sure no witnesses were around, then ran into the house, and, very frightened, locked the door in order to recover.

After that, she gathered her "subversive material" and quickly tried to bury it in the backyard of her house. She buried not only the material of for teaching reading but also the possibility of continuing the process, already advanced, of teaching people by making them aware and engaging them in politics, of teaching not only the man who had traveled from Angicos to Natal but also his fellows who had financed the trip hoping for the process of reading and writing to resume.

He returned without understanding that in his search to learn how to read and write it was his hope hidden and dream to become more. Meanwhile, the seed for awareness had been sown. History has shown that the process is irreversible.

The teacher clearly knew, during those days of terror in 1964, the reason why she could not return to Angicos. She had understood and felt in her bones what was being done in Brazil against the oppressed population.

That was the climate imposed not only on her, but on millions of Brazilians by the military regime, which was born in April 1964. It is good not to forget this.

In August 1993, when the teacher told me this story, all of us were convinced that reading had not stopped, rather, on the contrary, the reading of the oppressed world of Brazil had sharpened. From the world of prohibition against those who had been prohibited from learning to read themselves, we arrived at reading the word and the world.

Notes to the Fourteenth Letter

1. The student youth started to organize itself in Brazil from 1937 on, but it only gained its more authentic political form after the Second World War and fighting the dictatorship of Vargas.

From that climate of searching for freedom emerged the National Union of Students (UNE), which united the university students; the Metropolitan Union of Students (UME); the Brazilian Secondary Student Union (UBES); and the Student State Union (UEE) under the leadership of UNE.

The most important of these associations, UNE, was considered illegal in April 1964, although it continued to meet and act politically in secret

One of its clandestine meetings took place on October 1968, in Ibiuna in the interior of São Paulo. Showering denouncements on residents, eight hundred students were arrested and held for investigation. Many of them remained in prison, some for many years.

The UNE reemerged with the political openness of 1979, but only in 1992 did it begin to act in a more significant way, politically speaking. In 1992, the UNE organized university and high school students in the thousands, leading them onto the streets in rallies in the main cities of Brazil with faces painted green and yellow to show their disapproval of the lack of political ethics, government, and President Collor (see notes of the first, fifth, and twelfth letter).

Marching alongside the members of the most progressive institutions in Brazil–the Order of Lawyers of Brazil (OAB) and the Brazilian Press Association (ABI)–the political parties of the Left, some parties of the center, labor union leaders, church leaders, the working class, and people in general, those young people with painted faces yelled together, "Out, Collor!", "Down with corruption!", and "Ethics in politics!"

With laughter and tears; songs and hymns; historical leaders of OAB, ABI, and of the labor unions; speeches of repudiation and flag waving in the plazas and on the streets, the students with painted faces showed the nation that years of repression, distorted and "forgotten" history in the schools, and fear (which kept their parents and uncles silent), yielded contradictorily, an explosion in the vitality of youth.

By repudiating corruption and embracing the hope of building a better, more serious, and more just Brazil, the students demonstrated that they had gained the political force students possessed in the 1950s and 1960s.

The adolescents painted their faces as our Indians painted their bodies: to announce war. Indeed, they declared war on dishonesty, irresponsibility, and corruption.

Notes to the Fifteenth Letter

1. The central ideas of Paulo Freire's dissertation gave birth to his book *Education as the Practice of Freedom*, his first book, published when he lived in exile in Chile.

   The dissertation in question, "Education in Present-Day Brazil," was written so he could apply for a full professor's position at the College of Liberal Arts at the University of Recife.

   Having gained the position, which demanded the approval of a dissertation, he received his Ph.D. in History and Philosophy of Education and immediately after, according to the legislation in force at the time, the title of a full professor.

Notes to the Seventeenth Letter

1. At the beginning of the 1930s, Getúlio Vargas (see note of the fifth letter) was concerned about malnutrition in Brazil and wanted to introduce the use of the soybean, since that grain has more protein than the bean that is traditionally the main food in Brazil.

   Taste is one of the cultural manifestations of a people. Partly due to a lack of understanding, however, Brazilians rejected the less pleasant taste of the soybean.

   The feijoada is a typical bean stew much loved by the Brazilian people. It consists of pork—salted, smoked, and sausage style—cooked for hours on end together with black beans and jerked beef, and seasonings of garlic, onion, fresh herbs, and dry bay leaves. It is a dish of unbeatable taste. Strong, succulent, and generous as the Brazilian people, the dish is served with oranges, manioc flour, sautéed kale, a good cold beer, and a glass of sugarcane brandy.

   Traditionally enjoyed on Wednesdays or Saturdays around a table with many people discussing the taste of the feijoada and other national topics such as soccer and samba, this dish could not be prepared with soybeans.

   Today, Brazil is the largest producer of soybeans in the world. Soybeans are one of Brazil's major sources of income, producing vegetable oil, margarine, and animal feed, either for internal consumption or for export.

   Still, it is inconceivable to eat and enjoy a soybean feijoada.

2. If the "school failure" of the popular classes in Brazil has been startling (see note of the eleventh letter) within what I call the ideology of the prohibition of the body (see note 39 of Freire's book, *Pedagogy of Hope*) which has been growing and which our authoritarian, discriminatory, and elitist society perpetuates—when the same phenomena among the black population, has been even more striking.

   In Brazil, almost the entire black population belongs to the popular classes.

[236]

This is one of the inheritances that discriminatory elitism has left us. Consequently, the prohibitions of race and class cause the data about black "school failure" to be glaring.

According to data in the *Statistical Yearbook of Brazil* of 1992, the average number of years that people age ten or more have had in 1990 was 5.7 years for "whites," 3.4 years for "blacks," and 3.7 years for "mixed" race (p. 370).

Today, blacks, proud of their heritage, are no longer accepting those color markers. In 1990, approximately three to six years of school, therefore, one to two years less than "whites." This discrimination, and others, is translated into the cold statistical data of "school failure."

I also call attention to the fact that, 5.7, 3.7, or 3.4 years of schooling does not necessarily imply the same periods of schooling because the phenomena of grade retention (holding students back) is very high in Brazil (see note of the eleventh letter).

Other data that show the tendency to exclude blacks from the learning circle, to isolate them culturally, are those concerning illiteracy. In the majority of cases, illiteracy precedes "school failure" because most blacks never even started going to school. They were excluded from it before they had known of it.

The 1992 yearbook indicates that in 1990, 80.4 percent of the Brazilian population was literate; therefore, that 19.6 percent were illiterate.

The data showed that 87.9 percent (higher than average) of "whites" were literate and 12.1 percent (lower than average) were not. Among the "black" population, 69.9 percent were literate and 30.1 percent were not. Among the "mixed" population , 70.7 percent were literate and 29.3 percent were not. The latter were, thus, "superior" to blacks, who have the highest percentage of illiteracy and the lowest percentage of literacy in Brazil.

Notes to the Eighteenth Letter

1. One cannot talk about hunger without talking about Josué de Castro, a doctor, sociologist, anthropologist, writer, essayist, college professor, and geographer born in Pernambuco, Brazil in 1908. His work and his person deserve honor now even more than ever.

   His first study about the matter, *The Problem of Malnourishment in Brazil*, was published in 1933. Many came after, including the famous *Geography of Hunger* in 1946 and *Geopolitics of Hunger* in 1952. He was a founder and member of various international organizations connected to the hunger problem. He was the president of the United Nations Food and Agriculture Organization (FAO) from 1952 to 1956. As a witty scientist and generous soul concerned about those who were excluded from the world's food banks, he became a man without political rights in 1964 when, as the ambassador from Brazil to the United Nations in Geneva, he was fired by the military government. He died in exile in France in 1973 as a college professor at the University of Paris, a man respected by the world but forbidden to return to his own country.

   At the World Conference on the Human Environment in Stockholm in 1972, he said the following with the scientific political consciousness of a citizen of the world who is coherent and has dedicated almost all his life to bringing awareness of and fighting against world hunger:

> It is necessary to view the degradation of the economy of the underdeveloped countries as a contamination of their human environment caused by the economic abuses of the global economy; hunger, misery, high rates of illness, a minimum of hygiene, short average life expectancies—all of this is the product of the destructive action of world exploitation according to the model of the capitalist economy. . . .
>
> It is said that in the underdeveloped regions a concern for the qualitative aspects of life does not exist, only a concern for survival, that is, the battle against hunger, epidemic diseases, and ignorance. This attitude forgets that these are only the symptoms of a severe social illness: underdevelopment as a product of development (quoted in *Polis*, special edition on "The Fight Against Hunger," p. 31).

Josué de Castro, perhaps the greatest student of hunger in the world, a hunger that has afflicted two-thirds of the world population, knew about the political difficulty of finding a solution:

> In 1943, the delegates of the United Nations met in Hot Springs to discuss the problems of nourishment and nutrition. They signed a protocol establishing themselves as promoters of raising living standards and nutrition. At that time, they were far from evaluating the importance and complexity of their declaration. Only time confirmed the difficulty of structuring an effective policy for the FAO or organizing to end the problem in its universal expression (Josué de Castro, *Geopolitics of Hunger*, 4th ed., vol. 2 [Rio de Janeiro: Brasiliense Edition, 1952], p. 411).

The sharpness of Josué de Castro's thinking, in addition to his political, scientific, and humanist view of life, led him to publish the book *Geography of Hunger*, before his fortieth birthday, which addressed the theme of hunger, uprooted myths, and spread understanding of the phenomena of hunger in human life as a whole and its environment. He was the first to speak about and worry about hunger and its solutions in Brazil, while addressing related questions of ecological harmony and balance. About human beings and the environment, he had concerns for the survival of both.

> We do not want to say that our work is only about the geography of hunger in its more limited sense, laying aside the biological, medical, and hygienic aspects of the problem, but that we address these multiple aspects from the fundamental principles of geographic science, whose basic objective is to locate, delineate, and correlate the natural and cultural phenomena that occur on the surface of the earth. It is within these geographic principles of localizing, expanding, causing, correlating, and unifying the world that we intend to face the hunger phenomenon. In other words, we shall carry out the study of ecological nature

within a multifaceted concept of ecology, that is, the study of the actions and reactions of the living things in their environment (Ibid., p. 18).

He addressed the roots of hunger in Brazil. He understood hunger as a consequence of the political economic process of the country.

Hunger in Brazil is a product of its historical past, Brazil's human groups always in battle and almost never in harmony with nature. In certain cases, the battles were provoked by the aggressive environment, which openly initiated hostilities, but in most cases they were due to the colonizing element, indifferent to anything that would not mean direct and immediate advantage to their plans of direct and immediate commercial adventure. This unfolding adventure, successive cycles of a destructive economy, unbalanced the economic health of the nation through Brazilian wood, sugarcane, Indian hunting, mining, migrant labor of coffee, rubber extraction, and, finally, artificial industrialization based on the fiction of customs barriers and a regime of inflation (Ibid., p. 216).

Furthermore,

In the last analysis, economic and social unsuitability was the consequence of an inept political state serving to balance power between private and public interests. The incompetence of political power in managing the adventure of colonization and the social organization of the nation was at first due to its insignificance and potential weakness before the strength and independence of owners, who controlled their territories with closed gates and an indifference to the regulations and orders of the government that contradicted its interests; and then due to centralizing power by taking revenue and rights from the regional units in order to place them in the hands of central power, which was narrow-minded in spreading benefits. The government always acts with an inadequate notion of the use of political force in order to successfully administer such an extensive territory (Ibid., p. 218).

His studies tumbled the barriers to understanding the politics of hunger in Brazil, especially his book *Geopolitics of Hunger,* written in 1950, regarding the most diverse facets of hunger in the world. His book was translated into twenty-five languages and served, in great part, as the official politics of the FAO, although he modestly stated in the book:

This book is a small contribution to the indispensable collective work that aims to accelerate the maturity of this idea: the pressing need to initiate a global battle to end hunger (Josué de Castro, *Geopolitics of Hunger,* 8th ed., vol. 1 [Rio de Janeiro: Brasiliense Edition, 1952], p. 69).

He adds:

The first of our objectives is to demonstrate that hunger, in spite of being a universal phenomenon, is not a fact of nature. In studying hunger around the world, we will prove that, as a general rule, hunger is not the natural condition of human groups, but rather the result of certain cultural factors, errors, and flaws in social organization. Hunger caused by inclement nature is rare; meanwhile, hunger as a plague caused by man is habitual to many different regions of the earth: every land occupied by man has been transformed by him into a land of hunger (Ibid., p. 72).

Above political party, race, gender, and ideology, he saw the problem of hunger as the political humanist he was, without preconceived biases.

We shall consider the reality of hunger without preconceived notions about what political ideology will be capable of resolving the problem. We shall study hunger as a human problem, as the fiercest problem facing humanity and, therefore, all parties (Ibid., p. 71).

His polemic that most shocked elitist beliefs in Malthus's followers was a scientific study of the ideas of the philosopher and demographer T. Doubleday about the relationship between hunger and human reproduction.

The crucial point of our essay, which we try to demonstrate, is that it is not overpopulation that creates and maintains hunger in certain areas of the world, but hunger that creates overpopulation. This statement appears, without a doubt, paradoxical, since it is hunger that causes death and degradation, and which seems less favorable to provoking excessive demographic increase (Ibid., p. 73).

An optimist confident in the very human beings who created hunger, he said:

In order to fight the new theories of Malthus, which publicly proclaim that control of the birthrate is the only possible salvation for a world in supposed bankruptcy, we shall collect the actual knowledge of the geographic and social sciences, which can no longer accept any rigid determinism of nature. To admit that the earth has a fixed limit, insurmountable by any human force, is to return to the old theories of geographic determinism of Ratzel's times, according to which the natural environment controls the world, while man is no more than a passive piece in the game of nature, no creative force, no will, no possibility of escape before the overpowering impositions of natural forces. Man, with his creative and inventive techniques, is capable of escaping the imposed limits of nature by liberating himself from geographic determinism and claiming a social doctrine of possibilities (Ibid., p. 73).

He goes on to discuss his views of the supposed relationship between hunger and fertility, today no longer scientifically accepted, by insisting that hunger is a political, social, and economic problem.

Considering the world map of hunger and the factors that regulate regional distribution, it is obvious that collective hunger is a social phenomenon provoked, in general, by inadequate possibilities and natural resources or the poor distribution of goods. The facts show that it is no longer possible to view hunger as a natural phenomenon since it is conditioned more by economic nature than by geographic nature. The difficult truth is that the world daily disposes of recourses sufficient to provide adequate nourishment to all. And if, up until today, many of the guests of the earth continue without participating in its banquet, it is because all civilizations, including ours, have been structured and maintained on the basis of economic inequality (Ibid., vol. 2, p. 383).

If his estimations and calculations are no longer correct, his principles continue to be.

For the battle against hunger, he presented some technical and political solutions. First:

The first objective is, without a doubt, to significantly increase world food production. For that, it is necessary to enlarge agricultural areas through adequate use and elevating the productivity per capita and per area unit. The enlargement of world agricultural areas is a legitimate aspiration that can be obtained by incorporating extensive tropical zones and subpolar zones into agriculture. According to Robert Salter, arable soil covers about 28 percent of the surface of the earth but its use in agriculture does not exceed 1 percent (Ibid.)

Second:

The truth is that it is not enough to produce food with available techniques, it is also necessary that these foods be acquired and consumed by human groups who need them. If adequate distribution and expansion of consumption does not take place, agricultural excesses will immediately form, creating an acute problem of overproduction paired with underconsumption. Therefore, nourishment policies must address production as well as adequate distribution of food products and must, therefore, be planned on a global scale (Ibid., p. 408).

Third:

New concepts of soil fertility show the possibility of soil renovation and recent developments in the field of nuclear physics and chemistry encourage the artificial synthesis of food, helping us to gain against the new theories of Malthus believers and their macabre prophecies (Josué de Castro, *Geopolitics of Hunger*, 4th ed., vol. 1 [Rio de Janeiro: Brasiliense Edition, 1952], p. 39).

Being certain that the problem of hunger could be resolved through the political will of governments and world organizations, he anticipated what today is clear, the collapse of the North due to the hunger of the South:

The battle to eliminate hunger from the face of the earth is neither utopian, nor the fantasy of a fairy-tale world, but a perfectly feasible objective within the limits of human capacity and the earth's possibilities. What is necessary is to better distribute land to the peoples who occupy it and the benefits of the earth to all the people. At this moment, the battle against hunger is no longer a task of quixotic idealism, but rather a need that shines through any cold and realistic analysis of the actual political and economic situation of the world. On the results of this battle, depends the survival of our civilization, since it is only through the elimination of the forces of misery which sicken our world, that it will be possible for the economy to be whole, an economy we venture into so eagerly without paying attention to our lack of social preparedness. Without raising the living standards of the poor, who are two-thirds of humanity, it becomes impossible to maintain civilization for the remaining third. Civilization is based upon a high level of production, which always demands the continuous increase of markets, something made possible only by incorporating the two-thirds into the world economy instead of edging them out. Therefore, only by increasing the buying power and consumption capacity of such outsiders, will our civilization be able to survive and prosper within its actual economic and social structure (Ibid., vol. 2, p. 384).

Josué de Castro insists on the world economic imbalance as a mistake:

There are certain types of economic exploitation that invariably impose inhuman productivity beyond that needed for basic necessities of life; while these types of economic exploitation prevail, hunger will continue to undermine our civilization. The so-called colonial economy, which the industrialized powers are based upon, obtains raw materials in the colonies at a low price. It is one of the types of economic exploitation incompatible with the economic balance of the world (Ibid., p. 409).

Also:

It is necessary, before anything, to try to wipe from contemporary political thinking the erroneous concept of economy as a game in which some ought to lose all in order for others to gain all (Ibid., p. 385).

By stating that "hunger and war do not follow any natural law; they are, rather, human creations" (Ibid., vol. 1, p. 59), Josué de Castro invites us to reflect and become more human. He proposes that "the road to survival is in the decision to face the social reality courageously and surmount natural difficulties without unjustified fears" (Ibid., vol. 2, p. 419). He points to the concretization of utopia; that is, the democratic road in which all have the right to eat.

In order to maintain the democratic principles that would dignify the human condition, the world must, before anything, completely eliminate the degrading stigma of hunger (Ibid., p. 418).

Josué de Castro knew that the elites of the world would react against his theories and actions, but over his lifetime, his enthusiasm to fight for and his hope in a new society in which all would be able to eat never diminished. He tirelessly fought for a world in which there would be no more hungry people, for a real democratic world.

It is inconceivable that such an important book as that of Josué de Castro has fallen out of print at the very moment the world turns its attention toward Biafra and Somalia, and while Brazil is undertaking the greatest campaign against hunger in its history. The theoretical thinking (although no longer current) and practiced solutions (still relevant) pointed to by this remarkable Brazilian man are little known or found in the bookstores where we could have learned them with pride and faith that all must be aware of the terrible problem of hunger.

One cannot forget that it was a Brazilian who fearlessly demystified taboos and elitist beliefs and who gave status to scientific knowledge about the problem of hunger. He was a pioneer when he emphasized that the political, economic, social, and ecological be considered. He was also a pioneer in presenting feasible solutions—although they were not desired by the prevailing power—to the problem of hunger. For these reasons, we should and need to get to know the thinking of Josué de Castro.

Another Brazilian concerned about the problem of hunger is Melhem Adas. He published an important book about the topic in 1988 which asks an important question in its title, *Hunger: A Crisis or a Scandal?*

He states that from 1974 on the FAO had concluded (as Castro had argued in 1950) that "the quantity of food available is enough to offer the whole world an adequate diet." He emphasizes that the question of hunger has not been "discussed openly, it is hidden.... The political, social, economic, and cultural factors are underestimated or ignored ... although they, and not overpopulation, are responsible for hunger in the world" (p. 33). He follows and restates the pioneering thinking of Josué de Castro in regard to the problem of hunger. Adas didactically lists the true determinants of hunger today:

1. the concentration of income and land in the underdeveloped world;
2. the underexploitation of rural space by agrarian activities while millions of human beings are hungry and do not have enough land to grow crops on;
3. the use of land for commercial export agriculture, resulting in the loss of land for food agriculture and the international division of production maintained by the colonial metropolis of today through an unjust economic world order;
4. the unjust and antidemocratic agrarian structure, marked by land concentration in the hands of a few;
5. the difficult access to the resources of production by rural workers, those without land, and the population in general;
6. the progress of capitalism in agriculture, impoverishing the rural worker;
7. the influence of agribusiness transnationals on agricultural production and the food habits of Third World populations;
8. the use of agricultural power in "food diplomacy" as a weapon in relating to other countries;

9. the military-industrial complex of financial and human resources used for the production of wartime materials, while billions of human beings are malnourished and die of starvation;

10. the large consumption of cereals by livestock in the developed countries (60.6 percent) contrasted with the lack of food in the underdeveloped countries;

11. the relationship between external debt in the Third World and the deterioration of food availability;

12. the relationship between culture and food (pp. 33–34).

Hunger, a consequence of poverty and lack of food, results in a list of needs that dialectically perpetuates hunger and poverty.

We can verify this statement through a graph on health and nutrition in the World Bank's *Report on World Progress, 1990: Poverty* from which I collected some data about hunger and its fatal consequences.

Sweden and the United States, two countries with high average income, have, respectively, 390 and 470 people per doctor (in 1989); 100 and 70 people per nurse (in 1984); 100 percent of deliveries attended by a medical team (in 1985); and 4 percent and 7 percent of newborns with low birth weight (in 1985); 6 and 10 infant mortality death rate for every one thousand born alive (in 1988); and 3,064 and 3,645 per capita daily consumption calories(in 1986).

In Uruguay and Argentina, two countries with high average income, have 520 and 370 people per doctor (in 1984); "no information" and 980 people per nurse (in 1984); "no information" on deliveries attended by a medical team (in 1985); 8 percent and 6 percent of newborns with low birth weight (in 1985); 23 and 31 infant mortality rate for every one thousand born alive (in 1988); and 2,648 and 3210 per capita daily consumption calories (in 1986).

Brazil and Angola, two countries with low average income average, have 1,080 and 17,790 people per doctor (in 1984); 1,210 and 1,020 people per nurse (in 1984); 73 percent and 15 percent of deliveries attended by a medical team (in 1985); 8 percent and 17 percent of newborns with low birth weight (in 1985); 61 and 135 infant mortality rate for every one thousand born alive (in 1986); and 2,656 and 1,880 per capita daily consumption calories (in 1986).

Mozambique and Ethiopia, the two countries with the lowest average income have 37,960 and 78,970 people per doctor (in 1984); 5,760 and 5,400 people per nurse (in 1984); 28 percent and 58 percent of deliveries attended by a medical team (in 1985); 15 percent and "no information" of newborns with low birth weight (in 1985); 139 and 135 infant mortality rate for every one thousand born alive (in 1988); and 1,595 and 1,749 per capita daily consumption calories (in 1986).

The concentration of wealth in a few countries correlates with extremely generous averages in regard to doctors and nurses per person and a high caloric intake per day; it also corresponds with high infant mortality rates and insufficient caloric intake in all of the other countries, which do not have the high average incomes of the North, "owners of the world." Unfortunately, this proves what Josué de Castro denounced fifty years ago.

Of the list of high average income economies, only Japan (with 2,864), Singapore (with 2,840), and Hong-Kong (with 2,859) have daily caloric intakes of less than 3,000 calories per person, which is considered ideal. Of the low average income countries, daily caloric intake varies from China (with 2,630) to Mozambique (with 1,595). That is hunger! And it is the creation of human perversity! It is not the creation of those who do not eat, but of those who make two-thirds of humanity suffer from hunger.

In regard to income concentration and how polarization is connected to hunger, the Brazilian economist Ladislau Dowbor tells us:

> The polarization between rich and poor has reached, at the end of this century, a level unknown in past eras. The data in the *Report on World Progress,* published in 1992 by the World Bank, shows that the earth had in 1990, 5.3 billion inhabitants and a planetary income of twenty-two trillion dollars, which means 4,200 dollars per inhabitant. The planet already produces enough to provide a dignified life for all citizens. However, sixteen trillion of those dollars—that is, 72 percent— belong to eight hundred million inhabitants in the countries of the North—that is, 15 percent of the world population. The practical result is that our planet has three billion people with an average annual income of 350 dollars per person, less than half of the minimum Brazilian salary. The citizens of the North disposes, on average of sixty times more resources than the three billion poor people on the planet, although certainly they do not have sixty times more children to educate. It is easy to understand how this already catastrophic difference is deepening: in 1990, for example, the per capita income of the poor increased by 2.4 percent, which is 8 dollars, while that of the rich increased by 1.6 percent, which is 338 dollars. The population of the rich increased by four million per year, while that of the poor increased by fifty-nine million people ("The Space of Knowledge," *IPSO, the Technological Revolution and the New Paradigms of Society* [Belo Horizonte: Oficina de Livros, 1994], pp. 116–17).

Dowbor goes on to talk about—and I continue to cite him because his text emphasizes the ratio of income concentration to misery-hunger—the education category, a relationship Freire already denounced:

> The impact of this economic reality on the world of education is immediate. World expenses in education in 1988 were 1,024 billion dollars, about 5.5 percent of gross world product. The developed countries spent 898 billion of these resources, while the underdeveloped countries were limited to 126 billion. Since the population of the underdeveloped countries surpasses four billion inhabitants, the practical result is that, in 1988, the average annual cost per student was 2,888 dollars in the rich countries and 129 dollars in the underdeveloped countries, which is twenty-two times less (Ibid., p. 117. Data from the UNESCO report, *World Information about Education: 1991* [Paris: UNESCO, 1992]).

In regard to land concentration, Melhem Adas informs us about the "Latin America" data, since the countries of Latin America are grouped together by the

World Bank, which has two categories of low average income and high average income. All Latin American countries are considered high average income, with the exception of Haiti, which is considered low average income. This concentration of wealth is responsible for hunger (see the same graph in the World Bank report, pp. 238–39).

> According to data from CEPAL (Economic Commission for Latin America), the agrarian structure of Latin America at the end of the 1970s presented violent contrasts: a minority of rural land owners (1.2 percent) owned the majority of land used for rural enterprises (70.6 percent), while the majority of rural land owners (74.4 percent) owned little of the land used (2.9 percent). In the case of Guatemala, the land of the Mayas, the distribution was even more unequal: 0.1 percent of the land owners retained 40.8 percent of the occupied land, while 88.4 percent of the land owners owned only 14.3 percent of the land (see fig. 1).

Dimensional categories of properties	Percentage of businesses or of land owners	Percentages of total occupied land by businesses
from 1 to 20 hectares	74.4	2.9
from 21 to 100 hectares	18.0	6.8
from 101 to 1000 hectares	6.4	19.7
more than 1000 hectares	1.2	70.6

Source: Economic Commission for Latin America (Cepa)

Figure 1: The Agrarian Structure of Latin America, 1975

This situation not only is maintained today, but has gained new proportions, contributing to poverty, misery, and hunger in Third World populations. "The contradictions between the agrarian structure and hunger are becoming more profound" says Adas (*Hunger: A Crisis or a Scandal*, pp. 58–59).

We can easily conclude that a dominant force in the hunger and misery cycle, in dialectic relationship with it, is income and land concentration, which has determined, the lack of the following: public policies ensuring adequate housing, doctors, and basic hygiene; a division of land through agrarian reform, production, and more equitable distribution of food; and jobs and salaries that can sustain a minimum level of health. In the cycle of hunger, misery is present in illness and starvation; illiteracy and superstition; low life expectancy, stillbirths, and low birth weights; high birth rates and infant mortality rates; unemployment and apathy; and living without focus while wandering the cities hoping for divine gifts or landlords' munificence. Social injustice has been spreading these problems without reservation because of the high concentration of income and land, obviously a product of the first world countries economic exploitation of those of the Third World countries and, internally, by dominant classes exploiting the majority of the population.

We cannot continue to ignore reality. The countries of the North, formerly colonialists and today almost always imperialists, cannot continue to accuse those of the South, exploited and oppressed by their elites as well, for their high birth rates, supposed laziness or negligence, or intrinsic inferiority, which the North claims are the primary causes of their hunger.

We denounced these ideological interpretations of the elites—the rich countries and rich people—who, in reality, have been mercilessly punishing poor people and Third World countries with the wounds of economic-social inequalities, which determine the hunger of the world. This is indeed a scandal.

2. Betinho's Campaign emerged from the climate encouraged under President Collor when the "Movement for Ethics" unfolded into the "Movement of Citizensí Action Against Hunger and Misery and for Life," demonstrating once again that the claims about Brazilians' skepticism are not true.

That popular campaign started in April of 1993 and should have ended only when the "hunger and misery of 32 million people is rooted out, not before" as Betinho—also called Herbert José de Souza—intended and declared in an interview to the monthly newspaper *Much More* (March 1994, p. 12).

The optimist and critical sociologist says in his recent interview in 1993 that

Brazilian misery gained a name, face, and address. National hunger, the product of an extravagant society that excludes many and privileges few, reached its peak, exhibited its ugly face even to those who refused to look, inscribed itself on the national agenda and gained the status of an emergency (p. 12).

The campaign has made the population aware that hunger and misery are a problem for the whole society and not just "a question to be resolved among those who are hungry and those who represent the government, the power, and the state.... The campaign always discussed the difference between emergency and long-term action, as well as the need to discuss both dimensions and thoroughly examine them in order to attack the structural causes of hunger and misery (p. 12).

To give you an idea of the campaign, it has committees in twenty two of the twenty seven Brazilian states and the "participation of all the entities of civil society, including unions, businesses, universities, churches, as well the partnership of different spheres of government."

Briefly, from April to December 1993 the campaign distributed 1,000 tons of food in São Paulo through its committees and 30,520 food baskets through its "Christmas Without Hunger" campaign; 30 tons of foods to 50,000 families in Brasilía (D.F.); 470 tons of foods to 13,431 poor families in Londrina (Paraná), a progressive city in the west, a region known for its fertile lands and agricultural exports; 117 tons of foods, 19,000 pairs of shoes, and 18 tons of clothes distributed to twenty municipalities through the Archdiocese of Belem (Para); 100 tons of food to families of Salvador (Bahia); 200 tons of food to those of Recife (Pernambuco); 70 tons of food and Christmas toys and basic food baskets to those of Santos (São Paulo); 5,000 basic food baskets in the state of Rio de Janeiro.

Food distributions have been carried out throughout the whole country by the committees of the campaign, other organizations of civil society and even army soldiers.

On March 10, 1994, the "Movement of Citizens' Against Hunger and Misery and for Life" entered its second phase, that of creating new jobs.

The goal is modest concerning the salary of the jobs created, (the minimum Brazilian salary is actually 65 dollars), but the quantitative goal for jobs themselves is daring: nine million through a "combined effort, in partnership with public power and society and particularly of the 4,500 municipalities of the country, which can be the concrete road to accomplish this objective. To think of public works and public expenses from the employment perspective, to decide that at least once, the whole country is going to create nine million jobs. Only then is it possible to stop the insanity of destroying people through the most brutal process of social exclusion that we know of," declares Betinho (p. 12).

Indeed the statistical data on Brazil always show a difficult truth: we are a society that produces excluded, outlaw people.

At the request of Betinho, the IBGE compiled "Map of the Labor Market in Brazil" (published by Folha de São Paulo on March 11, 1994) in order to finance the campaign work.

Some of the data published there:

1. 5.2 million people work and are not paid; 2.4 million are unemployed; 12.3 receive less than the minimum monthly salary (65 dollars); 15 million receive the equivalent of one or two minimum monthly salaries; and 5 million earn more than ten minimum monthly salaries (pp. 1–15).
2. 64.5 million of the population is economically active, 6.2 million having some type of occupation; of these, 31 million do not contribute toward social security, as legislated, and therefore do not receive any benefits after retirement.
3. The monthly average salary is of 4.1 minimum salaries. The states with lower average monthly salaries are all from Northeast Brazil: Piauí (1.6), Maranhão (1.7) and Ceara (1.9). Those with higher average monthly salaries are São Paulo (6.1), Rio de Janeiro (4.8) and Brasília, the federal capital, (8.0) (pp. 1–15).
4. 64.5 of the working class has at least four years of school (not necessarily four years of schooling); 16.4 percent have zero to one year of school; 19.1 percent have one to three years of school; 32.9 percent has four to seven years of school; 12.2 percent have eight to ten years of school; and 19.4 percent have eleven or more years of school (pp. 1–16).
5. Some nonwage workers receive housing, land to till, and a few benefits. The states with the highest rates of nonwage workers are: Piauí (23.3 percent), Paran· (14.9 percent), and Santa Catarina (19.5 percent). The states with the lowest rates are Brasília (1.6 percent), Rio de Janeiro, (1.2 percent), and São Paulo (2.6 percent). The metropolitan region with the highest rate is Curitiba, and with the lowest rate is São Paulo (1.1 percent).
6. The 31 million people who do not contribute to social security are 49.9 percent of the people who have an occupation. Fourteen million work without a worker's permit signed by a land owner (34.7 percent), an illegal situation.
7. 14.2 percent of children from ten to thirteen years of age—that is, 1.9 million—are already in the work force even though the constitution prohibits

minors under the age of fourteen from working. The highest percentage of children from the ages of ten to thirteen who are working is in Piauí (28.4 percent), Maranhão (24.8 percent), and Paran· (20.1 percent). The states with the smallest concentration of working children are Brasilía (4.2 percent), Rio de Janeiro (5.6 percent), and São Paulo (7.3 percent).

8. Salaries differ by gender and race. Measured in average monthly income stated in minimum salaries, men receive 4.6 and women 2.6; white men receive 6.3 and black men or mixed men 2.9; white women receive 3.6 and black women or mixed women 1.7 (pp. 1–17).

In regard to this subject, Gilberto Dimenstein, a journalist with a São Paulo newspaper who has written about the exploitation of minors in Brazil, criticized the IBGE work by emphasizing that:

> Prostitution does not appear on the map of the IBGE as employment, but it is one of the main occupations of needy girls. Official data show that there are about 500,000 prostitutes, the majority living without any type of public or private support. Some of them live in practical slavery, jailed in whorehouses of North and Northeast Brazil, with the connivance of the police or even their participation. In the cities by the beaches, it is said, there is a sex industry for tourists through the police and hotels (pp. 1–17).

The great majority of these tourists are foreigners who come from the first world—the North of Germany, Italy, and France—who descend on the coastal region of Northeast Brazil openly seeking young girls, who sell themselves in the hope of better days.

If we want to create a real democratic society, we must do away with discrimination and the consequent discrepancies between classes, races, genders, and Brazilian regions, so visibly reported in the data. We must, if we do not want to see, with our very own eyes, a fettered Brazil.

Among the urgent tasks of building Brazilian democracy is what Betinho's Campaign has prioritized: the battle against hunger and unemployment.

3. The distribution of income in Brazil is terribly unjust and rebukes our elitist, discriminatory, and authoritarian society, which limits the great majority of the Brazilian population.

To prove this statement I add the sad, hard, and oppressive data written about in previous notes and taken from texts and charts of the organization responsible for Brazilian statistics, the IBGE.

The *Statistical Yearbook of Brazil*, dated 1992, states that the "distribution of income among families with private residences in 1989–1990. From a total of 38,002,452 families: 11.3 percent of them had a monthly family income of one minimum salary; 15.3 percent had one to two minimum salaries; 29.4 percent had between two and five minimum salaries; 20.1 percent had between five and ten minimum salaries; 12.4 percent had between ten and twenty minimum salaries; 8.1

percent had more than twenty minimum salaries; 2.2 percent had no income; and 1.1 percent did not answer.

If the minimum salary in Brazil has over the last few years varied between 50 to 80 dollars monthly, we can conclude that the most privileged group, consisting of 8.1 percent of the estimated population, had an average family income (a family being one to seven or more people) of between 1,000 to 1,600 dollars. In order to retain their previous level of income, they needed three or more employed people in the family.

The same chart reports the extreme poverty of those families with only one minimum monthly salary. Of those families, 21.5 percent consist of one to two people being (17.3 percent with one employed person and 5.1 percent with two employed persons); 9.6 percent were families with three persons whose income was one minimum salary (with one employed person was 11.3 percent, two persons was 3.9 percent, three employed persons was 4.0 percent); 6.7 percent were families with four people whose income was one minimum salary (with one employed person was 9.0 percent, two employed persons was 3.2 percent, and three or more employed persons was 3.3 percent); 6.5 percent were families with five or six people whose income was one minimum salary (with one employed person was 10.3 percent, two employed persons was 4.1 percent, and three or more employed persons was 3.1 percent); and the families of seven or more people whose income was one minimum salary (with one employed person was 19.3 percent, two employed persons was 8.7 percent, and three or more employed persons was 5.0 percent).

Therefore, the lowest paid people—receiving only one minimum salary—have in their family household 19.3 percent of heads of family—heads being an adult man or woman and sometimes minors—supporting families of seven or more people.

Other data, also from IBGE, clearly underscore the presence of income concentration in Brazil by indicating shares of national income in 1990. The poorest 50 percent of the country have only 12 percent of national income, while the richest 1 percent have 13.9 percent of the national income. The poorest 10 percent of the Brazilian population enjoyed the rights to only 0.9 percent of the national income, while the richest 10 percent possessed 48.1 percent of the national income (IBGE, PNAD, compiled by DIEESE). The World Bank, in its 1993 report, shows the income of the richest 10 percent in Brazil at 51.3 percent.

All these data show the extreme poverty of half of the Brazilian population, while 1 in 100 Brazilian citizens enjoy all the material and, consequently, cultural goods built by the whole society, placing us as the country with the most perverted concentration of income in the whole world.

4. Brazil has a fragile democratic system. Its previous elections are proof. During in the First Republic (1889–1930) the elections were fraudulent: votes were *cabresto* (farmer's were obliged to vote for the land owner's choice), bought, *bico de pena* (declared in a loud voice and noted down by public employees), and all kinds of hoaxes. Candidates not wanted by those in power were often decapitated.

From 1930 to 1945, we had Getúlio Vargas who bestowed power upon himself through the force of the military (in 1930), was elected by a Congress he manipulated (in 1934), and continued in power through a coup d'état (from 1937 to 1945) (see note of the fifth letter).

We had fairly free elections, not totally free of the above-mentioned deficiencies, in 1945, 1950, 1955, and 1960 when Generals Gaspar Dutra, Getúlio Vargas, Juscelino Kubischek, and Jânio Quadros were elected.

Dutra governed throughout the period for which he was elected (January 31, 1946 to January 31, 1951), Vargas assumed his first elected term in January 31, 1951, but committed suicide on August 24, 1954, to the despair of the people. To complete that term, Cafe Filho—who was the vice president, president of the House of Representatives, and president of the Senate—took office to protect the office to the newly elected president Kubischek, from a history of coups d'états by the right wing and counterplots by legalists. Kubischek governed from January 31, 1956 to January 31, 1961, and was one of the most dynamic and democratic governments we have known. He built Brasilía and transferred the capital of Rio de Janeiro to central Brazil on April 21, 1960. During his term, there were no political prisoners and the press was free.

Jânio Quadros, who succeeded him, was a political phenomenon, dictatorial but not authoritarian, and renounced the highest office in the nation after seven months in power (January 31, 1961 to August 25, 1961). Vice President João Goulart then assumed office, already marked by international imperialist forces and national military forces to be removed from power. He governed from September 7, 1961, until April 1, 1964 coup d'état.

Military governments continued without free elections until Tancredo Neves and José Sarney were elected by Congress on January 15, 1985. Tancredo became seriously ill on the eve of his inauguration. Therefore, the vice president assumed office as the president of the republic, elected by a restricted electoral rules (in spite of a large rally on the streets demanding "Direct immediately," that is, direct elections in 1985). With the death of Tancredo on April 21, 1985, he became president for the whole period for which he had been indirectly elected (March 15, 1985 to March 15, 1990).

In 1989, when we commemorated a century of the republic, the democratic inexperience of Brazilians, who voted for the first time in May 1933, lead them to elect Fernando Collor de Mello as president of the republic. He took office on March 15, 1990, and was impeached on September 29, 1992 (see notes of the fifth and twelfth letter).

Once more, we are being governed by a vice president elected on the same ticket as the deposed president, who shall be handed the presidential office on January 1, 1995.

The dream of holding presidential primaries on October 3, 1994 and of the most popular candidate obtaining 50 percent plus one of the votes in secondary voting on November 15, 1994, when the two most popular candidates of the primaries compete, already mobilizes a great part of civil society, who see elections as a necessary part of the exercise and constitution of a true democratic state. The first elections will also include an election for state governors, state and federal deputies, and senators.

The Labor Party (PT) candidate campaigning for the office of the president of the republic is the metallurgist Luíz Inacio Lula da Silva, who has been ahead in the polls with 40 percent of the electoral vote. Therefore, the other parties are already working to introduce their candidates and organize a rally to coalesce all the parties of the right and center to face the candidacy of Lula. Lula, who lost in the secondary elections in 1989, has been, since the majority of Brazil's thirty-five million voted for Collor, the most noted name to govern Brazil for four years according to the constitution, whose revision is today in force.

Index

Popular Action (AP), 203–204

Popular Institutes of Brazilian Studies (ISEB), 136

Popular Revolutionary Vanguard (VPR), 203

popular theater project, 130

practice, relationship with theory, 107–108

press, freedom of, 149

pressed ground floors, 124, 207, 230

prison massacre, 219–222

process of writing, 1–2, 80

professor's dilemma, 161

Professor Sim: Tia Não, 102, 159

progressive education, 86–87, 114, 116, 151, 153, 155. *See also* Education

punishment, corporal, 92

Quadros, Jânio, 251

Queiroz, Eça de, 51, 80

Quintas, Amaro, 63, 79

radicality, roots of, 14–15

Railway Band, 60

Ramos, Graciliano, 51, 80

reactionary postmodernity, 84

realist socialism, 165, 181, 188

Recife, return to, 77

religion, and oppressed classes, 54

respect for learner, in educational practice, 127

responsibility and freedom, 153

retention, in school, 90, 227, 236–237

Revolution of 1930, 42, 213–214

Revolutionary Movement of October 8 (MR-8), 202, 203

Ribeiro, Ernesto Carmeiro, 62

rights: political and pedagogical, 155; of subordinated social classes, 85

rituals, mourning, 74–75

river as recreational site, 52–54, 67

romance, forbidden, 65

roots of radicality, 14–15

Rosa e Silva, oligarchy of, 211

Rosas, Paulo, 107, 116, 119, 129–130, 231

Saint John's Eve, 37, 210

Sampaio, Cid, 81, 98

Sampaio, Plínio, 6

"Santa Claus Syndrome," 98

Santos, José Carlos Alves dos. *See* Alves dos Santos

Sarney, José, 251

Saul, Ana Maria, 170

school (grade) retention, 90, 227, 236–237

school failure among students of color, 174–176

Sebastiani, Eduardo, 208

SEC (Cultural Extension Service), 109, 131, 134–137

self-censorship, 7

"sentence forming," 29

Sérgio, Father, 229–230

SESI (Social Service of Industry), 81–82, 85, 87, 88, 91, 109, 122; clubs, 98–106; staff training seminars, 95–96

Severino (textile worker), and service charges, 105–106

sex education class, Swiss, 82–83

sexual repression, 32–34

Silva, José Dias da, 98

Silva, José Pessoa da, 50

Silva, Luíz Inacio Lula da. *See* Lula

soccer games, 66

social class, implications of, 21–22

social classes, relationships between, 83–84

Social Service of Industry. *See* SESI

socialism, 114, 136–137; realist socialism, 165, 181, 188

Souza, Herbert José de. *See* Betinho

soybeans, 236

space, importance for education and work, 123–126

Stela (sister), 23, 31, 75

stolen-chicken incident, 24, 209